THE

POETS' WORLD

An Anthology of English Poetry

OTHER BOOKS BY JAMES REEVES

ANTHOLOGIES

Heinemann's Junior Poetry Books: a collection of rhymes and poems for use in Primary Schools

1 *Yellow Wheels*
2 *Grey Goose and Gander*
3 *Green Broom*
4 *Strawberry Fair* (out of print)

The Merry-Go-Round (the above four books in one volume)
The Rhyming River, I–IV (four books for Secondary Schools)
Orpheus Book I (English poetry for 10–12-year-olds)
Orpheus Book II (English poetry for 13–15-year-olds)
The Speaking Oak (a miscellany of English prose and poetry)
Dialogue and Drama (a dramatic anthology) with Norman Culpan
A New Canon of English Poetry (with Martin Seymour-Smith)

PLAYS FOR YOUNG PLAYERS

Mulcaster Market
The King who took Sunshine

POEMS FOR CHILDREN

Hurdy-Gurdy
The Wandering Moon
Prefabulous Animiles with Edward Ardizzone
Ragged Robin

THE POETRY BOOKSHELF SERIES

Selections with introduction, notes and portraits

D. H. Lawrence
John Donne
Gerard Manley Hopkins
Jonathan Swift
John Clare
Chaucer: Lyric and Allegory
Emily Dickinson
Samuel Taylor Coleridge
Robert Browning
Andrew Marvell (with Martin Seymour-Smith)
Walt Whitman (with Martin Seymour-Smith)
The Modern Poets' World

OTHER TITLES

Commitment to Poetry
Teaching Poetry: Poetry in Class, Five to Fifteen
A Short History of English Poetry
Understanding Poetry
The Critical Sense
A First Bible
Inside Poetry (with Martin Seymour-Smith)
How to write Poems for Children
The Idiom of the People
The Everlasting Circle

THE POETS' WORLD

An Anthology of English Poetry

CHOSEN AND EDITED BY

JAMES REEVES

HEINEMANN EDUCATIONAL BOOKS LTD • LONDON

Heinemann Educational Books Ltd
LONDON EDINBURGH MELBOURNE TORONTO
SINGAPORE JOHANNESBURG AUCKLAND IBADAN NAIROBI
HONG KONG NEW DELHI KUALA LUMPAR

ISBN 0 435 14767 6

First published 1948
Reprinted fifteen times

Second Edition 1972

Published by
Heinemann Educational Books Ltd
48 Charles Street, London W1X 8AH
Printed in Great Britain by
Richard Clay (The Chaucer Press), Ltd.,
Bungay, Suffolk

TO

EDWARD THOMPSON

Contents

INTRODUCTION xxvii

ANONYMOUS
A Lyke-Wake Dirge 1
The Wife of Usher's Well 2
Edward 4
The Twa Corbies 6
Sir Patrick Spens 7
Helen of Kirconnell 10
The Daemon Lover 12
Lord Randal 14
The Old Cloak 15
I Sing of a Maiden 18
At the Setting of the Sun 19
An Old Soldier of the Queen's 20
Come, Come Away 21
Boney Was a Warrior 21
The Kerry Recruit 22
The Big Rock Candy Mountains 24
Alexander the Great 26

ANGLO-SAXON (*translated by* Gavin Bone)
Riddle on Moon and Sun 27
The Whale 27

JOHN GOWER (1325?–1408)
The Cave of Sleep 28

GEOFFREY CHAUCER (1340?–1400)
Now Welcome Summer (from *The Parlement of Foules*) 30
A Garden in a Dream (from *The Parlement of Foules*) 31
The Squire (from *The Canterbury Tales*) 32
The Chase (from *The Nun's Priest's Tale*) 33
Truth (*Ballade de Bon Conseyl*) 34

WILLIAM DUNBAR (1460?–1530)
Lament for the Makers 35

JOHN SKELTON (1460?–1529)
Poverty (from *Magnificence*) 39
Though Ye Suppose 40
To Mistress Isabel Pennell 40
To Mistress Margaret Hussey 41

MILES COVERDALE (1488–1568)
I Will Lift Up Mine Eyes (see under The Old Testament p. x) 80

SIR THOMAS WYATT (1503?–1542)
The Hind 43
To His Lady 43
Honesty 44

HENRY HOWARD, EARL OF SURREY (1517?–1547)
Youth and Age 45

WILLIAM STEVENSON (1530?–1575)
Jolly Good Ale and Old 46

SIR WALTER RALEGH (1552?–1618)
Walsingham 48

EDMUND SPENSER (1552?–1599)
When Flowered My Joyful Spring (from *The Shepheardes Calendar, December*) 50
One Day I Wrote Her Name Upon the Strand 51

GEORGE PEELE (1558?–1597?)
His Golden Locks Time Hath to Silver Turned 51

MICHAEL DRAYTON (1563–1631)
A Ballad of Agincourt 52

CHRISTOPHER MARLOWE (1564–1593)
Lament for Zenocrate (from *The Second Part of Tamburlaine the Great*) 57

WILLIAM SHAKESPEARE (1564–1616)
Blow, Blow, Thou Winter Wind (from *As You Like It*) 58
Where the Bee Sucks (from *The Tempest*) 59
Full Fathom Five (from *The Tempest*) 60
O Mistress Mine (from *Twelfth Night*) 60
Fear No More the Heat o' the Sun (from *Cymbeline*) 61
Shall I Compare Thee to a Summer's Day? 62
When to the Sessions of Sweet Silent Thought 62
Tired With All These for Restful Death I Cry 63
Since Brass, nor Stone, nor Earth, nor Boundless Sea 63
When in the Chronicle of Wasted Time 64
Let Me not to the Marriage of True Minds 65
A Dream (from *King Richard III*) 65
St. Crispin's Day (from *King Henry V*) 66
The Death of Kings (from *King Richard II*) 68
Sleep (from *King Henry IV Part 2*) 68
Music (from *The Merchant of Venice*) 69
Sounds and Sweet Airs (from *The Tempest*) 71

The Death of Cleopatra (from *Antony and Cleopatra*) 71
Irresolution (from *Hamlet*) 73

THOMAS CAMPIAN (1567?–1619)
Bessy and Jamie 74

THOMAS NASHE (1567–1601)
In Time of Pestilence 75

BEN JONSON (1573–1637)
Hymn to Diana 77
Inviting a Friend to Supper 78
That Women are but Men's Shadows 79
Song ('Still to be neat, still to be dressed') 80

THE OLD TESTAMENT: Authorised Version (1611)
I Will Lift Up Mine Eyes (*Psalm 121* in the Prayer Book version, attributed to Miles Coverdale) 80
The Earth is the Lord's (*Psalm 24*) 81
He is My Refuge (from *Psalm 91*) 82
Four Things (from *The Book of Proverbs*) 83
The War Horse (from *The Book of Job*) 83
David's Lament (from *The Second Book of Samuel*) 84
Vanity of Vanities (from *The Book of Ecclesiastes*) 85
The Valley of Dry Bones (from *The Book of Ezekiel*) 86

TOBIAS HUME (d. 1645)
Fain Would I Change that Note 87

JOHN DONNE (1576–1631)
Death, Be Not Proud 88
At the Round Earth's Imagined Corners 89
The Anniversary 89
The Expiration 90

A Valediction: forbidding Mourning 91
The Good-morrow 92

JOHN WEBSTER (1580?–1625?)
A Dirge 93

RICHARD CORBET (1582–1635)
To his Son 94

HENRY FARLEY
A Complaint 95

WILLIAM DRUMMOND (1585–1649)
This World a Hunting Is 96

ROBERT HERRICK (1591–1674)
To Anthea who may Command Him Any Thing 96
To Dianeme 97
Corinna's Going a Maying 98

GEORGE HERBERT (1593–1633)
Virtue 100
Jordan II 101
The Pulley 102
The Quip 102

JAMES SHIRLEY (1596–1666)
The Glories of our Blood and State 104

JOHN MILTON (1608–1674)
The Building of Pandemonium (from *Paradise Lost*, Book I) 105
They Err who Count it Glorious to Subdue (from *Paradise Regained*, Book III) 107
Samson Blind (from *Samson Agonistes*) 108
To the Lord General Cromwell, May 1652 110

RICHARD LOVELACE (1618–1658)
Gratiana Dancing and Singing 110

ABRAHAM COWLEY (1618–1667)
On the Death of Mr. William Hervey 111

ANDREW MARVELL (1621–1678)
The Mower to the Glow-worms 114
The Garden 115
To his Coy Mistress 118

HENRY VAUGHAN (1622–1695)
Man 119
The World of Light 120

JOHN HALL (1627–1656)
A Pastoral Hymn 122

JOHN DRYDEN (1631–1700)
Song for Saint Cecilia's Day 123
Achitophel (from *Absalom and Achitophel*) 125
Songs from *The Secular Masque* (1. Momus to Mars) 127
Songs from *The Secular Masque* (2. Momus to Diana, Mars and Venus) 127

HENRY ALDRICH (1647–1710)
A Catch 128

JOHN WILMOT, EARL OF ROCHESTER (1648–1680)
Love and Life 128

JONATHAN SWIFT (1667–1745)
Mary the Cook-Maid's Letter to Dr. Sheridan 129
A Description of a City Shower 131

ALEXANDER POPE (1688–1744)
Where'er You Walk (from *Summer, the Second Pastoral*) 133
The Faithless Lover (from *Autumn, the Third Pastoral*) 134
Sporus (from the *Epistle to Dr. Arbuthnot*) 136
Epistle to Miss Blount, on her leaving the Town, after the Coronation 137

SAMUEL JOHNSON (1709–1784)
On the Death of Mr. Robert Levet, a Practiser in Physic 139

THOMAS GRAY (1716–1771)
Elegy Written in a Country Churchyard 140

CHRISTOPHER SMART (1722–1771)
My Cat Jeoffry (from *Jubilate Agno*) 145

WILLIAM COWPER (1731–1800)
The Loss of the 'Royal George' 148
To Mary 149
The Shrubbery 151

WILLIAM BLAKE (1757–1827)
Laughing Song 152
The Little Black Boy 153
The Tyger 154
A Poison Tree 155
The Sword and the Sickle 156
And Did Those Feet in Ancient Time 156
Ah! Sun-flower 157
London 157
Holy Thursday (from *Songs of Experience*) 158
Holy Thursday (from *Songs of Innocence*) 159

ROBERT BURNS (1759–1796)
A Red, Red Rose 160

I Murder Hate by Field or Flood 161
Anna 162

ANONYMOUS
Waly Waly 164
The Seeds of Love 165
The Lowlands of Holland 166

WILLIAM WORDSWORTH (1770–1850)
Strange Fits of Passion Have I Known 167
She Dwelt Among the Untrodden Ways 168
I Travelled Among Unknown Men 169
Lines Written in Early Spring 169
To the Cuckoo 170
The Solitary Reaper 172
The World Is Too Much With Us 173
Skating (from *The Prelude*, Book I) 173
Nutting 175

SAMUEL TAYLOR COLERIDGE (1772–1834)
Kubla Khan 177
The Rime of the Ancient Mariner 179

WALTER SAVAGE LANDOR (1775–1864)
Well I Remember How You Smiled 201

PERCY BYSSHE SHELLEY (1792–1822)
A Widow Bird Sate Mourning for Her Love 202
Ozymandias 202
Ode to the West Wind 203

JOHN CLARE (1793–1864)
Pleasant Sounds 206
Autumn 207
Badger 207

Country Letter 209
I Am 210

JOHN KEATS (1795–1821)
Ode to Autumn 211
La Belle Dame sans Merci 212
In a Drear-nighted December 214
Written on a Blank Page in Shakespeare's Poems, facing *A Lover's Complaint* 215

HARTLEY COLERIDGE (1796–1849)
To a Friend 216
'Tis strange to me . . . 216

ALFRED, LORD TENNYSON (1809–1892)
The Splendour Falls on Castle Walls 217
Now Fades the Last Long Streak of Snow (from *In Memoriam*) 218
Tithonus 219
Ulysses 221

ROBERT BROWNING (1812–1889)
A Toccata of Galuppi's 224
My Last Duchess 227

EMILY BRONTË (1818–1848)
I am the only being whose doom ... 229

WALT WHITMAN (1819–1892)
Beginning My Studies 230
After the Sea-ship 230
Animals (from *Song of Myself*) 231
Native Moments 232
When I Heard the Learn'd Astronomer 232
A Sight in Camp in the Daybreak Gray and Dim 233
By the Bivouac's Fitful Flame 234

ARTHUR HUGH CLOUGH (1819–1861)
There is no God 234

HERMAN MELVILLE (1819–1891)
The Maldive Shark 236

MATTHEW ARNOLD (1822–1888)
The Gods are Happy (from *The Strayed Reveller*) 237
The Forsaken Merman 239

DANTE GABRIEL ROSSETTI (1828–1882)
Lovesight 244
On the Site of a Mulberry Tree 245

EMILY DICKINSON (1830–1886)
Success is counted sweetest 246
I know some lonely houses . . . 246
I like to see it lap the miles 248
It dropped so low in my regard 249
A narrow fellow in the grass 249

CHRISTINA ROSSETTI (1830–1894)
Summer 250

LEWIS CARROLL (1832–1898)
Jabberwocky 252

WILLIAM MORRIS (1834–1896)
The Burghers' Battle 253
In Prison 255

THOMAS HARDY (1840–1928)
Great Things 256
Old Furniture 257
Friends Beyond 259
Afterwards 261
Regret Not Me 262

GERARD MANLEY HOPKINS (1844–1889)
Hurrahing in Harvest 263
The Sea and the Skylark 264
Felix Randal 265
Thou Art Indeed Just, Lord 266
In Honour of St. Alphonsus Rodriguez 266
Spring and Fall 267

ALFRED EDWARD HOUSMAN (1859–1936)
In Valleys Green and Still 268
On Wenlock Edge 269
The chestnut casts his flambeaux . . . 270
Others, I am not the first 271
The laws of God, the laws of man 272

WILLIAM BUTLER YEATS (1865–1939)
The Hour Before Dawn 273
An Irish Airman Foresees his Death 276
The Three Monuments 277

WILLIAM HENRY DAVIES (1871–1940)
In the Country 278
The Heap of Rags 279
The Villain 280

WALTER DE LA MARE (1873–1956)
Farewell 281
By Order! 282
Dry August Burned 282
Drugged 283

ROBERT FROST (1875–1963)
The Rabbit Hunter 284
The Road Not Taken 285

Not to Keep 286
An Importer 287
Desert Places 288

JOHN MASEFIELD (1878–1967)
The Blowing of the Horn (from *The Song of Roland*) 289

EDWARD THOMAS (1878–1917)
The Owl 291
The New House 292
Cock-Crow 292

NICHOLAS VACHEL LINDSAY (1879–1931)
The Daniel Jazz 293

WALLACE STEVENS (1879–1955)
Disillusionment of Ten O'Clock 296

THOMAS ERNEST HULME (1883–1917)
Autumn 297
Above the Dock 297

EZRA POUND (b. 1883)
Salutation 298

DAVID HERBERT LAWRENCE (1885–1930)
Spray 298
Talk 299
Poverty 299
Bat 300
Piano 302

ANDREW YOUNG (1885–1971)
Last Snow 302

SIEGFRIED SASSOON (1886–1967)
The Dug-Out 303
To Any Dead Officer 304

EDWIN MUIR (1887–1959)
The Return 305

THOMAS STEARNS ELIOT (1888–1965)
Prelude 306
Rannoch, by Glencoe 307
The Journey of the Magi 308
Rhapsody on a Windy Night 309

JOHN CROWE RANSOM (b. 1888)
Old Man Playing With Children 312
Piazza Piece 313
Blue Girls 313

ARTHUR WALEY (1889–1966)
Fighting South of the Castle 314
Burial Songs 315
On the Birth of His Son 316
The Hat Given to the Poet by Li Chien 316
A Love Song 316
Plucking the Rushes 317

WILFRED OWEN (1893–1918)
Futility 317
Arms and the Boy 318
The Parable of the Old Man and the Young 318
Anthem for Doomed Youth 319

ROBERT GRAVES (b. 1895)
1805 320
To Lucia at Birth 321

EDMUND BLUNDEN (b. 1896)
The Ballast-Hole 322
Report on Experience 322

CECIL DAY LEWIS (b. 1904)
It Would Be Strange 323

NORMAN CAMERON (1905–1953)
The Compassionate Fool 324

JAMES REEVES (b. 1909)
Thoughts and Memories 325

DYLAN THOMAS (1914–1953)
The Force That Through the Green Fuse Drives the Flower 326

NOTES 329

INDEX OF FIRST LINES 385

Preface

To make of poetry a living voice, a voice that will continue to grow more moving and more revealing when other voices of the classroom and playing-field have become faint—this should be the chief object of teaching poetry in schools. To achieve this object, poetry must be read with enjoyment, but also with respect. Young readers respect studies accompanied by work, even hard work, more readily than those associated with mere relaxation. If poetry is regarded as a relaxation from harder studies, it will not be respected. Most good poetry demands study and interpretation; it cost its makers much effort of thought, imagination and feeling, and it is worthy of corresponding efforts by its readers. It is in making these efforts that young readers enlarge, not only their appreciation of poetry, but also their capacity for thought, imagination and feeling. The study of poetry is a training of the emotions—that is, a training for life.

A book of annotations to Palgrave's *Golden Treasury* published in 1904 furnishes the one hundred and fifty lines of Milton's *L'Allegro* with twenty-five closely printed pages of notes, and these the student was expected to 'get up.' It is against this sort of study that the present emphasis on 'enjoyment' is a reaction. If we subject both the method of indiscriminate 'notes' and the method of relaxed 'enjoyment', what approach are we to put in their place? It is, briefly, to study the poet's intentions and the means by which he carries them out. Every good poem has its own motivation, and makes its own enlargement of men's experience; these, and the poetic methods by which they are realised, are the proper objects of study. In the *Introduction* to this book, which is written for young readers, I have outlined the ways of thinking about poetry which I believe will be most helpful; and in the notes at the end of the book I have given such explanations as are necessary to the understanding of the poems, and such critical suggestions as I hope will guide the reader in forming his own judgement.

In making the choice of poems I have assumed that none but the best is good enough for reading in school. That some readers may have reached an appreciation of the best by way of the second and third best does not mean that this is necessarily the surest way. What is read at school has the stamp of authority, which may be accepted or rejected by the conscious mind, but which is never obliterated. 'The best', however, is an absolute standard impossible to apply with certainty; many poems are at the best in some, but not in all, respects. Of the large available volume of poetry in English, therefore, my choice has been limited by other considerations: first, the poems are intended to be suitable for the upper forms of secondary schools and for training colleges; a high proportion are well within the understanding of readers of fourteen or younger, while the more difficult require some skill in interpretation, even by fairly advanced readers of fifteen and over. Secondly, a good deal of attention has been given to a variety of technical accomplishment, since readers of fourteen and over can be encouraged to take an active interest in this essential part of the study of poetry. It is right, I am sure, for teachers to treat their pupils as makers, and not simply readers, of poetry. Thirdly, the consideration of space has made it necessary to quote only extracts from certain poems of great length; but some of the greatest poets remain among the most difficult to represent adequately. The selections from Chaucer, Spenser and Marlowe, for example, are no more than tokens of these poets' worth.

But what of the actual tastes and experience of adolescent

readers? Surely, it may be said, these should be given first consideration in making a choice of poems for schools. To answer this objection briefly, while many of the poems have immediate 'entertainment value', the first criterion has been that of poetic quality; for the tastes of adolescence change, and one of the purposes of teaching poetry is to direct the mind to the permanent aspects of existence. As for adolescent experience, especially emotional, that is something which is undergoing continuous enlargement in all directions, and poetry is an important agent in the process. To try to get young readers to appreciate poems just beyond their emotional reach is one of the surest ways of strengthening imagination and understanding. To grasp at what is just beyond the grasp is a manner of growing. Few poems in this book, after all, originate in emotional situations which are not dealt with, in one way or another, by the cinema.

The poems are arranged chronologically, except that all the anonymous poems have been placed at the beginning (except for three on pp. 164–166). The text represents a compromise not, I hope, offensive to scholarship, between the strict letter of the original and the needs of ordinary readers. An exception has been made in the case of a few medieval poems, where it was felt that something essential would have been lost by modernisation.

To many who have been laid under contribution for advice, suggestions and help of all kinds, I gratefully acknowledge my indebtedness—to my wife and others of my family and friends; to several fellow-members of the Society for Teachers of English; to several of my colleagues on the staff of Slough Grammar School, as well as to some of the pupils; to members of Eastbourne Training College; and to my publishers' educational staff and advisers.

Preface to the Second Edition

ALMOST twenty-five years have passed since this anthology first appeared. During this period fifteen reprints have been called for. Now, owing to changes in taste and in the needs of education, a new and revised edition seems to be required.

The changes I have made in the contents are aimed at strengthening the representation of certain poets formerly neglected in schools and at a revision of the treatment of certain periods. More space is given to the seventeenth century, in particular to Donne and Herbert; in the eighteenth century to Blake, and in the Romantic period to Clare. In the nineteenth century two American poets appear more prominently —Whitman and Emily Dickinson, not represented at all in the first edition. Other overall changes involved giving more emphasis to certain poets of the Tudor and medieval periods, and to a few twentieth century poets, in particular Wilfred Owen, who has steadily gained prestige with younger students. To make room for additions some poems, notably long narratives, have been left out. But the general picture here offered of English poetry from its beginnings until the outbreak of World War II remains substantially unchanged, and it is to be hoped that readers who are familiar with the original edition will easily find their way about this new one.

Lewes J. R.
1972

Acknowledgements

The Editor and Publishers wish to thank the following for permission to reprint copyright material:

Mr. Cameron and Messrs. J. M. Dent & Sons Ltd., for *The Compassionate Fool*, from *The Winter House*. Mr. C. Day Lewis and Messrs. Jonathan Cape Ltd., for *It Would Be Strange*, from *Word Over All*. Mr. Edmund Blunden and Messrs. Macmillan & Co., Ltd., for *The Ballast Hole*, from *Poems 1930–1940*. Mr. Robert Graves and Messrs. Cassell & Co., for *To Lucia at Birth* and *1805*. Mr. T. S. Eliot and Messrs. Faber & Faber for *Prelude*, *Rannoch by Glencoe*, *Journey of the Magi* and *Rhapsody on a Windy Night* from *Collected Poems 1909–1962*. Mr. Arthur Waley and Messrs. Constable & Co., Ltd., for *Fighting South of the Castle*, *Burial Songs*, *On the Birth of His Son*, *The Hat Given to the Poet*, *A Love Song* and *Plucking the Rushes* from *170 Chinese Poems*. Mr. Andrew Young and Messrs. Jonathan Cape Ltd., for *The Last Snow*, from *Collected Poems*. The Executors of the late D. H. Lawrence for *Spray*, *Talk*, *Poverty*, *Bat* and *Piano*. The Executors of the late J. E. Flecker and Messrs. Martin Secker & Warburg Ltd., for *Santorin*. Messrs. Kegan Paul, Trench & Trubner & Co., Ltd., for T. E. Hulme's *Autumn* and *Above the Dock* from *Speculations*. Messrs. Macmillan & Co., Ltd., for Vachel Lindsey's *Congo* and *The Daniel Jazz* from *Collected Poems*. Mr. John Masefield and The Society of Authors for *The Blowing of the Horn*. Messrs. Jonathan Cape Ltd., and the Estate of Robert Frost for *The Rabbit Hunter*, *The Road Not Taken*, *Not To Keep*, *An Importer* and *Desert Places* from *The Poetry of Robert Frost* edited by Edward Connery Letham. Mr. Walter de la Mare and Messrs. Faber & Faber for *Farewell*. The Society of Authors and The Literary Trustees of Walter de la Mare for *By Order*, *Dry August Burned* and *Drugged*. The Executors of the late W. H. Davies and Messrs. Jonathan Cape Ltd., for *In the Country*, *The Heap of Rags* and *The Villain*, from *The Collected Poems of W. H. Davies*. Messrs. Macmillan & Co., Ltd., and M. B. Yeats for *The Hour Before Dawn*, *An Irish Airman Foresees His Death* and *The Three Monuments* from *The Collected Poems of W. B. Yeats*. The Society of Authors for A. E. Housman's *In Valleys Green and Still*, *On Wenlock Edge*, *The Winds Out of the West Land Blow* and *When I Would Muse in Boyhood*; and The Society of Authors and Messrs Jonathan Cape Ltd., for *The Chestnut casts his flambeaux*, *Others, I am not the first* and *The laws of God, the laws of man* from *Collected Poems*. The Richards Press for John Davidson's *Song*. The Executors of the late Gerard Manley Hopkins and Messrs. The Oxford University Press for *Hurrahing in Harvest*, *The Sea and the Skylark*, *Felix Randal* and *Thou Art Indeed Just, Lord*, from *The Collected Poems of Gerard Manley Hopkins*. The Trustees of the late Thomas Hardy's Estate and Messrs. Macmillan & Co., Ltd., for *Great Things*, *Old Furniture*, *Friends Beyond*, *Afterwards* and *Regret Not Me*, from *The Collected Poems of Thomas Hardy*. Messrs. Longmans Green & Co., Ltd., for William Morris's *The Burghers' Battle* and *In Prison*. The Representatives of the late Lewis Carroll and Messrs. Macmillan & Co.,

Ltd., for *Jabberwocky*. The Curator of the Peterborough Museum for John Clare's *Pleasant Sounds*. Messrs. Eyre & Spottiswoode Ltd., for extracts from *The Authorized Version of the Bible*. Messrs. The Clarendon Press for Gavin Bone's translations: *Riddle on Moon and Sun*, *The Whale*, and *The Battle of Maldon*. Lady Coghill and Mr. Nevill Coghill for *The Kerry*. Mr. Wallace Stevens and Messrs. Faber & Faber for *Disillusionment of Ten O'Clock*, from *The Collected Poems of Wallace Stevens*. Mr. Ezra Pound and Messrs. Faber & Faber for *Salutation* from *Collected Shorter Poems*. Mr. Edwin Muir and Messrs. Faber & Faber for *The Return*, from *Collected Poems 1921–1958*. Messrs. J. M. Dent & Sons and the Trustees for the Copyrights of the late Dylan Thomas for *The Force that Through the Green Fuse Drives the Flower*, from *Collected Plays of Dylan Thomas*. Mr. James Reeves and Messrs. William Heinemann Ltd., for *Thoughts and Memories*, from *Collected Poems*. Mr. G. T. Sassoon for *To Any Dead Officer* and *The Dug-out* by Siegfried Sassoon. Mr. John Crowe Ransom and Messrs. Eyre & Spottiswoode for *Old Man Playing with Children*, *Piazza Piece* and *Blue Girls*. Mr. Harold Owen and Messrs. Chatto and Windus for *Futility*, *Arms and the Boy*, *The Parable of the Old Man and the Young* and *Anthem for Doomed Youth* by Wilfred Owen from *Collected Poems of Wilfred Owen*. Messrs. A. D. Peters for *Report on Experience* by Edmund Blunden.

Introduction

This book contains some of the best poems written in English from the time of the Saxons to the present day, a period of over 1000 years. The oldest poems in the book were, in fact, written not in modern English but in Anglo-Saxon, and so have had to be given in translation. The poems are arranged in chronological order according to when their authors were born, so that if you wish you can study the historical development of English poetry, and connect particular poets or poems with the corresponding periods in history. But this is important only in so far as it helps you to understand and appreciate the poems themselves; and that is the first thing you should try to do.

What poetry is

The enjoyment you can get from a poem at first or second reading is well worth having. You will probably find little difficulty in appreciating straight away such poems as *The Big Rock Candy Mountains* (p. 24). But the enjoyment you gain from having to work at a poem, to think about it, to puzzle out its meaning, is something much greater, and you will value it for having had to work for it. Andrew Marvell's *The Garden* (p. 115), for example, takes a good deal of understanding, but it is worth it. I do not mean to say that a difficult poem is always better than an easy one; I mean simply that you should not expect the reading of poetry to be easy; if you want to get all you can from it, you should be prepared to think hard when occasion demands. In this introduction I want to suggest some ways of thinking about poetry. But first let us consider the more general questions of what poetry is, and why people write and read it.

One of the universal instincts of all mankind is to make things. Another instinct is that of curiosity, the urge to find out about things. Animals do not seem to possess them in any marked degree, though it is true that birds build nest and cats are noted for curiosity. But if you watch any young child at play, you will see at once that these two instincts are the life and soul of much human activity. Some things that men make are for use and some for decoration, ornament, pleasure—call it what you like. It is a mistake to distinguish too sharply between these two sorts of creation. If a thing is useful it can give pleasure both to the maker and to the user, and if it is beautiful it can also be useful. A poem is a creation, something man makes. If a poem gives pleasure to the maker and also to the reader, there is no point in asking whether it is useful. Pictures and songs are some of the things that men make chiefly to give beauty to life. Poems are another. Pictures are made of shapes and colours, and music is made of sounds. What are poems made of?

The raw material of poetry

The obvious answer is that poems are made of words. But words also have a special use of their own, outside poetry. Words, unlike shapes, colours and sounds, express meanings; they express all the possible experiences and ideas which can occur to our minds—things, people, places, feelings, actions and processes. Words are the means by which we think about everything in life and about life itself. Although we may say, then, that poems are made of words, it is really truer to say that they are made of life.

Now what is the life of an ordinary human being? It is a

mass of actions, processes, sensations and emotions, some of them dull and mechanical, some of them exciting and—at least to the individual himself—important. Poetry is concerned especially with the exciting and important things. There are plenty of poems about trivial experiences, but on the whole these are not the ones that are longest remembered. Danger and disaster happen in most people's lives; love and anger are emotions we all feel; we are all capable of jealousy, joy, amusement, hunger and thirst, fear and reverence; most of us can be excited by murder, war and heroism; death may come to anyone we love and will come, we know, to ourselves. These are some of the experiences which poetry is made of. They are its raw material. We are always moved by them, and the instinct of curiosity leads us to want to know more about them as they affect other people. It is the poet's business to put all this material in such a form that it will be accessible to every one who is interested.

If you consider the nature of some of the things in life that move us—love, human beauty or the beauty of nature, courage and disaster—you will realise that they have one thing in common. They all pass away. In themselves they do not last. Because they move or excite us, we wish to make them last. We wish to make something permanent out of them. A poet is someone unusually aware of his emotions and perhaps unusually sensitive to feeling of all kinds, so that he feels most strongly the desire to communicate them to others. He is also especially conscious of their impermanence and so especially anxious to make something memorable out of them, in order that they shall not be lost to the world. Shakespeare, for example, in his sonnet *Shall I Compare Thee to a Summer's Day?* (p. 62), tells how the beauty of his lover will fade but will long be remembered in his poems. A proud boast, but as it happens, true.

Not only are our experiences in themselves impermanent, they are also private and individual. When we have a particularly valuable or exciting experience, or an unusually strong emotion, we feel a desire to tell people about it, to share it with others. A child says 'Look!' whenever anything pleases it. A poem is often nothing more than a more elaborate and interesting form of the child's exclamation. Not all of us are poets; that is, not all of us have the desire, the gift and the training to turn our experiences into poems. But we can all, if we will, train ourselves to read poems. We can appreciate and enjoy what poets have made of the emotions we feel. Poetry can in this way give us the sense of sharing our experiences, and can help us, if the experience is painful, to bear it more easily. Poetry makes us feel less alone in the world. It is the voice of all people. Let me quote one small example. Many of us must at some time have had a sense of being misunderstood and unappreciated; we have done our best and nobody is grateful. Now Shakespeare made this feeling of *man's ingratitude* into a song beginning *Blow, Blow, Thou Winter Wind* (p. 58), and if we know and love Shakespeare's poems, we shall often have a comforting sense, when some particular feeling depresses or exalts us, that he knew all about it. By knowing the best poems we make them part of our own lives and we make our lives richer and more full of meaning.

Worlds of the imagination

We have been considering why poems are made; before we begin thinking about how they are made, there is one other aspect of the poet's raw material which ought to be mentioned specially. Small children are curious about the small world in which they live. They explore the kitchen shelves, their mothers' work-baskets and dressing-tables, the cupboard under the stairs. As we get older, we begin to explore—in imagination—the world outside our own immediate surroundings: fairyland, King Arthur's Britain, the countries visited by Ulysses and Jason, Sherwood Forest, the scenes of ancient civilisations—Babylon and Tartary, the world under the sea, Heaven, Hell, the Garden of Eden, the whole shadowy region inhabited by ghosts and spirits, heroes and demons, witches and monsters. Some of these names may make you smile now, but they represent places real enough to most people at some time in their lives or at some stages in history. These worlds of romance, or of the imagination, are the attempts that men have made to realise the unknown tracts of experience which lie beyond our familiar world; they are attempts to explore the mysteries outside what men know of time and space. They may also satisfy a desire to create an ideal order of existence, in which the difficulties and perplexities of real life are straightened out. These are, especially, the poet's worlds. Poetry, then, can take us outside the familiar round of everyday experience. If you wish to know something of these worlds of pure imagination, read *The Wife of Usher's Well* (p. 2), *The Daemon Lover* (p. 12), the extract from *Paradise Lost* (p. 105), *Kubla Khan* (p. 177), and *The Forsaken Merman* (p. 239).

Poetic methods

Poetic technique—the methods by which poems are written and the devices used by poets to get their effects—this is something which should not be thought of as separate from the subject-matter of poetry. Yet in practice we sometimes have to talk about poetic method as if it were distinct from subject-matter. For example, we speak of metre, rhythm and rhyme, we speak of 'the sonnet form' or 'the ballad', as if they existed apart from the actual words of actual poems. But a poem is a creation, it is something made. The form and the subject-matter grow together in the poet's mind. It would be absurd to imagine Nature saying to itself, 'I will create a buttercup', and then saying, 'Now what shall it be like? How shall I make it?' You cannot, in other words, think of a flower apart from the form of the flower (though for the purposes of science you may dissect the flower and label each part). So it is with a poem. The ballad of *Sir Patrick Spens*, for example, is not only the story of Sir Patrick Spens, it is also a certain form of words. It is important to remember this, because people sometimes make the mistake of thinking that a poem is written simply to tell a story or express a thought. Then they naturally go on to ask why a poet should take all the trouble to 'turn the story into a poem', to put it in metre and make the words rhyme. In the end they come to regard poetry as a rather silly activity—they have no time for it, they can't be bothered with it. Thus they have missed the whole point of it. Other people miss the point by concealing too much on form; they think that when they have described the metre and worked out the rhyme-scheme and given names to the various figures of speech used in a poem, they have really said something about it. Thus poetic appreciation becomes a mere mechanical routine, and others would be justified in wondering why anybody bothered about it. When you think of *Sir Patrick Spens*, do not think of just the story, exciting though it is, and do not think of just the form; think of both together —that is, think of the words themselves:

The king sits in Dunfermline town
Drinking the blude-red wine.

If you have grasped this point, then it will do no harm to discuss the poetic and poetic form as if they existed apart from poems. One of the chief aims of studying poems is to understand why they are just as they are and not otherwise. When thinking about a poem, then, ask yourself 'Why did he write just those words, just like that?' In this way you can add immensely to your enjoyment of poetry.

The making of a ballad

At this point it will be well to examine a particular poem and discuss its form and technique. Let us consider the ballad *Edward* (p. 4). The story, briefly summarised, is this. A mother (we are not told her name) has a husband and a married son with children of his own. She appears to be ambitious for her son and indifferent about her husband, for she persuades her son (unlike her, he is a weak-willed person) to murder his father, probably for the sake of his property, in particular his castle or mansion. When the murder is done, the mother asks her son what he is going to do for himself, his wife and children, and—lastly—for her, his mother. The son is already bitter and full of remorse, and he tells her that he himself is going to run away overseas, his wife and children can beg and starve, and as for his mother—she can go to hell with his curse upon her.

This is a sordid and shocking story, not unlike many that you can find in newspapers, particularly the more sensational ones. But it is not the story that makes the poem, it is the poet's handling of the story. If you read of a tragedy like that in the papers, in commonplace newspaper language, even though heightened by some of the devices of journalese, you will not remember it very long; and if you read much of that sort of thing, you will not even be very impressed by it; nor will you have gained what you can gain from the poem and what countless readers have gained during the hundreds of years since the poem was first created—a profounder sense of the horror of human wickedness, the vanity of unlawful ambition, the bitterness of remorse for a crime which cannot be undone, and the awfulness of violating family ties which should be sacred. All that is in the ballad of *Edward*—not in the story, but in the poem as we have it. How has the poet used the story? How has he turned it into a poem?

The first thing to notice is that the poet does not *tell* the story at all; he composes a dialogue between mother and son, supposed to take place at a very important point in the story, the point where the son returns home with his sword still stained by his father's blood. The effect of this dialogue-form is to compress the story and cut out all unnecessary description. It makes the poem dramatic. Another highly dramatic effect is produced by keeping the first event in the story to the very end—that is, the advice given to Edward by his mother. The last line thus comes as a surprise. 'Sic counsels ye gave to me, O!' By keeping this information to the end, the poet is able to hold us in suspense. Why did Edward kill his 'father dear'? Why is he so bitter now? Why does he solemnly curse his mother and consign her to hell? All these uncertainties are resolved in the last line, and not till then.

The next thing to notice is that, although the poem is very compressed and gives no unnecessary details, there is nevertheless much repetition. What is the object of this? Why does the poet treat his dialogue in this way? Would the poem have been better without the repetitions? The effect of the repetitions is twofold. First, they slow down the poem and so add to the suspense. Secondly, they intensify or emphasise the various points in the dialogue. There is no possibility that any reader shall miss any of them. (I should say 'any *listener*', for undoubtedly this poem was meant to be sung or spoken aloud. You will not get the full effect of it unless you hear it. It is a good plan to read it in chorus, one group speaking the mother's words and the other Edward's.) Repetition is one of the most powerful means of securing emphasis and compelling attention—especially deliberate, rhythmical repetition. (This fact is of course well understood by composers of music; listen, for example, to the fourth movement of Beethoven's Fifth Symphony or Grieg's *In the Hall of the Mountain Kings*.) Another poem in this book which shows the effect of repetition most clearly is *A Lyke-Wake Dirge* (p. 1), which also should be read aloud, if possible in chorus. If you read and appreciate

Edward in the light of these suggestions, you will understand something of the way in which this unforgettable poem enlarges our experience of life. We must now go on to some more general questions of poetic form and technique.

Rhythm, rhyme and alliteration

When a poet writes a poem, he is saying something more important than the things said in everyday life. He wishes to make his poem memorable. He wishes to make his words striking, so as to impress the reader with the intensity of his own experience. One method of doing this is to write in a dramatic way, as we have seen, and another is rhythmic repetition. Now rhythm is, in itself, a form of repetition—the repetition of a particular pattern of light and heavy syllables. In
∪ / ∪ / ∪ / ∪ /
the line 'In Xanadu did Kubla Khan' you have first a light syllable 'in', then a heavy one 'Xan-', and this arrangement is repeated four times in all; the line has four stresses. There is another sound-pattern in this line, a rather subtle one; for notice that the vowel-sounds of the first two heavy syllables 'xAn' and 'dU' are repeated in reverse order in the last two heavy syllables 'kU' and 'khAn'. (Note that 'Khan' was pronounced by the writer of this poem to rhyme with 'ran' and 'man'.) Another form of repetition which is often found in poems is the choice of words beginning with the same letter (called alliteration).

In Xanadu did *K*hubla *K*han
  A stately pleasure *D*ome *D*ecree,
Where Alph, the sacred *R*iver, *R*an
Through caverns *M*easureless to *M*an
  Down to a *S*unless *S*ea.

Notice how there is one alliteration in each line. I do not know whether this was deliberate on the part of the writer; I think it is more likely to have been an unconscious part of the creative process as carried out by a poet with an abnormally sensitive ear. Another obvious form of repetition is what is called rhyme. 'Decree' rhymes with 'sea', and 'Khan' rhymes with 'ran' and 'man'. The rhymes of a good poet seem to arise naturally out of what he is saying in his poem. Examples of rhyme well used may be found in descriptions of *Achitophel* by Dryden (p. 125) and *Sporus* by Pope (p. 136). An example of a word very unsuitably used for the sake of the rhyme is found in the lines by an unknown poet on the death of Queen Victoria:

> Dust to dust, and ashes to ashes,
> Into the tomb the Great Queen dashes.

It is the same with alliteration. Where it seems to come naturally, and strengthens the atmosphere of the poem, it is a useful and legitimate device. Further on in *Kubla Khan* Coleridge describes the river as

> Five miles meandering with a mazy motion.

Here the repetition of the letter 'm' gives the line a slow, murmuring tone, and this reinforces the description. But a later poet, Swinburne, allowed himself to be carried away by this device; he often used words solely for the alliterative effect, with little regard for their meaning. Recognising this fault in his own work, he wrote an exaggerated imitation of it, a parody of himself at his worst. Here are the first two lines of *Nephelidia*:

> From the depth of the dreamy decline of the dawn through
> a notable nimbus of nebulous noonshine,
> Pallid and pink as the palm of the flag-flower that flickers
> with fear of the flies as they float . . .

This is the sort of thing that happens when a poet sacrifices meaning and surrenders himself to the 'music' of language!

On the other hand, in old English alliteration was the chief formal device used by poets, and many continued to write this form of verse right on until the fifteenth century. In the old alliterative verse there were no rhymes, there were four stresses in a line, and each line contained (as a rule) three words beginning with the same letter. There is no doubt that long after this form fell into disuse, the memory of it was very strong in English poetry: (e.g. Spenser's *When Flowered My Joyful Spring*, p. 50). The following is an example of alliterative verse from William Langland's *Piers the Plowman*, written in the fourteenth century. Some of the language of the original is obsolete and has here been modernised, but the rhythm and alliteration have been preserved.

GLUTTON AT THE TAVERN

Then goeth Glutton in, and great oaths after;
Cis the Shoemaker sat on the bench,
Wat the Warrener and his wife too,
Tim and Tinker and twain of his prentice,
Hick the Hackney-man[1] and Hugh the Needler,[2]
Clarice of Cock's Lane and the clerk of the church,
Davie the Ditcher and a dozen others,
Sir Piers of Pridie and Peronelle of Flanders,
A ribibour,[3] a rat-catcher, a raker[4] of Cheap,
A roper[5], a riding-man, and Rose who sold dishes,
Godfrey of Garlickhithe and Griffin the Welshman. . . .
There was laughing and louring[6] and 'Let go the cup!'
They sat so till evensong and sang for a while,
Till Glutton had guzzled a gallon and a gill.
He might neither step nor stand till he his staff had;
Then began he to go, like a gleeman's bitch,[7]
Sometimes sideways and sometimes backwards,

[1] hirer of horses [2] needle-seller [3] fiddler [4] scavenger
[5] rope-maker [6] scowling [7] blind street-singer's dog

As one who lays lines to catch little birds.
When he drew near the doorway his eyes grew dim;
He stumbled on the threshold and sank to the floor,
Clement the Cobbler caught him by the middle
For to lift him aloft and laid him on his knees
With all the woe in the world his wife and his wench
Bore him home to his bed and brought him therein,
And after his excess he had a fit of sloth;
He slept Saturday and Sunday till the sun went to rest.
Then woke he from his winking and wiped his eyes,
And the first word he uttered was 'Where is my breakfast?'

Now all these forms of repetition are practised by poets because they know that the human mind is naturally delighted by repetition; and what delights us is the more easily remembered. But do not forget that a poet uses the 'musical' qualities of language not only because we enjoy them; he uses them to help to get us into a state of mind in which we can the more readily grasp and appreciate the poem as a whole. A good poem consists of more than just pretty sounds. We must aim at appreciating the connection between the 'music' of a poem and its meaning.

Rhythm and metre

Before going on to consider some other aspects of poetic technique, there are a few more things to be said about rhythm. Rhythm is so fundamental to life and so universal in its appeal that it is far the most important element in the 'musical' part of poetic form. Rhythm in general means the alternation of periods of effort with periods of relaxation. The breaking of waves on the shore is rhythmical, so is the noise of a motor-engine; so are our breathing and our heart-beats. Dancing is rhythmical motion, music is rhythmical sound. A poet uses different rhythms to express different moods. He uses a long line and a slow rhythm to express a thoughtful and studious mood; for example, the sonnet *The World Is Too Much With Us* (p. 173). He uses a light, tripping rhythm to express a feeling of gaiety. In the line 'Merrily, merrily, shall I live now' there are two light syllables to each heavy one, and even the heavy ones are not very heavy; moreover, combined with this airy rhythm there are a number of light consonants (*m*, *r* and *l*) which slip easily from the lips and tongue; again, 'merrily' itself (twice repeated) is one of the merriest-sounding words imaginable, so that the whole line is the very essence of gaiety. It is spoken, remember, by Ariel (in *The Tempest*) who is the spirit of air.

The regular, mechanical pattern which underlies rhythm is called metre, and metres are given various names according to the number and position of the light and heavy syllables.

The chief metrical patterns in English poetry are:

(1) *Iambic*, consisting of a succession of iambuses, an iambus being one light syllable followed by one heavy one (e.g. again, at home). The metre of

Ĭn Xán|ădú | dĭd Kúb|lă Khán

is iambic, the line consisting of four iambuses.

(2) *Trochaic*, consisting of a succession of trochees, a trochee being one heavy syllable followed by one light one (e.g. gaily, sporting). The metre of

Quéen ănd | húntrĕss | cháste ănd | fáir

is trochaic, the line consisting of three trochees followed by a monosyllable.

(3) *Dactylic*, consisting of a succession of dactyls, a dactyl

being one heavy syllable followed by two light ones (e.g. merrily, certainly). The metre of

> Merrily, | merrily | shall I live | now

is dactylic, the line consisting of three dactyls followed by a monosyllable.

(4) *Anapaestic*, consisting of a succession of anapaests, an anapaest being two light syllables followed by one heavy one (e.g. a retreat, in a house). The metre of

> And the whis|pering sound | of the cool | colonnade|

is anapaestic, the line consisting of four anapaests.

These examples are simple, and show each metre used more or less regularly. But they are often used quite irregularly. Clare's *Autumn* (p. 207), for instance, is written in the anapaestic metre, but it contains no single line which is perfectly regular. Sometimes, too, there is a special advantage in varying the pattern. Dryden's *Song for St. Cecilia's Day* (p. 123) is a skilful combination of several different metres, each expressing a particular mood.

Metre, then, is a regular, mechanical pattern. The poet knows that just as this can give pleasure, so also it can become boring if it is too regular. So he varies the regular pattern, and this varied metre, which we call rhythm, is one of the chief sources of pleasure in poetry. There is no room here to go into all the kinds of variation possible. But notice the last line of the short passage from *Kubla Khan* quoted on p. xxxv. In 'Down to a sunless sea' the accent would normally fall on the second word 'to', but actually it falls on the first word 'down'. To make the first accent of an iambic line fall on the first syllable instead of the second is one of the commonest methods of varying the metre.

Free verse

But there is also poetry which has no metre at all, and which is still rhythmical. This is called 'free verse'. It is very commonly used by modern poets (e.g. in the Chinese translations of Arthur Waley, pp. 314–317), but it can also be recognised in the Authorised Version of the Bible (pp. 80–87). Just as the rhythm of a metrical poem can be compared to that of a motor-engine or a beating heart, so the rhythm of free verse is like that if the wind in the trees or the falling of a stream over stones. If you listen to either of these, you will hear a sort of rhythm—an irregular recurrence of louder and softer sounds; similarly you will hear an irregular rhythm if you listen to a person talking in a room where you cannot hear his actual words. This uneven rise and fall may be called 'speech-rhythm'; and it is the rhythms of ordinary speech which modern writers of free verse, such as D. H. Lawrence (pp. 298–302), have used. What are the advantages of this sort of technique, and what are the disadvantages? I will not try to answer this question here, but I suggest that you read some of the passages from the Bible (pp. 80–87), Clare's *Pleasant Sounds* (p. 206), Whitman's *Animals* (p. 231), Arnold's *The Gods Are Happy* (p. 237), Masefield's *The Blowing of the Horn* (p. 289) and some of the poems by Hulme, Lawrence, Waley and Eliot (pp. 297, 298–302, 314–317, 306–311)—then try to answer the question for yourself. I suggest, too, that you try to write some original poems in free verse; you will find you are able to concentrate on saying exactly what you want to without being tied down to a particular metre or rhyme-scheme.

Diction and imagery

We have said something of the story or idea behind a poem; we have considered metre and rhythm, and we have mentioned rhyme and alliteration. The other important aspects of the technique of poetry are summed up by the words 'diction' and 'imagery'. Diction means a poet's vocabulary or choice of words, considered for their meaning and associations as distinct from their sound-qualities. You would say that Whitman's or Lawrence's diction was on the whole familiar and conversational; that Spenser's was often archaic or old-fashioned; that Milton's was learned and scholarly, Pope's and Gray's often high-flown and artificial; Wordsworth aimed at simplicity, and Hopkins at originality. Nothing is more characteristic of a poet than his diction. The poems of Keats abound in words expressing vivid colours and attractive tastes and sounds; those of Shelley in words suggesting speed and light.

As a rule, however, poets do not think of words singly; they think of, and choose them, as part of a group of words expressing a thought or an image. An image is a picture called up in the mind by a group of words. In discussing poetry, we may extend the term to include, not only pictures, but also sounds and other sense-impressions. Notice that an image is not a thing, nor is it the words used to denote the thing, it is the consciousness of the thing called up in the mind of the reader by the words. For example, in Shirley's *The Glories of our Blood and State* (p. 104), there is a line

Death lays his icy hand on kings.

We call the words 'icy hand' an image, but the image is really the picture or the feeling of a cold, white, thin hand which your mind receives when you read the words. Perhaps you picture Death as a bent, bony figure clutching the shoulder of a king dressed in his royal robes and sitting on his throne of state. The 'meaning' of the line is that even people as high and mighty as kings have to die in time just like anybody else. But how vividly the poet is able to convey this thought to you by means of his imagery! Notice, too, that the word 'icy' is in itself almost an image, and much more vivid than 'cold' or 'chilly' would be. Good poems always contain fresh or striking imagery, not stale or commonplace imagery that makes no impression on your mind. When D. H. Lawrence in his poem *Bat* (p. 300) wanted to create in the mind of the reader a striking picture of the bats as he saw them at evening in Florence, he used a series of original images which force you to see them as vividly as he saw them: 'serrated wings against the sky', 'a black glove thrown up against the light', 'bits of umbrella', 'an old rag'.

Another modern poet, T. E. Hulme, wrote a series of very short poems made up of nothing but images. He did not try to express a thought or an idea, in the ordinary sense; he simply aimed at producing unforgettable images. Read his poem *Autumn* (p. 297), which has only seven short lines. There is little but the two images, in which the large, low harvest moon is compared to a red-faced farmer looking over a hedge, and the stars are compared to the white faces of town children. 'Well, what is there in that?' you may ask. The answer is that Hulme did not wish to express any thoughts or ideas about autumn, he wanted to convey as directly and economically as he could the *feeling* of a particular autumn night; if you think about the poem, and about a similar autumn scene in the country as you may have noticed it yourself, you will realise that it is a *true* picture, and a striking one because it makes you think of nature in an entirely new way. You will recognise that the contrast between the healthy, red-faced country farmer and the pale town children gives a very clear impression of the difference between the warm, homely harvest moon and the pale, far-away stars. Hulme seems to be saying to us, 'If you too look at nature in this fresh and original way, you will gain new and valuable experience; you will see things in a new way, and that will make life more interesting and exciting.' And all this in seven lines! Hulme had a poet's eyes, and you have them too if you choose to open them.

The ways in which different poets employ imagery is one of the most interesting things in the study of poetry. A poet such as Hulme or John Clare, who wrote mainly descriptive poems (see pp. 297, 206, 207), used imagery more or less for its own sake, with the object of conveying to the reader their impressions of nature. But poets may also use imagery in two other ways: in what we might call a *symbolic* way, to express a truth without stating it directly; and in a decorative or *illustrative* way, to make a story or a thought more striking. As an example of the symbolic use of imagery, read Blake's poem *The Sword and the Sickle* (p. 156). Here the sword stands for war and strife and the 'barren heath' for the wastefulness and death which strife produces; the sickle and 'the fruitful field' stand for productive labour, life and growth; and when Blake says that the sword could not make the sickle yield, he means that however hard war tries to overcome life, life is in the end victorious. A prose statement of this idea might be merely commonplace, but Blake's poem remains in our memory and impresses our imagination. The images of the sword and the sickle give the thought dignity and nobility. Blake cannot *prove* that life will be triumphant over death, but he can express his conviction, as a poet and a prophet, that ultimately it will be so.

An example of the illustrative or decorative use of imagery is Skelton's poem *Though ye suppose all jeopardies are passed* (p. 40). Here he states more or less straightforwardly that danger is never past and that you may always have a stroke of ill-luck; then he illustrates this idea with the image of the sore festering under the skin and liable to break out at any moment, and the image of the 'lizard' (by which he means a poisonous snake) lurking in the grass and able to dart out and bite you when you least expect it. The poem is a warning against complacency, against taking things too easily, and the images bring home this meaning in a way in which mere statement would not.

Understanding poetry

Poetry is concerned with the beauty of the world, and with truth about life, and with the splendour of man's imagination. Truth, beauty and imagination are inexhaustible and many-sided. There are many kinds of poem; indeed, every good poem has a separate beauty and truth of its own, and it is the object of poetic appreciation to recognise and value these qualities, which thereby enrich our own lives. It is not enough to ask 'What does a poem *say*?' We must also ask what the poem *is*: is it vital, true, memorable, beautiful, moving? If it is some of these things, it is good; if it is all of them, it is very good indeed. When we have read and thought about a poem, we should then ask ourselves: Does it add to our experience of life? Has it made us think or feel more deeply? Is it worth knowing well, or shall I be content to forget it? The answers to these questions will depend, of course, mainly on the merit of the poem, but partly on the understanding we have brought to it. We ought not to throw aside a poem until we are quite sure we have got all there is to be got out of it. Sometimes it is difficult to know how to begin thinking about a poem. A good way is to ask ourselves, What was the poet trying to do? What is the purpose of the poem?

To test this method and see how it helps, let us consider from this point of view one more short poem, a very well known one, Shakespeare's song *Full Fathom Five* (p. 60). A casual reading will make us feel that here is, at any rate, a very melodious and rather dreamy poem, full of beautiful diction and imagery and a suggestion of the 'rich and strange' world under the sea. We shall notice the muffled alliteration of 'Full Fathom Five thy Father lies' and the half-rhyme 'five' and 'lies'; we shall appreciate the change of rhythm at the line 'But doth suffer a sea-change', and the unearthly beauty of the submerged bell rung by the sea-nymphs. We may acknowledge that no poet was ever more master than Shakespeare of the music of words and the magic of their associations. But there is more than this in *Full Fathom Five*, which is not merely music and painting, but drama as well. It is in the dramatic purpose of the poem that its poetic depth lies. For in Shakespeare's play *The Tempest* this song is sung by Ariel to the young man Ferdinand shortly after he has been wrecked on an island. Ferdinand has been grieving for his father, who he fears is lost in the wreck. His father is in fact alive, but Shakespeare does not want Ferdinand to find him till later on in the play; nor does he want him to spend time looking for his father, because the next thing Ferdinand has to do is to meet and fall in love with Miranda. Accordingly Ariel, a spirit of the island, sings a song to Ferdinand, partly to make him follow the music and so be led towards Miranda, and partly to convince him his father is drowned. 'Full fathom five thy father lies'. So one thing to notice about Ariel's song is that beautiful though it is, it is a lie. But it is a lie with a purpose. Now it is all very well to persuade Ferdinand that his father is drowned, so that it is useless to go searching for him: will not Ferdinand be so shocked and grieved that he will be in no frame of mind to fall in love with Miranda, however charming and attractive she may be? So Ariel has not only to tell the young man his father is dead, he must at the same time soften the shock and calm his grief. This is where Shakespeare's artistry comes in. This is the dramatic reason for the beauty of the music and the imagery. The drowned father is not a horrible corpse floating about on the sea, perhaps to be washed up later; he is five full fathoms down and transformed into something rich and beautiful over which the sea-nymphs ring the passing bell. In this way Ferdinand's mind is distracted from his loss, and his grief is calmed as he thinks of the images of fantastic and unearthly beauty of which Ariel sings.

The history of English poetry is something quite different from the poetry itself; and as I said earlier, it is something which no reader need trouble about until he has some knowledge and appreciation of the individual poems and poets. At the same time the development of poetic technique is a fascinating subject, and there is enough material in this book for you to be able at least to make a start with it. One feature of the history of poetry is not very difficult to study, and that is the way in which poets have continually gone back to the past in search of ideas. The way in which science progresses is, generally speaking, by building on and then rejecting the ideas of the past; but no discovery in poetry is ever really out of date. Poetry often progresses by looking backwards, and carrying on some tradition from the older poets which has for a time been forgotten. Thus towards the end of the eighteenth century the poets of what is called the Romantic Movement, Wordsworth and Coleridge, became interested in the old ballads and imitated them, partly to get away from the way of writing poetry which had been common since the time of Dryden and Pope three-quarters of a century before. Notice how Coleridge in *The Rime of the Ancient Mariner* (p. 179) and Keats in *La Belle Dame sans Merci* (p. 212) copied some of the features of the old ballads; notice how Gerard Manley Hopkins (pp. 263–267), a poet of the Victorian period, to some extent revived a kind of diction that had not been in use since the time of the Anglo-Saxon poets; and notice how Walt Whitman, a nineteenth-century American, was influenced by some of the rhythms of the Bible, and in turn influenced modern writers of free verse, such as D. H. Lawrence. Poetry is a living tradition, not a mere inheritance of dead museum-pieces, and the poems of the past are a source of continual inspiration to the poets of more recent times.

As has been said earlier, the raw material of poetry is life itself, and as life is infinitely varied, so poetry is of many different kinds. This book gives you a small part of the great wealth which English poetry offers. You will not be able to enjoy fully any great part of that wealth unless you are ready to take trouble. You must know poetry well and think about it much. I have tried to suggest some of the ways in which you may begin to think about poetry; but neither I nor any other teacher or writer can do the work of appreciation for you. It is by your own efforts that you will best learn how to appreciate and enjoy poetry. Poetry can be compared to the view from the top of a mountain. The view is the same whether you climb the mountain on foot or whether you are carried up on a mountain-railway. But your enjoyment of the prospect will be infinitely greater if it comes as the reward of effort. So do not fight shy of poems which look difficult. They may prove to be the most rewarding in the end.

One point more: no study is complete unless the student himself practices, however little and however unsuccessfully, the subject he is studying. You do not study woodwork or cookery in a purely theoretical way; you study science in the laboratory as well as the classroom. You draw and paint, you do not merely study pictures by great artists. So try to write poems yourself, not only because you will in this way add to your enjoyment and understanding of poetry, but you may also help to shape the future of English poetry.

Anonymous

A Lyke-Wake Dirge

THIS ae nighte, this ae nighte,
—Every nighte and alle,
Fire and fleet and candle-lighte,
And Christe receive thy saule.

When thou from hence away art past,
—Every nighte and alle,
To Whinny-muir thou com'st at last;
And Christe receive thy saule.

If ever thou gavest hosen and shoon,
—Every nighte and alle,
Sit thee down and put them on;
And Christe receive thy saule.

If hosen and shoon thou ne'er gav'st nane
—Every nighte and alle,
The whinnies[1] sall prick thee to the bare bane;
And Christe receive thy saule.

From Whinny-muir when thou may'st pass,
—Every nighte and alle,
To Brig o' Dread thou com'st at last;
And Christe receive thy saule.

[1] gorse

If ever thou gavest meat or drink,
—Every nighte and alle,
The fire sall never make thee shrink;
And Christe receive thy saule.

If meat or drink thou ne'er gav'st nane,
—Every nighte and alle,
The fire will burn thee to the bare bane;
And Christe receive thy saule.

This ae nighte, this ae nighte,
—Every nighte and alle,
Fire and fleet and candle-lighte,
And Christe receive thy saule.

The Wife of Usher's Well

THERE lived a wife at Usher's Well,
And a wealthy wife was she;
She had three stout and stalwart sons,
And sent them o'er the sea.

They hadna been a week from her,
A week but barely ane,
When word came to the carlin[1] wife,
That her three sons were gane.

They hadna been a week from her,
A week but barely three,
When word came to the carlin wife,
That her sons she'd never see.

[1] old

'I wish the wind may never cease,
Nor fashes[1] in the flood,
Till my three sons come hame to me,
In earthly flesh and blood!'

It fell about the Martinmas,
When nights are lang and mirk,
The carlin wife's three sons came hame,
And their hats were o' the birk.[2]

It neither grew in dyke nor ditch,
Nor yet in ony sheugh[3];
But at the gates o' Paradise,
That birk grew fair eneugh.

. . . .

'Blow up the fire, my maidens,
Bring water from the well!
For a' my house shall feast this night,
Since my three sons are well.'

And she has made to them a bed,
She's made it large and wide;
And she's ta'en her mantle her about,
Sat down at the bedside.

. . . .

Up then crew the red red cock,
And up and crew the gray;
The eldest to the youngest said,
''Tis time we were away.'

[1] troubles [2] birch [3] trench

The cock he hadna craw'd but once,
  And clapp'd his wings at a',
When the youngest to the eldest said,
  'Brother, we must awa.

The cock doth craw, the day doth daw,
  The channerin'[1] worm doth chide;
Gin we be mist out o' our place,
  A sair pain we maun bide.

'Fare ye weel, my mother dear!
  Fareweel to barn and byre!
And fare ye weel, the bonny lass,
  That kindles my mother's fire.'

. . . .

Edward

'WHY does your brand sae drop wi' blude,
    Edward, Edward?
Why does your brand sae drop wi' blude,
  And why sae sad gang ye, O?'—
'O I hae kill'd my hawk sae gude,
    Mither, mither;
O I hae kill'd my hawk sae gude,
  And I had nae mair but he, O.'

'Your hawk's blude was never sae red,
    Edward, Edward;
Your hawk's blude was never sae red,
  My dear son, I tell thee, O.'—

[1] fretting

'O I hae kill'd my red-roan steed,
Mither, mither;
O I hae kill'd my red-roan steed,
That erst was sae fair and free, O.'

'Your steed was auld, and ye hae got mair,
Edward, Edward;
Your steed was auld, and ye hae got mair;
Some other dule ye dree,[1] O.'
'O I hae kill'd my father dear,
Mither, mither;
O I hae kill'd my father dear,
Alas, and wae is me, O!'

'And whatten penance will ye dree[1] for that,
Edward, Edward?
Whatten penance will ye dree for that?
My dear son, now tell me, O.'—
'I'll set my feet in yonder boat.
Mither, mither;
I'll set my feet in yonder boat,
And I'll fare over the sea, O.'

'And what will ye do wi' your tow'rs and your ha',
Edward, Edward?
And what will ye do wi' your tow'rs and your ha',
That were sae fair to see, O?'—
'I'll let them stand till they doun fa',
Mither, mither;
I'll let them stand till they doun fa',
For here never mair maun I be, O.'

[1] undergo

'And what will ye leave to your bairns and your wife,
Edward, Edward?
And what will ye leave to your bairns and your wife,
When ye gang owre the sea, O?'—
'The warld's room: let them beg through life,
Mither, mither;
The warld's room: let them beg through life;
For them never mair will I see, O.'

'And what will ye leave to your ain mither dear,
Edward, Edward?
And what will ye leave to your ain mither dear,
My dear son, now tell me, O?'—
'The curse of hell frae me sall ye bear,
Mither, mither;
The curse of hell frae me sall ye bear:
Sic counsels ye gave to me, O!'

The Twa Corbies

As I was walking all alane
I heard twa corbies making a mane:[1]
The tane unto the tother say,
'Whar sall we gang and dine to-day?'

'In behint yon auld fail-dyke,
I wot there lies a new-slain knight;
And naebody kens that he lies there
But his hawk, his hound, and his lady fair.

[1] moan

'His hound is to the hunting gane,
His hawk to fetch the wild-fowl hame,
His lady's ta'en anither mate,
So we may mak our dinner sweet.

'Ye'll sit on his white hause-bane,[1]
And I'll pike out his bonnie blue e'en;
Wi' ae lock o' his gowden hair
We'll theek[2] our nest when it grows bare.

'Mony a one for him maks mane,
But nane sall ken whar he is gane;
O'er his white banes, when they are bare,
The wind sall blow for evermair.'

Sir Patrick Spens

THE king sits in Dunfermline town
  Drinking the blude-red wine,
'O whare will I get a skeely[3] skipper
  To sail this new ship o' mine?'

O up and spak an eldern knight,
  Sat at the king's right knee;
'Sir Patrick Spens is the best sailor
  That ever sailed the sea.'

Our king has written a braid[4] letter,
  And seal'd it with his hand,
And sent it to Sir Patrick Spens,
  Was walking on the strand.

[1] neck-bone [2] thatch [3] skilful [4] broad, plain

The first word that Sir Patrick read
  So loud, loud laugh'd he;
The next word that Sir Patrick read
  The tear blinded his e'e.

'O wha is this has done this deed
  And tauld the king o' me,
To send us out, at this time o' year,
  To sail upon the sea?

'Be it wind, be it weet, be it hail, be it sleet,
  Our ship must sail the faem;
The king's daughter o' Noroway,
  'Tis we must fetch her hame.'

They hadna been a week, a week,
  In Noroway but twae,
When that the lords o' Noroway
  Began aloud to say:

'Ye Scottish men spend a' our king's gowd,
  And a' our queenis fee.'
'Ye lee, ye lee, ye leears loud,
  Fu' loud I hear ye lee!

'For I brought as much o' the white monie
  As gane[1] my men and me,
And a half-fou[2] o' the gude red gowd,
  Out ower the sea with me.

[1] suffices [2] half-bushel

'Mak' ready, mak' ready, my merry men a'!
Our gude ship sails the morn.'
'Now ever alack, my master dear,
I fear a deadly storm.

'I saw the new moon late yestreen
Wi' the auld moon in her arm;
And if we gang to sea, master,
I fear we'll come to harm.'

They hadna sail'd a league, a league,
A league but barely three,
When the lift[1] grew dark, and the wind blew loud,
And gurly[2] grew the sea.

The ankers brak, and the topmast lap,[3]
It was sic a deadly storm:
And the waves cam owre the broken ship
Till a' her sides were torn.

They fetch'd a web o' the silken claith,[4]
Another o' the twine,[5]
And they wapp'd[6] them round that gude ship's side,
But still the sea came in.

O laith[7], laith were our gude Scots lords
To wet their cork-heel'd shoon;
But lang or a' the play was play'd
They wat their hats aboon.[8]

[1] sky [2] rough [3] cracked [4] cloth [5] sacking [6] packed
[7] loath [8] above

And mony was the feather bed
  That flatter'd[1] on the faem;
And mony was the gude lord's son
  That never mair cam hame.

O lang, lang may the ladies sit,
  Wi' their fans into their hand,
Before they see Sir Patrick Spens
  Come sailing to the strand!

And lang, lang may the maidens sit
  Wi' their gowd kames[2] in their hair,
A-waiting for their ain dear loves!
  For them they'll see nae mair.

Half-owre,[3] half-owre to Aberdour,
  'Tis fifty fathoms deep;
And there lies gude Sir Patrick Spens,
  Wi' the Scots lords at his feet!

Helen of Kirconnell

I WISH I were where Helen lies,
Night and day on me she cries:
O that I were where Helen lies,
  On fair Kirconnell lea!

Curst be the heart that thought the thought,
And curst be the hand that fired the shot,
When in my arms burd[4] Helen dropt,
  And died to succour me!

[1] floated [2] golden combs [3] half-way over [4] maid

O think na ye my heart was sair,
When my Love dropt and spak nae mair?
There did she swoon wi' meikle[1] care,
On fair Kirconnell lea.

As I went down the waterside
None but my foe to be my guide,
None but my foe to be my guide,
On fair Kirconnell lea;

I lighted down, my sword to draw,
I hackèd him in pieces sma',
I hackèd him in pieces sma',
For her sake that died for me.

O Helen fair, beyond compare!
I'll mak a garland o' thy hair,
Shall bind my heart for evermair,
Until the day I die.

O that I were where Helen lies!
Night and day on me she cries;
Out of my bed she bids me rise,
Says, 'Haste, and come to me!'

I wish my grave were growing green,
A winding-sheet drawn owre my een,
And I in Helen's arms lying
On fair Kirconnell lea.

[1] much

The Daemon Lover

'O WHERE have you been, my long, long love,
This long seven years and more?'
'O I'm come to seek my former vows
Ye granted me before.'

'O hold your tongue of your former vows,
For they will breed sad strife;
O hold your tongue of your former vows,
For I am become a wife.'

He turned him right and round about,
And the tear blinded his e'e;
'I would never ha' trodden on Irish ground,
If it had na' been for thee.

'I might ha' had a king's daughter,
Far, far beyond the sea;
I might have had a king's daughter,
Had it not been for love o' thee.'

'If ye might ha' had a king's daughter
Yourself ye had to blame;
Ye might ha' taken the king's daughter
For ye kenned that I was nane!

'If I was to leave my husband dear,
And my two babes also,
O what have you to take me to,
If I with you should go?'

'I ha' seven ships upon the sea;
  The eighth brought me to land,
With four and twenty bold mariners,
  And music on every hand.'

She has taken up her two little babes,
  Kissed them both cheek and chin;
'O fare ye well, my own two babes,
  For I'll never see you again.'

She set her foot upon the ship;
  No mariners could she behold,
But the sails were 'o the taffety,
  And the masts o' the beaten gold.

She had not sailed a league, a league,
  A league but barely three,
When dismal grew his countenance,
  And drumlie[1] grew his e'e.

They had not sailed a league, a league,
  A league but barely three,
Until she espied his cloven foot,
  And she wept right bitterly.

'O hold your tongue of your weeping,' says he
  'Of your weeping now let me be;
I will show you how the lillies grow
  On the banks of Italy!'

'O what hills are yon, yon pleasant hills,
  That the sun shines sweetly on?'
'O yon are the hills of heaven,' he said,
  'Where you will never win.'

[1] gloomy

'O whaten a mountain is yon,' she said,
  'All so dreary wi' frost and snow?'
'O yon is the mountain of hell,' he cried,
  'Where you and I will go.'

He struck the topmast wi' his hand,
  The foremast wi' his knee,
And he brake that gallant ship in twain,
  And sank her in the sea.

Lord Randal

'O WHERE hae ye been, Lord Randal, my son?
O where hae ye been, my handsome young man?'
'I hae been to the wild wood; mother, make my bed
    soon,
For I'm weary wi' hunting, and fain wad lie down.'

'Where gat ye your dinner, Lord Randal, my son?
Where gat ye your dinner, my handsome young man?'
'I dined wi' my true-love; mother, make my bed soon,
For I'm weary wi' hunting, and fain wad lie down.'

'What gat ye to your dinner, Lord Randal, my son?
What gat ye to your dinner, my handsome young man?'
'I gat eels boiled in broth; mother, make my bed soon,
For I'm weary wi' hunting, and fain wad lie down.'

'And wha gat your leavings, Lord Randal, my son?
And wha gat your leavings, my handsome young man?'
'My hawks and my hounds; mother, make my bed soon,
For I'm weary wi' hunting, and fain wad lie down.'

'What became of your bloodhounds, Lord Randal, my
son?
What became of your bloodhounds, my handsome young
man?'
'O they swelled and they died; mother, make my bed
soon,
For I'm weary wi' hunting, and fain wad lie down.'

'O I fear ye are poisoned, Lord Randal, my son!
O I fear ye are poisoned, my handsome young man!'
'O yes! I am poisoned; mother, make my bed soon,
For I'm sick at the heart and I fain wad lie down.'

The Old Cloak

THIS winter's weather it waxeth cold,
And frost it freezeth on every hill,
And Boreas blows his blasts so bold
That all our kine he is like to kill.
Bell, my wife, she loves no strife;
She said unto me quietly,
Rise up, and save cow Crumbock's life!
Man, put thine old cloak about thee!

He

O Bell my wife, why dost thou flyte[1]?
Thou kens my cloak is very thin;
It is so sore and over wore,
A crickë[2] thereon cannot rin.[3]

[1] scold [2] cricket [3] run

Then I'll no longer borrow nor lend,
  For once I'll new apparelled be;
To-morrow I'll to town and spend;
  For I'll have a new cloak about me.

She

Cow Crumbock is a very good cow;
  She has been always good to the pail;
She has helped us to butter and cheese, I trow
  And other things she will not fail.
I would be loth to see her pine.
  Good husband, counsel take of me;
It is not for us to go so fine.
  Man, take thine old cloak about thee!

He

My cloak it was a very good cloak,
  It hath been always good to the wear;
It hath cost me many a groat;
  I have had it this four and forty year.
Sometime it was of the cloth in grain[1];
  It is now but a sigh clout,[2] as you may see;
It will neither hold out wind nor rain;
  And I'll have a new cloak about me.

[1] scarlet [2] rag for straining

She

It is four and forty years ago
  Sine the one of us the other did ken;
And we have had, betwixt us two,
  Children either nine or ten;
We have brought them up to women and men;
  In the fear of God I trow they be.
And why wilt thou thyself misken?
  Man, take thine old cloak about thee!

He

O Bell my wife, why dost thou flyte?
  Now is now, and then was then.
Seek all the world now throughout,
  Thou kens not clowns from gentleman;
They are clad in black, green, yellow, and blue,
  So far above their own degree.
Once in my life I'll take a view;
  For I'll have a new cloak about me.

She

King Stephen was a worthy peer;
  His breeches cost him but a crown;
He held them sixpence all too dear,
  Therefore he called the tailor lown.[1]
He was a wight of high renown,
  And thou's but of a low degree.
It's pride that puts this country down:
  Man, put thy old cloak about thee!

[1] rogue

He

Bell my wife, she loves not strife,
  Yet she will lead me if she can:
And to maintain an easy life,
  I oft must yield, though I'm good-man.
It's not for a man with a woman to threap,[1]
  Unless he first give o'er the play.
As we began, so will we keep;
  And I'll have mine old cloak about me.

I Sing of a Maiden

I SING of a maiden
  That is makeles,[2]
King of all kinges
  To her sone sche ches.[3]
He cam also[4] stille
  There his moder was,
As dew in Aprille
  That falleth on the grass.
He cam also stille
  To his moderes bour,
As dew in Aprille
  That falleth on the flour.
He cam also stille
  There his moder lay,
As dew in Aprille
  That falleth on the spray.

[1] argue [2] without a mate (*or* matchless) [3] chose [4] as

Moder and maiden
  Was never none but sche;
Well may swich a lady
  Godes moder be.

At the Setting of the Sun

COME all you young fellows that carry a gun,
Beware of late shooting when daylight is done,
For 'tis little you reckon what hazards you run,
I shot my true love at the setting of the sun.

In a shower of rain as my darling did hie[1]
All under the bushes to keep herself dry,
With her head in her apron I thought her a swan,
And I shot my true love at the setting of the sun.

I'll fly from my country, I nowhere find rest,
I've shot my true love like a bird in her nest.
Like lead on my heart lies the deed I have done,
I shot my true love at the setting of the sun.

In the night the fair maid as a white swan appears,
She says, O my true love, quick dry up your tears,
I freely forgive you, I have Paradise won,
I was shot by my love at the setting of the sun.

O the years as they pass leave me lonely and sad,
I can ne'er love another and naught makes me glad.
I wait and expect till life's little span done
I meet my true love at the rising of the sun.

[1] go

An Old Soldier of the Queen's

Of an old soldier of the Queen's,
With an old motley coat, and a Maumsie nose,
And an old jerkin that's out at the elbows,
And an old pair of boots, drawn on without hose
Stuft with rags instead of toes;
    And an old soldier of the Queen's,
    And the Queen's old soldier.

With an old rusty sword that's hackt with blows,
And an old dagger to scare away the crows,
And an old horse that reels as he goes,
And an old saddle that no man knows,[1]
    And an old soldier of the Queen's,
    And the Queen's old soldier.

With his old gun, and his bandoliers,
And an old head-piece to keep warm his ears,
He's now rid to Bohemia to fight with his foes,
And he swears by his valour he'll have better clothes,
Or else he'll lose legs, arms, fingers, and toes,
And he'll come again, when no man knows,
    And an old soldier of the Queen's,
    And the Queen's old soldier.

[1] would recognise

Come, Come Away

COME, come away, to the tavern I say,
For now at home 'tis washing day;
Leave your prittle-prattle, and fill us a pottle,
You are not so wise as Aristotle.
Drawer come away, let's make it holy day:
Anon, anon, anon, Sir, what is't you say?

Boney Was a Warrior

BONEY was a warrior,
  Way-ay yah,
Boney was a warrior,
  John Fran-swah.

Boney beat the Prooshians,
Boney beat the Rooshians.

Boney went to Moscow,
Moscow was afire.

Boney he came back again,
Boney he came back again.

Boney went to Elbow,
Boney went to Elbow.

Boney went to Waterloo,
Boney was defeated.

Boney was a prisoner,
'Board the Billy Ruffian.

Boney he was sent away,
'Way to St. Helena.

Boney broke his heart and died,
Boney broke his heart and died.

Boney was a warrior,
  Way-ay yah,
Boney was a warrior,
  John Fran-swah.

The Kerry Recruit

One fine morning in May I was tilling the land
With me hat on me head and me spade in me hand
When says I to meself, 'Tis a pity to see
A young fellow like me digging spuds in Tralee!'

Chorus Kerry-i-ay, fol-lol-de-rol-lay,
Kerry-i-ay, fol-lol-de-rol-lay.

So I buttered[1] me brogues and shook hands with me spade
And I off to the Fair like a sporting young blade,
When up comes a Sergeant and axed me to 'list—
Sergeant O'Grath shoves a bob in me fist.

He tipped me a shilling, and said he'd no more,
If I'd come to Headquarters he'd give me a score,
'Headquarters?' says I, 'Yerrah! Sergeant, good-bye,
Faith I'll not be quartered for fear I might die!'

[1] polished

'Yerrah! Paddy, be aisy, why can't you abide?
Headquarter's the place where we all do reside.'
I soon found his meaning and went with good grace
To take up my quarters in that Royal Place.

Then up came the Captain, a man of great fame,
He axed me me country, I tould him me name,
I ups with me story and tould him again
That me father and mother was both Kerry men.

The first thing they gave me, it was a red coat,
With a strip of black leather to tie round me throat,
They gave me a queer thing, I axed them 'What's that?'
'Wisha! Honea ma diaoul![1] a cockade for your hat!'

The next thing they gave me, it was a big gun,
And under the trigger they put my first thumb,
And first she spits fire, and then she spits smoke,
With a noise like great thunder me shoulder she broke,

The next thing they gave me, it was a white horse,
With saddle and bridle me two legs across,
I gave her the whip and I gave her the steel,
Sure, Honea ma diaoul! she ran down like an eel!

The first place they brought me was down to the say,
On board a big ship bound for the Cri-me-ay,
Three sticks in the middle all covered with sheet,
Sure, she walks through the water without any feet.

One morning we landed at Balaclava, all sound,
Both wet, cold and hungry we lay on the ground,
Next morning for action the bugle did call
And we made a hot breakfast off powder and ball.

[1] Go to the devil!

But the shots was so thick and the day was so hot,
That I lay in the trenches for fear I'd be shot,
And oft did I think of me mam all alone
And the fun I had digging pittayties at home.

Now me five years are over, thank God it's not tin,
I'll go back to old Ireland and dig praties agin,
And I'll butter me brogues and shake hands with me spade,
For I find that this fighting's the Divil's own trade.

The Big Rock Candy Mountains

ONE evenin' as the sun went down
And the jungle fire was burnin',
Down the track came a hobo[1] hikin',
And he said: 'Boys, I'm not turnin',
I'm headed fer a land that's far away
Beside the crystal fountains,
So come with me, we'll all go see
The Big Rock Candy Mountains.'

In the Big Rock Candy Mountains,
There's a land that's fair and bright,
Where the handouts grow on bushes,
And you sleep out every night.
Where the boxcars are all empty,
And the sun shines every day
On the birds and the bees and the cigarette trees,
And the lemonade springs where the bluebird sings,
In the Big Rock Candy Mountains.

[1] tramp

In the Big Rock Candy Mountains,
All the cops have wooden legs,
The bulldogs all have rubber teeth,
And the hens lay soft-boiled eggs,
The farmers' trees are full of fruit,
And the barns are full of hay.
Oh, I'm bound to go where there ain't no snow,
Where the rain don't pour, the wind don't blow,
In the Big Rock Candy Mountains.

In the Big Rock Candy Mountains,
You never change your socks,
And the little streams of alcohol
Come tricklin' down the rocks.
There the brakemen have to tip their hats
And the railroad bulls are blind.
There's a lake of stew and of whisky too,
You can paddle all around 'em in a big canoe,
In the Big Rock Candy Mountains.

In the Big Rock Candy Mountains,
All the jails are made of tin,
And you can bust right out again
As soon as you are in.
There ain't no short-handled shovels,
No axes, saws or picks.
I'm goin' to stay where you sleep all day,
Where they hung the Turk that invented work,
In the Big Rock Candy Mountains.

Alexander the Great

FOUR men stood by the grave of a man,
The grave of Alexander the Proud:
They sang words without falsehood
Over the prince from fair Greece.

Said the first man of them:
'Yesterday there were around the king
The men of the world—a sad gathering!
Though to-day he is alone.'

'Yesterday the king of the brown world
Rode upon the heavy earth:
Though to-day it is the heavy earth
That rides upon his neck.'

'Yesterday,' said the third wise author,
'Philip's son owned the whole world:
To-day he has nought
Save seven feet of earth.'

'Alexander the liberal and great
Was wont to bestow silver and gold:
To-day,' said the fourth man,
'The gold is here, and it is nought.'

Thus truly spoke the wise men
Around the grave of the high king:
It was not foolish women's talk
What those four sang.

Anglo-Saxon

(translated by GAVIN BONE)

Riddle on Moon and Sun

'I SAW a creature sally with booty,
Between its horns bearing treasures amazing.
'Twas a bright cup of the air, a brave, pipkin-thing
Adorned with delicate, darting rays.
This plunder gay for a bower it would take
Spoil of the air, to its palace dim,
And, cunning, would build a room of its own in heaven.
Over the wall an arrogant being
Sprang up, though common to all men's sight is he.
He snatched the booty, drove the other home,
Wisp of a pilgrim; and westwards itself
The cruel creature went careering on.
Dust blew up. Dew came down.
The night followed after. But never a man
Knew where the wandering thing had gone.'

The Whale

To explain the nature of fishes in craft of verse—
And first, the Great Whale. A grim purpose is his;
Mariners often find him against their will
Floating on eternal ocean.

His name is Fastitocolon,
His coat is like rough stone,
Like a huge sea-knot of wrack, ringed with sand-dunes,
That floats by the shore.
  Now when wave-borne men trust their eyes for an island,
And moor their high-beaked ships to the fraudy shore,
Tether their sea-horses at the brink of ocean
And roam up the island to explore:
While the keels lie at the tide-mark
The tired sailors make their camp,
They wake a fire on the island,
Happy are the men, and tired—glad to encamp.
But he is crafty and treacherous; when he feels
The travellers properly planted and set
Taking the pretty weather—Instantly down
Darts the oceanic animal,
And locks drowning in the hall of death
Both ships and souls!

John Gower

The Cave of Sleep

(from *Confessio Amantis*)

UNDER an hill there is a cave
Which of the sonnë may nought have,
So that no man may knowe aright
The point between the day and night.

There is no fire, there is no sparke,
There is no dorë which may charke,[1]
Whereof an eyë shulde unshet,[2]
So that inward there is no let.[3]
And for to speke of that withoute,
That stant no great tre nigh aboute,
Whereon there mightë crowe or pie
Alightë for to clepe[4] or crie.
There is no cock to crowë day,
Ne bestë none which noisë may
The hille, but all aboute round
There is growend[5] upon the ground
Poppy, which bereth the sede of slepe,
With other herbës suche an hepe.
A stillë water for the nonës[6]
Rennend[7] upon the smallë stonës,
Which hight[8] of Lethës the river,
Under that hille in such maner
There is, which yiveth[9] great appetite
To slepe. And thus ful of delite
Slepe hath his hous, and of his couche
Within this chambre if I shall touche,[10]
Of hebenus that slepy tre
The bordës all aboutë be,
And for[11] he shuldë slepë softe
Upon a fether bed alofte
He lith with many a pilwe of doun:
The chambre is strowëd up and doun
With swevenes[12] many a thousand fold.

[1] creak [2] open [3] hindrance (to sleep) [4] call out
[5] growing [6] on that occasion [7] running [8] is called
[9] giveth [10] speak [11] in order that [12] dreams

Geoffrey Chaucer

Now Welcome Summer

(from *The Parlement of Foules*)

Now welcom somer, with thy sonnë softe,
That hast this wintres weders over-shake,[1]
And driven awey the longë nightës blake![2]

Seynt Valentyn, that art ful hy on-lofte;—
Thus singen smalë foulës for thy sake—
Now welcom somer, with thy sonnë softe,
That has this wintres weders over-shake.

Wel han they causë for to gladen ofte,
Sith ech of hem recovered hath his make;[3]
Ful blisful may they singen whan they wake;
Now welcom somer, with thy sonnë softe,
That hast this wintres weders over-shake,
And driven awey the longë nightës blake.

[1] shaken off [2] black [3] mate

A Garden in a Dream

(from *The Parlement of Foules*)

WITH that my hond[1] in his he took anoon,
Of which I comfort caughte, and wente in faste;
But lord! so I was glad and wel begoon![2]
For over-al, wher that I myn eyen caste,
Were treës clad with leves that ay shal laste,
Eche in his kinde, of colour fresh and grene
As emeraude, that joyë was to sene.

The bilder ook, and eek the hardy asshe;
The piler elm, the cofre[3] unto careyne;[4]
The boxtree piper;[5] holm[6] to whippës lasshe;
The sayling firr; the cipres, deth to pleyne;[7]
The sheter[8] ew, the asp[9] for shaftës pleyne;[10]
The olyve of pees, and eek the drunken vyne,
The victor palm, the laurer to devyne.[11]

A garden saw I, ful of blosmy bowes,
Upon a river, in a grenë mede,
Ther as that swetnesse vermore y-now is,
With flourës whytë, blewe, yelowe, and rede;
And coldë wellë-stremës, no-thing dede,
That swommen ful of smalë fisshes lighte,
With finnës rede and scalës silver-brighte.

On every bough the briddës herde I singe,
With voys of aungel in hir armonye,
Som besyed[12] hem hir briddës[13] forth to bringe;
The litel conyes[14] to hir pley gunne hye,[15]

[1] hand [2] contented [3] coffin [4] corpse [5] suitable for pipes
[6] evergreen oak [7] mourn [8] shooter (for bows) [9] aspen
[10] smooth [11] prophesy by [12] busied [13] young [14] rabbits
[15] began to go

And further al aboute I gan espye
The dredful[1] roo, the buk, the hert and hinde,
Squerels, and bestës smale of gentil kinde.

Of instruments of strengës[2] in acord
Herde I so pleye a ravisshing swetnesse,
The god, that maker is of al and lord,
Ne herdë never better, as I gesse;
Therwith a wind, unnethe[3] hit might be lesse,
Made in the levës grene a noisë softe
Acordant to the foulës songe on-lofte.

The air of that place so attempre[4] was
That never was grevaunce of hoot ne cold;
Ther wex[5] eek every holsom spyce and gras,
Ne no man may ther wexë[6] seek ne old;
Yet was ther joyë more a thousand fold
Then[7] man can telle; ne never wolde it nighte
But ay[8] cleer day to any mannës sighte.

The Squire

(from *The Prologue to The Canterbury Tales*)

WITH him ther was his sone, a yong Squyer,
A lovyere and a lusty bacheler,
With lokkës cruel,[9] as they were leyd in presse.
Of[10] twenty yeer of age he was, I gesse.
Of his stature he was of evene[11] lengthe,
And wonderly deliverd[12] and greet of strengthe;

[1] timid [2] strings [3] scarcely [4] mild [5] grew [6] sick
[7] than [8] always [9] curly [10] about [11] normal [12] nimble

And he had been somtyme in chivachye,[1]
In Flaundrës, in Artoys and Picardye,
And born him wel, as of so litel space,
In hope to stonden in his lady grace.
Embrouded was he, as it were a mede
Al ful of fresshë flourës whyte and rede;
Singinge he was or floytynge[2] al the day;
He was as fresh as is the month of May.
Short was his gowne, with slevës longe and wyde.
Wel coude he sitte on hors, and fairë ryde;
He coudë songës make and wel endite,
Juste[3] and eek[4] daunce and wel purtreye[5] and write.
So hote he lovëde that by nightertale[6]
He sleep no more than doth a nightingale.
Curteys he was, lowly and servisable,
And carf[7] biforn his fader at the table.

The Chase

(from *The Nun's Priest's Tale*)

This sely widwe, and eek hir doghtres two,
Herden thise hennes crye and maken wo,
And out at dores sterten they anoon,
And seyen the fox toward the grove goon,
And bar upon his bak the cok away;
And cryden, 'Out! harrow! and weylaway!
Ha, ha, the fox!' and after him they ran,
And eek with staves many another man;
Ran Colle our dogge, and Talbot, and Gerland,
And Malkin, with a distaf in hir hand;
Ran cow and calf, and eek the verray hogges
So were they fered for berking of the dogges

[1] cavalry expeditions [2] fluting [3] joust [4] also [5] draw
[6] at night [7] carved

And shouting of the men and wimmen eke,
They ronne so, hem thoughte hir herte breke.
They yelleden as feendes doon in helle;
The dokes cryden as men wolde hem quelle;
The geese for fere flowen over the trees;
Out of the hyve cam the swarm of bees;
So hidous was the noyse, a! *benedicite!*
Certes, he Jakke Straw, and his meynee,
Ne made never shoutes half so shrille,
Whan that they wolden any Fleming kille,
As thilke day was maad upon the fox.
Of bras they broghten bemes, and of box,
Of horn, of boon, in which they blewe and pouped,
And therwithal thay shryked and they houped;
It seemed as that heven sholde falle.

Truth

Ballade de bon conseyl

Flee fro the prees, and dwelle with sothfastnesse,
Suffyce unto thy good, though hit be smal;
For hord hath hate, and climbing tikelnesse,
Prees hath envye, and wele blent overal;
Savour no more than thee bihove shal;
Werk wel thy-self, that other folk canst rede;
And trouthe shal delivere, hit is no drede.

Tempest thee noght al croked to redresse,
In trust of hir that turneth as a bal:
Gret reste stant in litel besinesse;
And eek be war to sporne ageyn an al;
Stryve noght, as doth the crokke with the wal.
Daunte thy-self, that dauntest otheres dede;
And trouthe shal delivere, hit is no drede.

That thee is sent, receyve in buxumnesse,
The wrastling for this worlde axeth a fal.
Her nis non hoom, her nis but wildernesse:
Forth, pilgrim, forth! Forth, beste, out of thy stal!
Know thy contree, look up, thank God of al;
Hold the hye wey, and lat thy gost thee lede:
And trouthe shal delivere, hit is no drede.

Envoy

Therfore, thou vache, leve thyn old wrecchednesse
Unto the worlde; leve now to be thral;
Crye him mercy, that of his goodnesse
Made thee of noght, and in especial
Draw unto him, and pray in general
For thee, and eek for other, hevenlich mede;
And trouthe shal delivere, hit is no drede.

William Dunbar

Lament for the Makers

When he was sick

I THAT in heill[1] was and gladness
Am trublit now with great sickness
And feblit[2] with infirmitie:—
Timor Mortis conturbat me.

[1] health [2] enfeebled

Our plesance here is all vain glory,
This fals world is but transitory,
The flesh is bruckle,[1] the Feynd is slee:—[2]
Timor Mortis conturbat me.

The state of man does change and vary,
Now sound, now sick, now blyth, now sary,
Now dansand mirry, now like to die:—
Timor Mortis conturbat me.

No state in Erd here standis sicker;[3]
As with the wynd wavis the wicker[4]
So wannis[5] the world's vanitie:—
Timor Mortis conturbat me.

Unto the Death gois all Estatis,
Princis, Prelatis, and Potestatis,
Baith rich and poor of all degree:—
Timor Mortis conturbat me.

He takis the knichtis in to the field
Enarmit[6] under helm and scheild;
Victor he is at all mellie:—[7]
Timor Mortis conturbat me.

That strong unmerciful tyrand
Takis, on the motheris breast sowkand,[8]
The babe full of benignite:—
Timor Mortis conturbat me.

He takis the campion[9] in the stour,[10]
The captain closit in the tour,
The lady in bour full of bewtie:—
Timor Mortis conturbat me.

[1] brittle, frail [2] sly [3] sure [4] willow [5] wanes [6] armed
[7] battle [8] sucking [9] champion [10] battle

He spairis no lord for his piscence,[1]
Na clerk[2] for his intelligence;
His awful straik[3] may no man flee:—
Timor Mortis conturbat me.

Art-magicianis and astrologgis,
Rethoris, logicianis, and theologgis,
Them helpis no conclusionis slee:—
Timor Mortis conturbat me.

In medecine the most practicianis
Leechis, surrigianis, and physicianis,
Themself fra death may not supplee:—[4]
Timor Mortis conturbat me.

I see that makaris[5] amang the lave[6]
Playis here their padyanis,[7] syne[8] gois to grave;
Sparit[9] is nocht their facultie:—[10]
Timor Mortis conturbat me.

He has done petuously devour
The noble Chaucer, of makaris flour,
The Monk of Bury, and Gower, all three:—
Timor Mortis conturbat me.

The good Sir Hew of Eglintoun,
Ettrick, Heriot, and Wintoun,
He has tane out of this cuntrie:—
Timor Mortis conturbat me.

That scorpion fell has done infeck
Maister John Clerk, and James Affleck,
Fra ballat-making and tragedie:—
Timor Mortis conturbat me.

[1] power [2] scholar [3] stroke [4] save [5] makers, i.e. poets
[6] rest [7] pageants [8] then [9] spared [10] craft

Holland and Barbour he has berevit
Alas! that he not with us levit
Sir Mungo Lockart of the Lee:—
Timor Mortis conturbat me.

Clerk of Tranent eke he has tane,
That made of anteris[1] of Gawaine;
Sir Gilbert Hay endit has he:—
Timor Mortis conturbat me.

He has Blind Harry and Sandy Traill
Slain with his schour of mortal hail,
Quhilk Johnstoun might nocht flee:—
Timor Mortis conturbat me.

He has reft Merseir his endite,
That did in luve so lively write,
So short, so quick, of sentence hie:—
Timor Mortis conturbat me.

He has tane Rowll of Aberdene,
And gentill Rowll of Corstorphine;
Two better fallowis did no man see:—
Timor Mortis conturbat me.

In Dunfermline he has tane Broun
With Maister Robert Henrysoun;
Sir John the Ross enbrast has he:—
Timor Mortis conturbat me.

And he has now tane, last of a,
Good gentil Stobo and Quintin Shaw,
Of quhom all wichtis[2] hes pitie:—
Timor Mortis conturbat me.

[1] adventures [2] people

Good Maister Walter Kennedy
In point of death lies verily;
Great ruth it were that so suld be:—
Timor Mortis conturbat me.

Sen he has all my brether tane,
He will nocht let me live alane;
Of force[1] I man his next prey be:—
Timor Mortis conturbat me.

Since for the death remeid is none,
Best is that we for death dispone,[2]
After our death that live may we:—
Timor Mortis conturbat me.

John Skelton

Poverty

(from *Magnificence*)

Ah, my bones ache, my limbs be sore;
Alas, I have the sciatica full evil in my hip!
Alas, where is youth that was wont for to skip?
I am lousy, and unliking, and full of scurf,
My colour its tawny, coloured as turf.
I am Poverty, that all men doth hate,
I am baited with dogs at every man's gate;
I am ragged and rent, as ye may see;
Full few but they have envy at me.

[1] necessity [2] prepare

Though Ye Suppose

THOUGH ye suppose all jeopardies are passed,
 And all is done that ye looked for before,
Ware yet, I rede [1] you, of Fortune's double cast,
 For one false point she is wont to keep in store,
 And under the fell [2] oft festered is the sore:
That when ye think all danger for to pass
Ware of the lizard lieth lurking in the grass.

To Mistress Isabel Pennell

BY Saint Mary, my lady,
Your mammy and your daddy
Brought forth a goodly baby.

My maiden Isabel,
Reflaring rosabel,[3]
The flagrant [4] camamel,

The ruddy rosary,[5]
The sovereign rosemary,
The pretty strawberry,

The columbine, the nept,[6]
The jeloffer [7] well set,
The proper [8] violet;

[1] advise [2] skin [3] scented rose [4] fragrant [5] rose-garden
[6] nepeta (catmint) [7] clove-pink [8] fine

Ennewèd[1] your colour
Is like the daisy flower
After the April shower.

Star of the morrow[2] gray,
The blossom on the spray,
The freshest flower of May,

Maidenly demure,
Of womanhood the lure;
Wherefore I you assure,

It were an heavenly health,
It were an endless wealth,
A life for God himself,

To hear this nightingale
Among the birdes smale
Warbling in the vale,

'Dug, dug! Jug, jug!
Good year and good luck!'
With 'Chuck, chuck, chuck, chuck!'

To Mistress Margaret Hussey

MERRY Margaret,
As midsummer flower,
Gentle as falcon,
Or hawk of the tower;

[1] shaded, tinted [2] morning

With solace and gladness,
Much mirth and no madness,
All good and no badness;
So joyously,
So maidenly,
So womanly,
Her demeaning,
In every thing,
Far, far passing
That I can indite,
Or suffice to write,
Of Merry Margaret,
As midsummer flower,
Gentle as falcon,
Or hawk of the tower;
As patient and as still,
And as full of good will,
As fair Isiphil,
Coliander,
Sweet pomander,
Good Cassander;
Stedfast of thought,
Well made, well wrought,
Far may be sought,
Erst that ye can find
So courteous, so kind,
As Merry Margaret,
This midsummer flower,
Gentle as falcon,
Or hawk of the tower.

Sir Thomas Wyatt

The Hind

Whoso list to hunt, I know where is an hind,
  But as for me, *helas!* I may no more.
  The vain travail hath wearied me so sore,
I am of them that furthest come behind.
Yet may I, by no means, my wearied mind
  Draw from the deer; but as she fleeth afore
  Fainting I follow. I leave off therefore,
Since in a net I seek to hold the wind.
Who list her hunt, I put him out of doubt,
  As well as I, may spend his time in vain;
There is written, her fair neck round about,
    '*Noli me tangere*, for Caesar's I am,
    And wild for to hold, though I seem tame.'

To His Lady

MADAM, withouten many words,
  Once, I am sure, ye will or no.
And if the will, then leave your bourds
  And use your wit and show it so,

And with a beck ye shall me call;
  And if of one, that burneth alway,
Ye have any pity at all,
  Answer him fair with yea, or nay.

If it be yea, I shall be fain;
  If it be nay, friends as before;
Ye shall another man obtain,
  And I mine own and yours no more.

Honesty

THROUGHOUT the world if it were sought,
  Fair words enough a man shall find;
They be good cheap, they cost right nought,
  Their substance is but only wind.
    But well to say, and so to mean,
    This sweet accord is seldom seen.

Henry Howard, Earl of Surrey

Youth and Age

Laid in my quiet bed, in study as I were,
I saw within my troubled head a heap of thoughts appear.
And every thought did show so lively in mine eyes,
That now I sigh'd, and then I smiled, as cause of thought
did rise.
I saw the little boy in thought how oft that he
Did wish of God to 'scape the rod, a tall young man to be.
The young man, eke, that feels his bones with pains opprest,
How he would be a rich old man, to live and lie at rest.
The rich old man, that sees his end draw on so sore,
How he would be a boy again, to live so much the more.
Whereat full oft I smiled, to see how all these three,
From boy to man, from man to boy, would chop and
change degree.
And, musing thus, I think the case is very strange
That man from wealth, to live in woe, doth ever seek to
change.
Thus thoughtful as I lay, I saw my wither'd skin,
How it doth show my dinted jaws, the flesh was worn so
thin.
And eke my toothless chaps, the gates of my right way,
That opes and shuts as I do speak, do thus unto me say:
'Thy white and hoarish hairs, the messengers of age,
That show, like lines of true belief, that this life doth
assuage,

Bid thee lay hand and feel them hanging on thy chin;
The which do write two ages past, the third now coming in.
Hang up therefore the bit of thy young wanton time:
And thou that therein beaten art, the happiest life define.'
Whereat I sigh'd, and said: 'Farewell, my wonted joy!
Truss up thy pack, and trudge from me to every little boy,
And tell them thus from me: their time most happy is,
If, to their time, they reason had to know the truth of this.'

William Stevenson

Jolly Good Ale and Old

I CANNOT eat but little meat,[1]
    My stomach is not good;
But sure I think that I can drink
    With him that wears a hood.
Though I go bare, take ye no care,
    I nothing am a-cold;
I stuff my skin so full within
    Of jolly good ale and old.
        Back and side go bare, go bare;
        Both foot and hand go cold;
        But, belly, God send thee good ale enough,
        Whether it be new or old.

I love no roast but a nut-brown toast,
    And a crab laid in the fire;
A little bread shall do me stead;
    Much bread I not desire.

[1] food

No frost nor snow, no wind, I trow,
Can hurt me if I wold;
I am so wrapp'd and thoroughly lapp'd
Of jolly ale and old.
Back and side go bare, go bare, &c.

And Tib, my wife, that as her life
Loveth well good ale to seek,
Full oft drinks she till ye may see
The tears run down her cheek:
Then doth she trowl[1] to me the bowl
Even as a maltworm[2] should,
And saith, 'Sweetheart, I took my part
Of this jolly good ale and old.'
Back and side go bare, go bare, &c.

Now let them drink till they nod and wink,
Even as good fellows should do;
They shall not miss to have the bliss
Good ale doth bring men to;
And all poor souls that have scour'd bowls
Or have them lustily troll'd,
God save the lives of them and their wives,
Whether they be young or old.
Back and side go bare, go bare;
Both foot and hand go cold;
But, belly, God send thee good ale enough,
Whether it be new or old.

[1] pass [2] drinker

Sir Walter Ralegh

Walsingham

'As you came from the holy land
  Of Walsingham,
Met you not with my true love
  By the way as you came?'

'How shall I know your true love,
  That have met many one
As I went to the holy land,
  That have come, that have gone?'

'She is neither white nor brown,
  But as the heavens fair,
There is none hath a form so divine
  In the earth or the air.'

'Such an one did I meet, good Sir,
  Such an angelic face,
Who like a queen, like a nymph did appear
  By her gait, by her grace.'

'She hath left me here all alone,
  All alone as unknown,
Who sometimes did me lead with herself,
  And me loved as her own.'

'What's the cause that she leaves you alone
   And a new way doth take,
Who loved you once as her own
   And her joy did you make?'

'I have loved her all my youth,
   But now old as you see,
Love likes not the falling fruit
   From the withered tree.

'Know that Love is a careless child,
   And forgets promise past;
He is blind, he is deaf when he list
   And in faith never fast.

'His desire is a dureless content
   And a trustless joy;
He is won with a world of despair
   And is lost with a toy.

'Of womenkind such indeed is the love
   Or the word love abused,
Under which many childish desires
   And conceits are excused.

'But love is a durable fire
   In the mind ever burning;
Never sick, never old, never dead,
   From itself never turning.'

Edmund Spenser

When Flowered My Joyful Spring

(from *The Shepheardes Calendar: December*)

Whilome[1] in youth, when flowered my joyful spring,
Like swallow swift I wandered here and there:
For heat of headless lust[2] me so did sting
That I of doubted danger had no fear:
  I went the wasteful[3] woods and forests wide,
  Withouten dread of wolves to been espied.

I wont to range amid the mazy thicket,
And gather nuts to make me Christmas game,
And joyèd oft to chase the trembling pricket,[4]
Or hunt the heartless[5] hare till she were tame.
  What reckèd I of wintry age's waste?—
  Tho[6] deemèd I my spring would ever last.

How often have I scaled the craggy oak,
All to dislodge the raven of her nest?
How have I wearièd with many a stroke
The stately walnut-tree, the while the rest
  Under the tree fell all for nuts at strife?
  For ylike[7] to me were liberty and life.

[1] formerly [2] pleasure [3] lonely [4] buck [5] timid
[6] then [7] alike

One Day I Wrote Her Name Upon the Strand

ONE day I wrote her name upon the strand,
But came the waves and washèd it away:
Again I wrote it with a second hand,
But came the tide and made my pains his prey.
'Vain man,' said she, 'that dost in vain assay
A mortal thing so to immortalise,
For I myself shall like to this decay,
And eek[1] my name be wipèd out likewise.'
'Not so,' quod[2] I, 'let baser things devise
To die in dust, but you shall live by fame:
My verse your virtues rare shall eternise,
And in the Heavens write your glorious name.
  Where whenas death shall all the world subdue,
  Our love shall live and later life renew.'

George Peele

His Golden Locks Time Hath to Silver Turned

HIS golden locks Time hath to silver turned;
  O Time too swift, O swiftness never ceasing!
His youth 'gainst time and age hath ever spurned,

[1] also [2] quoth, said

But spurned in vain; youth waneth by increasing:
Beauty, strength, youth are flowers but fading seen;
Duty, faith, love are roots, and ever green.

His helmet now shall make a hive for bees,
And, lovers' sonnets turned to holy psalms,
A man-at-arms must now serve on his knees,
And feed on prayers, which are Age's alms:
But though from court to cottage he depart,
His Saint is sure of his unspotted heart.

And when he saddest sits in homely cell,
He'll teach his swains this carol for a song,
'Blest be the hearts that wish my Sovereign well,
Curst be the souls that think her any wrong!'
Goddess, allow this aged man his right
To be your beadsman[1] now that was your knight.

Michael Drayton

A Ballad of Agincourt

Fair stood the wind for France
When we our sails advance,
Nor now to prove our chance
Longer will tarry;

[1] one who prays for another's soul

But putting to the main,
At Caux, the mouth of Seine,
With all his martial train
  Landed King Harry.

And taking many a fort,
Furnish'd in warlike sort,
Marcheth tow'rds Agincourt
  In happy hour;
Skirmishing day by day
With those that stopp'd his way.
Where the French gen'ral lay
  With all his power.

Which, in his height of pride,
King Henry to deride,
His ransom to provide
  To the King sending;
Which he neglects the while
As from a nation vile,
Yet with an angry smile
  Their fall portending.

And turning to his men,
Quoth our brave Henry then,
'Though they to one be ten
  Be not amazèd:
Yet have we well begun;
Battles so bravely won
Have ever to the sun
  By fame been raisèd.

'And for myself (quoth he)
This my full rest shall be:
England ne'er mourn for me
  Nor more esteem me:
Victor I will remain
Or on this earth lie slain,
Never shall she sustain
  Loss to redeem me.

'Poitiers and Cressy tell
When most their pride did swell,
Under our swords they fell:
  No less our skill is
Than when our grandsire great,
Claiming the regal seat,
By many a warlike feat
  Lopp'd the French lilies.'

The Duke of York so dread
The eager vaward[1] led;
With the main Henry sped
  Among his henchmen.
Excester had the rear,
A braver man not there;
O Lord, how hot they were
  On the false Frenchmen!

They now to fight are gone,
Armour on armour shone,
Drum now to drum did groan,
  To hear was wonder.
That with the cries they make
The very earth did shake:
Trumpet to trumpet spake,
  Thunder to thunder.

[1] vanguard

Well it thine age became,
O noble Erpingham,
Which didst the signal aim
  To our hid forces!
When from a meadow by,
Like a storm suddenly
The English archery
  Stuck the French horses.

With Spanish yew so strong
Arrows a cloth-yard long
That like to serpents stung,
  Piercing the weather;
None from his fellow starts,
But playing manly parts,
And like true English hearts
  Stuck close together.

When down their bows they threw,
And forth their bilbos[1] drew,
And on the French they flew,
  Not one was tardy;
Arms were from shoulders sent,
Scalps to the teeth were rent,
Down the French peasants went—
  Our men were hardy.

This while our noble king,
His broadsword brandishing,
Down the French host did ding[2]
  As to o'erwhelm it;
And many a deep wound lent,
His arms with blood besprent,[3]
And many a cruel dent
  Bruisèd his helmet.

[1] swords [2] knock [3] spattered

Gloster, that duke so good,
Next of the royal blood,
For famous England stood
  With his brave brother;
Clarence, in steel so bright,
Though but a maiden knight,
Yet in that furious fight
Scarce such another.

Warwick in blood did wade,
Oxford the foe invade,
And cruel slaughter made
  Still as they ran up;
Suffold his axe did ply,
Beaumont and Willoughby
Bare them right doughtily,
  Ferrers and Fanhope.

Upon Saint Crispin's Day
Fought was this noble fray,
Which fame did not delay
  To England to carry.
O when shall English men
With such acts fill a pen?
Or England breed again
  Such a King Harry?

Christopher Marlowe

Lament for Zenocrate

(from *The Second Part of Tamburlaine the Great*)

BLACK is the beauty of the brightest day;
The golden ball of heaven's eternal fire,
That danced with glory on the silver waves,
Now wants the fuel that inflamed his beams;
And all with faintness, and for foul disgrace,
He binds his temples with a frowning cloud,
Ready to darken earth with endless night.
Zenocrate, that gave him light and life,
Whose eyes shot fire from their ivory brows,
And tempered every soul with lively heat,
Now by the malice of the angry skies,
Whose jealousy admits no second mate,
Draws in the comfort of her latest breath,
All dazzled with the hellish mists of death.
Now walk the angels on the walls of heaven,
As sentinels to warn th' immortal souls
To entertain divine Zenocrate:
Apollo, Cynthia, and the ceaseless lamps
That gently look'd upon this loathsome earth,
Shine downwards now no more, but deck the heavens
To entertain divine Zenocrate:
The crystal springs, whose taste illuminates
Refinèd eyes with an eternal sight,
Like trièd silver run through Paradise
To entertain divine Zenocrate:

The cherubins and holy seraphins,
That sing and play before the King of Kings,
Use all their voices and their instruments
To entertain divine Zenocrate;
And, in this sweet and curious[1] harmony,
The god that tunes this music to our souls
Holds out his hand in highest majesty
To entertain divine Zenocrate.
Then let some holy trance convey my thoughts
Up to the palace of th' empyreal heaven,
That this my life may be as short to me
As are the days of sweet Zenocrate.

William Shakespeare

Blow, Blow, Thou Winter Wind

(from *As You Like It*)

Blow, blow, thou winter wind,
    Thou art not so unkind
    As man's ingratitude;
    Thy tooth is not so keen
    Because thou art not seen,
    Although thy breath be rude.

[1] elaborate

Heigh ho! sing heigh ho! unto the green holly:
Most friendship is feigning, most loving mere folly:
Then, heigh ho, the holly!
This life is most jolly.

Freeze, freeze, thou bitter sky,
Thou dost not bite so nigh
As benefits forgot:
Though thou the waters warp,[1]
Thy sting is not so sharp
As friend remember'd not.
Heigh ho! sing heigh ho! unto the green holly:
Most friendship is feigning, most loving mere folly:
Then, heigh ho, the holly!
This life is most jolly.

Where the Bee Sucks

(from *The Tempest*)

WHERE the bee sucks, there suck I:
In a cowslip's bell I lie;
There I couch when owls do cry.
On the bat's back I do fly
After summer merrily.
Merrily, merrily shall I live now
Under the blossom that hangs on the bough.

[1] shrivel, contract

Full Fathom Five

(from *The Tempest*)

FULL fathom five thy father lies:
  Of his bones are coral made;
Those are pearls that were his eyes
  Nothing of him that doth fade
But doth suffer a sea-change
Into something rich and strange.
Sea-nymphs hourly ring his knell:
                Ding-dong.
Hark! now I hear them: Ding-dong, bell.

O Mistress Mine

(from *Twelfth Night*)

O MISTRESS mine, where are you roaming?
O! stay and hear, your true-love's coming,
  That can sing both high and low:
Trip no further, pretty sweeting;
Journeys end in lovers meeting,
  Every wise man's son doth know.

What is love? 'tis not hereafter;
Present mirth hath present laughter;
  What's to come is still unsure:
In delay there lies no plenty
Then come kiss me, sweet-and-twenty!
  Youth's a stuff will not endure.

Fear No More the Heat o' the Sun

(from *Cymbeline*)

FEAR no more the heat o' the sun,
  Nor the furious winter's rages;
Thou thy worldly task hast done,
  Home art gone, and ta-en thy wages:
Golden lads and girls all must,
  As chimney-sweepers, come to dust.

Fear no more the frown o' the great;
  Thou art past the tyrant's stroke;
Care no more to clothe and eat;
  To thee the reed is as the oak;
The sceptre, learning, physic, must
All follow this and come to dust.

Fear no more the lightning-flash,
  Nor the all-dreaded thunder-stone;
Fear not slander, censure rash;
  Thou hast finished joy and moan:
All lovers young, all lovers must
Consign to thee and come to dust.

No exorciser harm thee!
Nor no witchcraft charm thee!
Ghost unlaid forbear thee!
Nothing ill come near thee!
Quiet consummation have;
And renownèd be thy grave!

Shall I Compare Thee to a Summer's Day?

SHALL I compare thee to a summer's day?
Thou art more lovely and more temperate:
Rough winds do shake the darling buds of May,
And summer's lease hath all too short a date:
Sometime too hot the eye of heaven shines,
And often is his gold complexion dimm'd:
And every fair from fair sometime declines,
By chance, or nature's changing course untrimm'd.
But thy eternal summer shall not fade
Nor lose possession of that fair thou owest;
Nor shall Death brag thou wander'st in his shade,
When in eternal lines to time thou growest:
So long as men can breathe, or eyes can see,
So long lives this, and this gives life to thee.

When to the Sessions of Sweet Silent Thought

WHEN to the sessions of sweet silent thought
I summon up remembrance of things past,
I sigh the lack of many a thing I sought,
And with old woes new wail my dear time's waste:
Then can I drown an eye, unused to flow,
For precious friends hid in death's dateless night,
And weep afresh love's long since cancelled woe.
And moan the expense of many a vanished sight.
Then can I grieve at grievances foregone,
And heavily from woe to woe tell o'er

The sad account of fore-bemoanèd moan,
Which I new pay as if not paid before.
  But if the while I think on thee, dear friend,
  All losses are restored and sorrows end.

Tired With All These For Restful Death I Cry

Tired with all these for restful death I cry,
As to behold desert a beggar born,
And needy nothing trimm'd in jollity,
And purest faith unhappily forsworn,
And gilded honour shamefully misplaced,
And maiden virtue rudely strumpeted,
And right perfection wrongfully disgraced,
And strength by limping sway disabled,
And art made tongue-tied by authority,
And folly, doctor-like, controlling skill,
And simple truth miscall'd simplicity,
And captive good attending captain ill:
  Tired with all these, from these would I be gone,
  Save that to die, I leave my love alone.

Since Brass, nor Stone, nor Earth, nor Boundless Sea

Since brass, nor stone, nor earth, nor boundless sea,
But sad mortality o'er-sways their power,
How with this range shall beauty hold a plea,
Whose action is no stronger than a flower?

O, how shall summer's honey breath hold out
Against the wreckful siege of battering days,
When rocks impregnable are not so stout,
Nor gates of steel so strong, but Time decays?
O fearful meditation! where, alack
Shall Time's best jewel from Time's chest lie hid?
Or what strong hand can hold his swift foot back?
Or who his spoil of beauty can forbid?
O, none, unless this miracle have might,
That in black ink my Love may still shine bright.

When in the Chronicle of Wasted Time

WHEN in the chronicle of wasted time
I see descriptions of the fairest wights,
And beauty making beautiful old rime,
In praise of ladies dead and lovely knights:
Then in the blazon of sweet beauty's best,
Of hand, of foot, of lip, of eye, of brow,
I see their antique pen would have exprest
Even such a beauty as you master now.
So all their praises are but prophecies
Of this our time, all you prefiguring;
And, for they looked but with divining eyes,
They had not skill enough your worth to sing:
For we which now behold these present days,
Have eyes to wonder, but lack tongues to praise.

Let Me not to the Marriage of True Minds

LET me not to the marriage of true minds
Admit impediments. Love is not love
Which alters when it alteration finds,
Or bends with the remover to remove:
O no, it is an ever fixèd mark
That looks on tempests and is never shaken;
It is the star to every wand'ring bark,
Whose worth's unknown, although his height be taken.
Love's not Time's fool, though rosy lips and cheeks
Within his bending sickle's compass come;
Love alters not with his brief hours and weeks,
But bears it out even to the edge of doom.
  If this be error and upon me proved,
  I never writ, nor no man ever loved.

A Dream

(from *King Richard III*)

LORD, Lord! methought, what pain it was to drown!
What dreadful noise of waters in mine ears!
What ugly sights of death within mine eyes!
Methought I saw a thousand fearful wracks;
Ten thousand men that fishes gnaw'd upon;
Wedges of gold, great anchors, heaps of pearl,
Inestimable stones, unvalued jewels,
All scattered in the bottom of the sea:
Some lay in dead men's skulls; and, in those holes

Where eyes did once inhabit, there were crept,
As 'twere in scorn of eyes, reflecting gems,
Which woo'd the slimy bottom of the deep,
And mock'd the dead bones that lay scattered by.

St. Crispin's Day

(from *King Henry V*)

Westmoreland. O that we now had here
But one ten thousand of those men in England
That do no work to-day!
King Henry. What's he that wishes so?
My cousin Westmoreland? No, my fair cousin:
If we are mark'd to die, we are enow
To do our country loss; and if to live,
The fewer men, the greater share of honour.
God's will! I pray thee, wish not one man more.
By Jove, I am not covetous for gold,
Nor care I who doth feed upon my cost;
It yearns[1] me not if men my garments wear;
Such outward things dwell not in my desires;
But if it be a sin to covet honour,
I am the most offending soul alive.
No, faith, my coz, wish not a man from England:
God's peace! I would not lose so great an honour,
As one man more, methinks, would share from me,
For the best hope I have. O, do not wish one more!
Rather proclaim it, Westmoreland, through my host,

[1] grieves

That he which hath no stomach to this fight,
Let him depart; his passport shall be made,
And crowns for convoy put into his purse:
We would not die in that man's company
That fears his fellowship to die with us.
This day is call'd the feast of Crispian:
He that outlives this day, and comes safe home,
Will stand a tip-toe when this day is named,
And rouse him at the name of Crispian.
He that shall live this day, and see old age,
Will yearly on the vigil[1] feast his neighbours,
And say 'To-morrow is Saint Crispian:'
Then will he strip his sleeve and show his scars,
And say 'These wounds I had on Crispin's day.'
Old men forget; yet all shall be forgot,
But he'll remember with advantages
What feats he did that day: then shall our names,
Familiar in his mouth as household words,—
Harry the king, Bedford and Exeter,
Warwick and Talbot, Salisbury and Gloucester,—
Be in their flowing cups freshly remember'd.
This story shall the good man[2] teach his son;
And Crispin Crispian shall ne'er go by,
From this day to the ending of the world,
But we in it shall be remembered,
We few, we happy few, we band of brothers;
For he to-day that sheds his blood with me
Shall be my brother; be he ne'er so vile,
This day shall gentle his condition:
And gentlemen in England now a-bed
Shall think themselves accursed they were not here,
And hold their manhoods cheap whiles any speaks
That fought with us upon Saint Crispin's day.

[1] eve [2] master of the house

The Death of Kings

(from *King Richard II*)

FOR God's sake, let us sit upon the ground,
And tell sad stories of the death of kings:—
How some have been deposed; some slain in war;
Some haunted by the ghosts they have deposed;
Some poison'd by their wives; some sleeping kill'd;
All murder'd:—for within the hollow crown
That rounds the mortal temples of a king
Keeps Death his court; and there the antick[1] sits,
Scoffing his state, and grinning at his pomp;
Allowing him a breath, a little scene,
To monarchize, be fear'd, and kill with looks;
Infusing him with self and vain conceit,—
As if this flesh, which walls about out life,
Were brass impregnable; and humour'd thus,
Comes at the last, and with a little pin
Bores through his castle-wall, and—farewell king!

Sleep

(from *King Henry IV, Part 2*)

How many thousand of my poorest subjects
Are at this hour asleep! O sleep, O gentle sleep,
Nature's soft nurse, how have I frighted thee,
That thou no more wilt weigh my eyelids down,
And steep my senses in forgetfulness?

[1] buffoon

Why rather, sleep, liest thou in smoky cribs,
Upon uneasy pallets stretching thee,
And hushed with buzzing night-flies to thy slumber,
Than in the perfumed chambers of the great,
Under the canopies of costly state,
And lulled with sounds of sweetest melody?
O thou dull god, why liest thou with the vile
In loathsome beds, and leav'st the kingly couch
A watch-case, or a common 'larum-bell?
Wilt thou upon the high and giddy mast
Seal up the ship-boy's eyes, and rock his brains
In cradle of the rude imperious surge,
And in the visitation of the winds,
Who take the ruffian billows by the top,
Curling their monstrous heads, and hanging them
With deafening clamour in the slippery shrouds,
That, with the hurly, death itself awakes?—
Canst thou, O partial sleep, give thy repose
To the wet sea-boy in an hour so rude;
And, in the calmest and most stillest night,
With all appliances and means to boot,
Deny it to a king? Then, happy low, lie down!
Uneasy lies the head that wears a crown.

Music

(from *The Merchant of Venice*)

Lorenzo. How sweet the moonlight sleeps upon this bank!
Here will we sit, and let the sounds of music
Creep in our ears: soft stillness and the night

Become the touches of sweet harmony.
Sit, Jessica: look, how the floor of heaven
Is thick inlaid with patens of bright gold:
There's not the smallest orb which thou behold'st
But in his motion like an angel sings,
Still quiring to the young-eyed cherubins;
Such harmony is in immortal souls;
But, whilst this muddy vesture of decay
Doth grossly close it in, we cannot hear it.
Come, ho! and wake Diana with a hymn:
With sweetest touches pierce your mistress' ear,
And draw her home with music. [*Music.*

Jessica. I am never merry when I hear sweet music.

Lorenzo. The reason is, your spirits are attentive:
For do but note a wild and wanton herd,
Or race of youthful and unhandled colts,
Fetching mad bounds, bellowing and neighing loud,
Which is the hot condition of their blood;
If they but here perchance a trumpet sound,
Or any air of music touch their ears,
You shall perceive them make a mutual stand,
Their savage eyes turn'd to a modest gaze
By the sweet power of music: therefore the poet
Did feign that Orpheus drew trees, stones, and floods;
Since nought so stockish, hard, and full of rage,
But music for the time doth change his nature.
The man that hath no music in himself,
Nor is not mov'd with concord of sweet sounds,
Is fit for treasons, stratagems, and spoils;
The motions of his spirit are dull as night,
And his affections dark as Erebus:
Let no such man be trusted. Mark the music.

Sounds and Sweet Airs

(from *The Tempest*)

Be not afeard, the isle is full of noises,
Sounds, and sweet airs, that give delight and hurt not;
Sometimes a thousand twangling instruments
Will hum about mine ears; and sometime voices,
That, if I then had waked after long sleep,
Will make me sleep again: and then, in dreaming,
The clouds methought would open, and show riches
Ready to drop upon me, that when I waked
I cried to dream again.

The Death of Cleopatra

(from *Antony and Cleopatra*)

Cleopatra. Give me my robe, put on my crown, I have
Immortal longings in me. Now no more
The juice of Egypt's grape shall moist this lip.
Yare,[1] yare, good Iras; quick. Methinks I hear
Anthony call: I see him rouse himself
To praise my noble act. I hear him mock
The luck of Cæsar, which the gods give men
To excuse their after wrath. Husband, I come:
Now to that name my courage prove my title.
I am fire, and air; my other elements
I give to baser life. So, have you done?

[1] quickly

Come then, and take the last warmth of my lips.
Farewell kind Charmian, Iras, long farewell.
[*Kisses them. Iras falls and dies.*
Have I the aspic in my lips? Dost fall?
If thou and nature can so gently part,
The stroke of death is as a lover's pinch,
Which hurts, and is desired. Dost thou lie still?
If thus thou vanishest, thou tell'st the world
It is not worth leave-taking.
Charmian. Dissolve thick cloud, and rain, that I may say
The gods themselves do weep.
Cleopatra. This proves me base:
If she first meet the curled Antony,
He'll make demand of her, and spend that kiss
Which is my heaven to have. Come, thou mortal wretch,
[*To an asp, which she applies to her breast.*
With thy sharp teeth this knot intrinsicate
Of life at once untie: poor venomous fool,
Be angry, and dispatch. O, couldst thou speak,
That I might hear thee call great Cæsar ass
Unpolicied.
Charmian. O, eastern star.
Cleopatra. Peace, peace:
Dost thou not see my baby at my breast,
That sucks the nurse asleep?
Charmian. O break! O break!
Cleopatra. As sweet as balm, as soft as air, as gentle.
O Antony! Nay, I will take thee too:
[*Applying another asp to her arm.*
What should I stay— [*Dies.*
Charmian. In this vile world? So fare thee well:
Now boast thee, death, in thy possession lies
A lass unparallel'd. Downy windows close,
And golden Phœbus never be beheld
Of eyes again so royal: your crown's awry;
I'll mend it, and then play.

Irresolution

(from *Hamlet*)

How all occasions do inform against me,
And spur my dull revenge! What is a man,
If his chief good and market of his time
Be but to sleep and feed? a beast, no more.
Sure, he that made us with such large discourse,
Looking before and after, gave us not
That capability and godlike reason
To fust in us unused. Now, whether it be
Beastial oblivion, or some craven scruple
Of thinking too precisely on th' event,—
A though which, quarter'd, hath but one part wisdom
And ever three parts coward,—I do not know
Why yet I live to say 'This thing's to do;'
Sith I have cause, and will, and strength, and means
To do't. Examples, gross as earth, exhort me:
Witness this army, of such mass and charge,
Led by a delicate and tender prince;
Whose spirit, with divine ambition puff'd,
Makes mouths at the invisible event;
Exposing what is mortal and unsure
To all that fortune, death, and danger dare,
Even for an egg-shell. Rightly to be great
Is not to stir without great argument,
But greatly to find quarrel in a straw
When honour's at the stake. How stand I then,
That have a father kill'd, a mother stain'd,
Excitements of my reason and my blood,
And let all sleep? while, to my shame, I see
The imminent death of twenty thousand men,
That for a fantasy and trick of fame

Go to their graves like beds; fight for a plot
Whereon the numbers cannot try the cause,
Which is not tomb enough and continent
To hide the slain?—O, from this time forth,
My thoughts be bloody, or be nothing worth!

Thomas Campian

Bessy and Jamie

It fell on a summer's day,
While sweet Bessy sleeping lay
In her bower, on her bed,
Light with curtains shadowed,
Jamie came: she him spies,
Op'ning half her heavy eyes.

Jamie stole in through the door,
She lay slumb'ring as before;
Softly to her he drew near,
She heard him, yet would not hear,
Bessy vow'd not to speak,
He resolv'd that dumpe to break.

First a soft kiss he doth take,
She lay still, and would not wake;
Then his hands learn'd to woo,
She dream'd not what he would do,

But still slept, while he smil'd
To see love by sleep beguil'd.

Jamie then began to play,
Bessy as one buri'd lay,
Gladly still through this sleight
Deceiv'd in her own deceit,
And since this trance began,
She sleeps every afternoon.

Thomas Nashe

In Time of Pestilence

ADIEU! farewell earth's bliss!
This world uncertain is:
Fond are life's lustful joys,
Death proves them all but toys.
None from his darts can fly:
I am sick, I must die—
Lord, have mercy on us!

Rich men, trust not in wealth,
Gold cannot buy you health;
Physic himself must fade;
All things to end are made;
The plague full swift goes by:
I am sick, I must die—
Lord, have mercy on us!

Beauty is but a flower
Which wrinkles will devour:
Brightness falls from the air;
Queens have died young and fair,
Dust hath closed Helen's eye:
I am sick, I must die—
  Lord, have mercy on us!

Strength stoops unto the grave,
Worms feed on Hector brave;
Swords may not fight with fate;
Earth still holds ope her gate;
Come! Come! the bells do cry:
I am sick, I must die—
  Lord, have mercy on us!

Wit with his wantonness,
Tasteth death's bitterness;
Hell's executioner
Hath no ears for to hear
What vain art can reply.
I am sick, I must die—
  Lord, have mercy on us!

Haste, therefore, each degree
To welcome destiny!
Heaven is our heritage;
Earth but a player's stage.
Mount we unto the sky!
I am sick, I must die—
  Lord, have mercy on us!

Ben Jonson

Hymn to Diana

QUEEN and huntress, chaste and fair,
Now the sun is laid to sleep,
Seated in thy silver chair,
State in wonted manner keep:
Hesperus entreats thy light,
Goddess excellently bright.

Earth, let not thy envious shade
Dare itself to interpose;
Cynthia's shining orb was made
Heaven to clear when day did close:
Bless us then with wishèd sight,
Goddess excellently bright.

Lay thy bow of pearl apart,
And thy crystal-shining quiver;
Give unto the flying hart
Space to breathe, how short soever:
Thou that mak'st day of night—
Goddess excellently bright.

Inviting a Friend to Supper

To-night, grave sir, both my poor house, and I
  Do equally desire your company:
Not that we think us worthy such a guest,
  But that your worth will dignify our feast,
With those that come; whose grace may make that seem
  Something, which, else, could hope for no esteem.
It is the fair acceptance, Sir, creates
  The entertainment perfect: not the cates.
Yet shall you have, to rectify your palate,
  An olive, capers, or some better salad
Ush'ring the mutton; with a short-leg'd hen,
  If we can get her, full of eggs, and then,
Lemons, and wine for sauce: to these, a coney
  Is not to be despair'd of, for our money;
And, though fowl now be scarce, yet there are clerks,
  The sky not falling, think we may have larks.
I'll tell you of more, and lie, so you will come:
  Of partridge, pheasant, wood-cock, of which some
May yet be there; and godwit, if we can;
  Knat, raile, and ruff too. How so e'er, my man
Shall read a piece of Virgil, Tacitus,
  Livy, or some better book to us,
Of which we'll speak our minds, amidst our meat;
  And I'll profess no verses to repeat:
To this, if ought appear, which I know not of,
  That will the pastry, not my paper, show of.
Digestive cheese, and fruit there sure will be;
  But that, which most doth take my *Muse*, and me,
Is a pure cup of rich *Canary*-wine,
  Which is the *Mermaid's*, now, but shall be mine:
Of which had Horace, or Anacreon tasted,

Their lives, as do their lines, till now had lasted.
Tabacco, *Nectar*, or the *Thespian* spring,
Are all but Luther's beer, to this I sing.
Of this we will sup free, but moderately,
And we will have no *Pooly*, or *Parrot* by;
Nor shall our cups make any guilty men:
But, at our parting, we will be, as when
We innocently met. No simple word,
That shall be utter'd at our mirthful board,
Shall make us sad next morning: or affright
The liberty, that we'll enjoy tonight.

That Women are but Men's Shadows

Follow a shadow, it still flies you,
Seem to fly it, it will pursue:
So court a mistress, she denies you;
Let her alone, she will court you.
Say, are not women, truly, then,
Styl'd but the shadows of us men?
At morn, and even, shades are longest;
At noon, they are short, or none:
So men at weakest, they are strongest,
But grant us perfect, they're not known.
Say, are not women, truly, then,
Styl'd but the shadows of us men?

Song

Still to be neat, still to be dressed,
As you were going to a feast;
Still to be powder'd, still perfum'd:
Lady, it is to be presum'd,
Though Art's hid causes are not found,
All is not sweet, all is not sound.

Give me a look, give me a face,
That makes simplicity a grace;
Robes loosely flowing, hair as free:
Such sweet neglect more taketh me,
Than all th'adulteries of Art;
They strike mine eyes, but not my heart.

The Old Testament

I Will Lift Up Mine Eyes

(*Psalm 121* in the Prayer Book version, attributed to Miles Coverdale)

I WILL lift up mine eyes unto the hills: from whence cometh my help.

My help cometh even from the Lord: who hath made heaven and earth.

He will not suffer thy foot to be moved: and he that keepeth thee will not sleep.

Behold, he that keepeth Israel: shall neither slumber nor sleep.

The Lord himself is thy keeper: the Lord is thy defence upon thy right hand;

So that the sun shall not burn thee by day: neither the moon by night.

The Lord shall preserve thee from all evil: yea, it is even he that shall keep thy soul.

The Lord shall preserve thy going out, and thy coming in: from this time forth for evermore.

The Earth is the Lord's

(Psalm 24)

THE earth is the Lord's, and the fulness thereof;
The world, and they that dwell therein.
For he hath founded it upon the seas,
And established it upon the floods.
Who shall ascend into the hill of the Lord?
Or who shall stand in his holy place?
He that hath clean hands, and a pure heart;
Who hath not lifted up his soul unto vanity, nor sworn deceitfully.
He shall receive the blessing from the Lord,
And righteousness from the God of his salvation.
This is the generation of them that seek him,
That seek thy face, O Jacob.

Lift up your heads, O ye gates;
And be ye lift up, ye everlasting doors;
And the King of glory shall come in.
Who is this King of glory?
The Lord strong and mighty,
The Lord mighty in battle.
Lift up your heads, O ye gates;
Even lift them up, ye everlasting doors;
And the King of glory shall come in.
Who is this King of glory?
The Lord of hosts,
He is the King of glory.

He is My Refuge

(from *Psalm 91*)

He that dwelleth in the secret place of the most High
Shall abide under the shadow of the Almighty.
I will say of the Lord, He is my refuge and my fortress:
My God; in him will I trust.
Surely he shall deliver thee from the snare of the fowler,
And from the noisome pestilence.
He shall cover thee with his feathers,
And under his wings shalt thou trust:
His truth shall be thy shield and buckler.

Thou shalt not be afraid for the terror by night;
Nor for the arrow that flieth by day;
Nor for the pestilence that walketh in darkness;
Nor for the destruction that wasteth at noonday.
A thousand shall fall at thy side,
And ten thousand at thy right hand:
But it shall not come nigh thee.

Four Things

(from *The Book of Proverbs*)

THERE be four things which are little upon the earth, but they are exceeding wise:
The ants are a people not strong, yet they prepare their meat in the summer:
The conies are but a feeble folk, yet make they their houses in the rocks;
The locusts have no king, yet go they forth all of them by bands;
The spider taketh hold with her hands, and is in king's palaces.

The War Horse

(from *The Book of Job*)

HAST thou given the horse strength?
Hast thou clothed his neck with thunder?
Canst thou make him afraid as a grasshopper?
The glory of his nostrils is terrible.
    He paweth in the valley, and rejoiceth in his strength:
    He goeth on to meet the armed men.
    He mocketh at fear, and is not affrighted;
    Neither turneth he back from the sword.
    The quiver rattleth against him,
    The glittering spear and the shield.
    He swalloweth the ground with fierceness and rage:
    Neither believeth he that it is the sound of the trumpet.
He saith among the trumpets, Ha, ha;
And he smelleth the battle afar off,
The thunder of the captains, and the shouting.

David's Lament

(from *The Second Book of Samuel*)

AND David lamented with this lamentation over Saul and over Jonathan his son:

The beauty of Israel is slain upon thy high places:
How are the mighty fallen!
Tell it not in Gath,
Publish it not in the streets of Askelon;
Lest the daughters of the Philistines rejoice,
Lest the daughters of the uncircumcised triumph.
Ye mountains of Gilboa,
Let there be no dew, neither let there be rain upon you nor fields of offerings:
For there the shield of the mighty is vilely cast away,
The shield of Saul as though he had not been anointed with oil.
From the blood of the slain, from the fat of the mighty,
The bow of Jonathan turned not back,
And the sword of Saul returned not empty.
Saul and Jonathan were lovely and pleasant in their lives,
And in their death they were not divided:
They were swifter than eagles,
They were stronger than lions.
Ye daughters of Israel, weep over Saul,
Who clothed you in scarlet, with other delights,
Who put on ornaments of gold upon your apparel.
How are the mighty fallen in the midst of the battle!
O Jonathan, thou wast slain in thine high places.
I am distressed for thee, my brother Jonathan:
Very pleasant hast thou been unto me:
Thy love to me was wonderful,
Passing the love of women.
How are the mighty fallen,
And the weapons of war perished!

Vanity of Vanities

(from *The Book of Ecclesiastes*)

REMEMBER now thy Creator in the days of thy youth:
While the evil days come not,
Nor the years draw nigh when thou shalt say, I have no pleasure in them;
While the sun,
  Or the light,
  Or the moon,
  Or the stars,
Be not darkened,
Nor the clouds return after the rain:

In the days when the keepers of the house shall tremble,
And the strong men shall bow themselves,
And the grinders cease because they are few,
And those that look out of the windows be darkened,
And the doors shall be shut in the streets,
When the sound of the grinding is low,
And he shall rise up at the voice of the bird,
And all the daughters of music shall be brought low;
Also when they shall be afraid of that which is high,
  And fears shall be in the way,
  And the almond tree shall flourish,
  And the grasshopper shall be a burden,
    And desire shall fail:
Because man goeth to his long home,
And the mourners go about the streets:

  Or ever the silver cord be loosed,
  Or the golden bowl be broken,
  Or the pitcher be broken at the fountain,
  Or the wheel broken at the cistern.

Then shall the dust return to the earth as it was
And the spirit shall return unto God who gave it.

Vanity of vanities, saith the preacher: all is vanity.

The Valley of Dry Bones

(from *The Book of Ezekiel*)

THE hand of the Lord was upon me, and carried me out in the spirit of the Lord, and set me down in the midst of the valley which was full of bones, and caused me to pass by them round about: and, behold, there were very many in the open valley; and, lo, they were very dry.

And he said unto me, Son of man, can these bones live? And I answered, O Lord God, thou knowest.

Again he said unto me, Prophesy upon these bones, and say unto them, O ye dry bones, hear the word of the Lord. Thus saith the Lord God unto these bones: Behold, I will cause breath to enter into you, and ye shall live: and I will lay sinews upon you, and cover you with skin, and put breath in you, and ye shall live; and ye shall know that I am the Lord.

So I prophesied as I was commanded: and as I prophesied, there was a noise, and behold a shaking, and the bones came together, bone to his bone. And when I beheld, lo, the sinews and the flesh came up upon them, and the skin covered them above: but there was no breath in them.

Then said he unto me, Prophesy unto the wind, prophesy, son of man, and say to the wind, Thus saith the Lord God; Come from the four winds, O breath, and breathe upon these slain, that they may live.

So I prophesied as he commanded me, and the breath came

into them, and they lived, and stood up upon their feet, an exceeding great army.

Then he said unto me, Son of man, these bones are the whole house of Israel: behold, they say, Our bones are dried, and our hope is lost: we are cut off for our parts. Therefore prophesy and say unto them, Thus saith the Lord God; Behold, O my people, I will open your graves, and cause you to come up out of your graves, and bring you into the land of Israel. And ye shall know that I am the Lord, when I have opened your graves, O my people, and brought you up out of your graves, and shall put my spirit in you, and ye shall live, and I shall place you in your own land: then shall ye know that I the Lord have spoken it, and performed it, saith the Lord.

Tobias Hume

Fain Would I Change that Note

FAIN would I change that note
  To which fond love hath charmed me
Long, long to sing by rote,
  Fancying that that harmed me.
Yet when this thought doth come,
'Love is the perfect sum
    Of all delight,'
I have no other choice
Either for pen or voice
    To sing or write.

O love! they wrong thee much
  That say thy sweet is bitter,
When thy ripe fruit is such
  As nothing can be sweeter.
Fair house of joy and bliss
Where truest pleasure is,
    I do adore thee:
I know thee what thou art,
I serve thee with my heart
    And fall before thee.

John Donne

Death, Be Not Proud

DEATH, be not proud, though some have called thee
Mighty and dreadful, for thou art not so;
For those whom thou think'st thou dost overthrow
Die not, poor Death; nor yet canst thou kill me.
From rest and sleep, which but thy pictures be,
Much pleasure; then from thee much more must flow;
And soonest our best men with thee do go,
Rest of their bones and souls' delivery!
Thou'rt slave to fate, chance, kings, and desperate men,
And dost with poison, war, and sickness dwell,
And poppy or charms can make us sleep as well
And better than thy stroke; why swell'st thou then?
One short sleep past, we wake eternally,
And Death shall be no more: Death, thou shalt die!

At the Round Earth's Imagined Corners

At the round earth's imagined corners, blow
Your trumpets, angels, and arise, arise
From death, you numberless infinities
Of souls, and to your scattered bodies go;
All whom the flood did, and fire shall o'erthrow,
All whom war, dearth, age, agues, tyrannies,
Despair, law, chance hath slain, and you, whose eyes
Shall behold God, and never taste death's woe.
But let them sleep, Lord, and me mourn a space;
For, if above all these my sins abound,
'Tis late to ask abundance of Thy grace,
When we are there. Here on this lowly ground,
Teach me how to repent, for that's as good
As if thou hadst seal'd my pardon with thy blood.

The Anniversary

All Kings, and all their favourites,
All glory of honours, beauties, wits,
The Sun itself, which makes times, as they pass,
Is elder by a year, now, than it was
When thou and I first one another saw:
All other things, to their destruction draw,
Only our love hath no decay;
This, no tomorrow hath, nor yesterday,
Running, it never runs from us away,
But truly keeps his first, last, everlasting day.
Two graves must hide thine and my corse,
If one might, death were no divorce.

Alas, as well as other Princes, we,
(Who Prince enough in one another be,)
Must leave at last in death, these eyes, and ears,
Oft fed with true oaths, and with sweet salt tears;
    But souls where nothing dwells but love
(All other thoughts being inmates) then shall prove
This, or a love increased there above,
When bodies to their graves, souls from their graves remove.

    And then we shall be throughly blest,
    But we no more, than all the rest;
Here upon earth, we'are Kings, and none but we
Can be such Kings, nor of such subjects be.
Who is so safe as we? where none can do
Treason to us, except one of us two.
    True and false fears let us refrain,
Let us love nobly, and live, and add again
Years and years unto years, till we attain
To write threescore: this is the second of our reign.

The Expiration

So, so, break off this last lamenting kiss,
  Which sucks two souls, and vapours both away,
Turn thou ghost that way, and let me turn this,
  And let ourselves benight our happiest day,
We ask'd none leave to love; nor will we owe
  Any, so cheap a death, as saying, Go;
Go; and if that word hath not quite kill'd thee,
  Ease me with death, by bidding me go too.
Oh, if it have, let my word work on me,

And a just office on a murderer do.
Except it be too late, to kill me so,
Being double dead, going, and bidding, go.

A Valediction: Forbidding Mourning

As virtuous men pass mildly away,
And whisper to their souls, to go,
Whilst some of their sad friends do say,
The breath goes now, and some say, no:

So let us melt, and make no noise,
No tear-floods, nor sigh-tempests move,
T'were profanation of our joys
To tell the laity our love.

Moving of th'earth brings harms and fears,
Men reckon what it did and meant,
But trepidation of the spheres,
Though greater far, is innocent.

Dull sublunary lovers' love
(Whose soul is sense) cannot admit
Absence, because it doth remove
Those things which elemented it.

But we by a love, so much refin'd,
That our selves know not what it is
Inter-assured of the mind,
Care less, eyes, lips, and hands to miss.

Our two souls therefore, which are one,
  Though I must go, endure not yet
A breach, but an expansion,
Like gold to airy thinness beat.

If they be two, they are two so
  As stiff twin compasses are two,
Thy soul the fix'd foot, makes no show
  To move, but doth, if th'other do.

And though it in the centre sit,
  Yet when the other far doth roam,
It leans, and hearkens after it,
  And grows erect, as that comes home.

Such wilt thou be to me, who must
  Like th'other foot, obliquely run;
Thy firmness draws my circle just,
  And makes me end, where I begun.

The Good-morrow

I WONDER by my troth, what thou, and I
Did, till we lov'd? were we not wean'd till then?
But suck'd on country pleasures, childishly?
Or snorted we in the seven sleepers' den?
T'was so; But this, all pleasures fancies be.
If ever any beauty I did see,
Which I desir'd, and got, t'was but a dream of thee.

And now good morrow to our waking souls,
Which watch not one another out of fear;
For love, all love of other sights controls,
And makes one little room, an every where.

Let sea-discoverers to new worlds have gone,
Let Maps to others, worlds on worlds have shown,
Let us possess one world, each hath one, and is one.

My face in thine eye, thine in mine appears,
And true plain hearts do in the faces rest,
Where can we find two better hemispheres,
Without sharp North, without declining West?
What ever dies, was not mix'd equally;
If our two loves be one, or, thou and I
Love so alike, that none do slacken, none can die.

John Webster

A Dirge

CALL for the robin-redbreast and the wren,
Since o'er shady groves they hover,
And with leaves and flowers do cover
The friendless bodies of unburied men.
Call unto his funeral dole[1]
The ant, the field-mouse, and the mole,
To rear him hillocks that shall keep him warm,
And (when gay tombs are robb'd) sustain no harm;
But keep the wolf far thence, that's foe to men,
For with his nails he'll dig them up again.

[1] mourning

Richard Corbet

To His Son

VINCENT CORBET, on his birthday, November 10, 1630,
being then three years old.

WHAT I shall leave thee none can tell,
But all shall say I wish thee well;
I wish thee, Vin, before all wealth,
Both bodily and ghostly[1] health:
Not too much wealth, nor wit, come to thee,
So much of either may undo thee.
I wish thee learning, not for show,
Enough for to instruct, and know;
Not such as gentlemen require,
To prate at table, or at fire.
I wish thee all thy mother's graces,
Thy father's fortunes, and his places.
I wish thee friends, and one at Court,
Not to build on, but support;
To keep thee, not in doing many
Oppressions, but from suffering any.
I wish thee peace in all thy ways,
Nor lazy nor contentious days;
And when thy soul and body part,
As innocent as now thou art.

[1] spiritual

Henry Farley

A Complaint

To see a strange outlandish fowl,
A quaint baboon, an ape, an owl,
A dancing bear, a giant's bone,
A foolish engine move alone,
A morris-dance, a puppet-play,
Mad Tom to sing a roundelay,
A woman dancing on a rope,
Bull-baiting also at the Hope,
A rimer's jests, a juggler's cheats,
A tumbler showing cunning feats,
Or players acting on a stage,—
There goes the bounty of our age!
But unto any pious motion
There's little coin and less devotion.

William Drummond

This World a Hunting Is

THIS world a hunting is,
The prey poor man, the Nimrod fierce is Death;
His speedy greyhounds are
Lust, sickness, envy, care,
Strife that ne'er falls amiss,
With all those ills which haunt us while we breathe.
Now, if by chance we fly
Of these the eager chase,
Old age with stealing pace
Casts up his nets, and there we panting die.

Robert Herrick

To Anthea who may Command Him Any Thing

BID me to live, and I will live
  Thy Protestant to be:
Or bid me love, and I will give
  A loving heart to thee.

A heart as soft, a heart as kind,
  A heart as sound and free
As in the whole world thou canst find,
  That heart I'll give to thee.

Bid that heart stay, and it will stay,
  To honour thy decree:
Or bid it languish quite away,
  And't shall do so for thee.

Bid me to weep, and I will weep
  While I have eyes to see:
And, having none, yet I will keep
  A heart to weep for thee.

Bid me despair, and I'll despair
  Under that cypress tree:
Or bid me die, and I will dare
  E'en Death, to die for thee.

Thou art my life, my love, my heart,
  The very eyes of me,
And hast command of every part,
  To live and die for thee.

To Dianeme

Sweet, be not proud of those two eyes
Which starlike sparkle in their skies;
Nor be you proud, that you can see
All hearts your captives; yours yet free:

Be you not proud of that rich hair
Which wantons with the lovesick air;
Whenas that ruby which you wear,
Sunk from the tip of your soft ear,
Will last to be a precious stone
When all your world of beauty's gone.

Corinna's Going a Maying

GET up, get up for shame, the blooming morn
Upon her wings presents the god unshorn.
See how Aurora throws her fair
Fresh-quilted colours through the air:
Get up, sweet slug-a-bed, and see
The dew-bespangled herb and tree.
Each flower has wept and bow'd toward the east,
Above an hour since, yet you not drest;
Nay! not so much as out of bed?
When all the birds have matins said,
And sung their thankful hymns, 'tis sin,
Nay, profanation to keep in,
Whenas a thousand virgins on this day
Spring, sooner than the lark, to fetch in May.

Rise, and put on your foliage, and be seen
To come forth, like the spring-time, fresh and green,
And sweet as Flora. Take no care
For jewels for your gown or hair:
Fear not; the leaves will strew
Gems in abundance upon you:
Besides, the childhood of the day has kept,
Against you come, some orient pearls unwept.

Come, and receive them while the light
Hangs on the dew-locks of the night,
And Titan on the eastern hill
Retires himself, or else stands still
Till you come forth. Wash, dress, be brief in praying:
Few beads are best when once we go a Maying.

Come, my Corinna, come; and coming, mark
How each field turns a street, each street a park,
Made green and trimm'd with trees: see how
Devotion gives each house a bough
Or branch: each porch, each door, ere this
An ark, a tabernacle is,
Made up of white-thorn neatly interwove,
As if here were those cooler shades of love.
Can such delights be in the street
And open fields, and we not see 't?
Come, we'll abroad: and let's obey
The proclamation made for May,
And sin no more, as we have done, by staying;
But, my Corinna, come, let's go a Maying.

There's not a budding boy or girl this day
But is got up and gone to bring in May.
A deal of youth, ere this, is come
Back, and with white-thorn laden home.
Some have dispatch'd their cakes and cream,
Before that we have left to dream:
And some have wept and woo'd, and plighted troth,
And chose their priest, ere we can cast off sloth:
Many a green-gown has been given,
Many a kiss, both odd and even:
Many a glance, too, has been sent
From out the eye, love's firmament:
Many a jest told of the keys betraying
This night, and locks pick'd: yet y'are not a Maying.

Come, let us go, while we are in our prime,
And take the harmless folly of the time:
    We shall grow old apace, and die
    Before we know our liberty.
    Our life is short, and our days run
    As fast away as does the sun.
And, as a vapour or a drop of rain,
Once lost, can ne'er be found again,
    So when or you or I are made
    A fable, song, or fleeting shade,
    All love, all liking, all delight
    Lies drowned with us in endless night.
Then, while time serves, and we are but decaying,
Come, my Corinna, come, let's go a Maying.

George Herbert

Virtue

SWEET day, so cool, so calm, so bright,
The bridal of the earth and sky,
The dew shall weep thy fall to-night;
    For thou must die.

Sweet rose, whose hue angry and brave
Bids the rash gazer wipe his eye,
Thy root is ever in its grave;
    And thou must die.

Sweet spring, full of sweet days and roses,
A box where sweets compacted lie,
My music shows ye have your closes,
And all must die.

Only a sweet and virtuous soul,
Like seasoned timber, never gives;
But though the whole world turn to coal,
Then chiefly lives.

Jordan II

When first my lines of heav'nly joys made mention,
Such was their lustre, they did so excel,
That I sought out quaint words, and trim invention;
My thoughts began to burnish, sprout, and swell,
Curling with metaphors a plain intention,
Decking the sense, as if it were to sell.

Thousands of notions in my brain did run,
Off'ring their service, if I were not sped:
I often blotted what I had begun;
This was not quick enough, and that was dead.
Nothing could seem too rich to clothe the sun,
Much less those joys that trample on his head,

As flames do work and wind, when they ascend,
So did I weave my self into the sense.
But while I bustled, I might hear a friend
Whisper, *How wide is all this long pretence*!
There is in love a sweetness ready penn'd
Copy out only that, and save expense.

The Pulley

WHEN God at first made man,
Having a glass of blessings standing by,
Let us (said he) pour on him all we can.
Let the world's riches, which dispersed lie
Contract into a span.

So strength first made a way,
Then beauty flow'd, then wisdom, honour, pleasure.
When almost all was out, God made a stay,
Perceiving that alone of all his treasure
Rest in the bottom lay.

For if I should (said he)
Bestow this jewel also on my creature,
He would adore my gifts instead of me,
And rest in Nature, not the God of Nature.
So both should losers be.

Yet let him keep the rest,
But keep them with repining restlessness.
Let him be rich and weary, that at least,
If goodness lead him not, yet weariness
May toss him to my breast.

The Quip

The merry world did on a day
With his train-bands and mates agree
To meet together where I lay,
And all in sport to jeer at me.

First, Beauty crept into a rose;
  Which when I pluck'd not, Sir, said she,
Tell me, I pray, whose hands are those?
  But thou shalt answer, Lord, for me.

Then Money came, and chinking still,
  What tune is this, poor man? said he,
I heard in Music you had skill.
  But thou shalt answer, Lord, for me.

Then came brave Glory puffing by
  In silks that whistled, who but he?
He scarce allow'd me half an eye.
  But thou shalt answer, Lord, for me.

Then came quick Wit and Conversation,
  And he would needs a comfort be,
And, to be short, made an oration.
  But thou shalt answer, Lord, for me.

Yet when the hour of thy design
  To answer these fine things shall come,
Speak not at large, say, I am thine;
  And then they have their answer home.

James Shirley

The Glories of our Blood and State

THE glories of our blood and state
  Are shadows, not substantial things,
There is no armour against fate,
  Death lays his icy hand on kings;
      Sceptre and crown
      Must tumble down,
And in the dust be equal made
With the poor crooked scythe and spade.

Some men with swords may reap the field,
  And plant fresh laurels where they kill,
But their strong nerves at last must yield,
  They tame but one another still;
      Early or late,
      They stoop to fate,
And must give up their murmuring breath,
When they, pale captives, creep to death.

The garlands wither on your brow,
  Then boast no more your mighty deeds,
Upon Death's purple altar now,
  See, where the victor-victim bleeds;
      Your heads must come
      To the cold tomb;
Only the actions of the just
Smell sweet, and blossom in their dust.

John Milton

The Building of Pandemonium

(from *Paradise Lost*, Book I)

There stood a hill not far, whose grisly top
Belched fire and rolling smoke; the rest entire
Shone with a glossy scurf—undoubted sign
That in his womb was hid metallic ore,
The work of sulphur. Thither, winged with speed,
A numerous brigad hastened: as when bands
Of pioneers, with spade and pickaxe armed,
Forerun the royal camp, to trench a field,
Or cast a rampart. Mammon led them on—
Mammon, the least erected Spirit that fell
From Heaven; for even in Heaven his looks and thoughts
Were always downward bent, admiring more
The riches of Heaven's pavement, trodden gold,
Than aught divine or holy else enjoyed
In vision beatific. By him first
Men also, and by his suggestion taught,
Ransacked the Centre, and with impious hands
Rifled the bowels of their mother Earth
For treasures better hid. Soon had his crew
Opened into the hill a spacious wound,
And digged out ribs of gold. Let none admire
That riches grow in Hell; that soil may best
Deserve the precious bane. And here let those
Who boast in mortal things, and wondering tell

Of Babel and the works of Memphian kings,
Learn how their greatest monuments of fame,
And strength, and art, are easily outdone
By Spirits reprobate, and in an hour
What in an age they, with incessant toil
And hands innumerable, scarce perform.
Nigh on the plain, in many cells prepared,
That underneath had veins of liquid fire
Sluiced from the lake, a second multitude
With wondrous art founded the massy ore,
Severing each kind, and scummed the bullion-dross.
A third as soon had formed within the ground
A various mould, and from the boiling cells
By strange conveyance filled each hollow nook;
As in an organ, from one blast of wind,
To many a row of pipes the sound-board breathes.
Anon out of the earth a fabric huge
Rose like an exhalation, with the sound
Of dulcet symphonies and voices sweet—
Built like a temple, where pilasters round
Were set, and Doric pillars overlaid
With golden architrave; nor did there want
Cornice or frieze, with bossy sculptures graven:
The roof was fretted gold. Not Babylon
Nor great Alcairo such magnificence
Equalled in all their glories, to enshrine
Belus or Serapis their gods, or seat
Their kings, when Egypt with Assyria strove
In wealth and luxury. The ascending pile
Stood fixed her stately highth; and straight the doors,
Opening their brazen folds discover, wide
Within, her ample spaces o'er the smooth
And level pavement: from the archèd roof,
Pendent by subtle magic, many a row
Of starry lamps and blazing cressets, fed

With naphtha and asphaltus, yielded light
As from a sky. The hasty multitude
Admiring entered; and the work some praise,
And some the architect. His hand was known
In Heaven by many a towered structure high,
Where sceptred Angels held their residence,
And sat as Princes, whom the supreme King
Exalted to such power, and gave to rule
Each in his hierarchy, the Orders bright.
Nor was his name unheard or unadored
In ancient Greece; and in Ausonian land
Men called him Mulciber; and how he fell
From Heaven they fabled, thrown by angry Jove
Sheer o'er the crystal battlements: from morn
To noon he fell, from noon to dewy eve,
A summer's day, and with the setting sun
Dropt from the zenith, like a falling star,
On Lemnos, the Ægæan isle. Thus they relate,
Erring; for he with this rebellious rout
Fell long before; nor aught availed him now
To have built Heaven high towers; nor did he scape
By all his engines, but was headlong sent,
With his industrious crew, to build in Hell.

They Err who Count it Glorious to Subdue

(from *Paradise Regained*, Book III)

THEY err who count it glorious to subdue
By conquest far and wide, to overrun
Large countries, and in field great battles win,
Great cities by assault. What do these worthies
But rob and spoil, burn, slaughter, and enslave

Peaceable nations, neighbouring or remote,
Made captive, yet deserving freedom more
Than those their conquerors, who leave behind
Nothing but ruin wheresoe'er they rove,
And all the flourishing works of peace destroy;
Then swell with pride, and must be titled Gods,
Great Benefactors of mankind, Deliverers,
Worshipped with temple, priest, and sacrifice?
One is the son of Jove, of Mars the other;
Till conqueror Death discover them scarce men,
Rolling in brutish vices, and deformed,
Violent or shameful death their due reward.
But, if there be in glory aught of good,
It may by means far different be attained,
Without ambition, war, or violence—
By deeds of peace, by wisdom eminent,
By patience, temperance. I mention still
Him whom thy wrongs, with saintly patience borne,
Made famous in a land and times obscure;
Who names not now with honour patient Job?
Poor Socrates (who next more memorable?),
By what he taught and suffered for so doing,
For truth's sake suffering death unjust, lives now
Equal in fame to proudest conquerors.

Samson Blind

(from *Samson Agonistes*)

But, chief of all,
O loss of sight, of thee I most complain!
Blind among enemies! O worse than chains,
Dungeon, or beggary, or decrepit age!

Light, the prime work of God, to me is extinct,
And all her various objects of delight
Annulled, which might in part my grief have eased.
Inferior to the vilest now become
Of man or worm, the vilest here excel me:
They creep, yet see; I, dark in light, exposed
To daily fraud, contempt, abuse and wrong,
Within doors, or without, still as a fool,
In power of others, never in my own—
Scarce half I seem to live, dead more than half.
O dark, dark, dark, amid the blaze of noon,
Irrecoverably dark, total eclipse
Without all hope of day!
O first-created beam, and thou great Word,
'Let there be light, and light was over all,'
Why am I thus bereaved thy prime decree?
The sun to me is dark
And silent as the Moon,
When she deserts the night,
Hid in her vacant interlunar cave.
Since light so necessary is to life,
And almost life itself, if it be true
That light is in the soul,
She all in every part, why was the sight
To such a tender ball as the eye confined,
So obvious and so easy to be quenched,
And not, as feeling, through all parts diffused,
That she might look at will through every pore?
Then had I not been thus exiled from light,
As in the land of darkness, yet in light,
To live a life half dead, a living death,
And buried; but, O yet more miserable!
Myself my sepulchre, a moving grave.

To the Lord General Cromwell, May 1652

Cromwell, our chief of men, who through a cloud
Not of war only, but detractions rude,
Guided by faith and matchless fortitude,
To peace and truth thy glorious way hast ploughed,
And on the neck of crowned Fortune proud
Hast reared God's trophies, and his work pursued,
While Darwen stream, with blood of Scots imbrued,
And Dunbar field, resounds thy praises loud,
And Worcester's laureate wreath: yet much remains
To conquer still; Peace hath her victories
No less renowned than War: new foes arise,
Threatening to bind our souls with secular chains.
Help us to save free conscience from the paw
Of hireling wolves, whose Gospel is their maw.

Richard Lovelace

Gratiana Dancing and Singing

SEE! with what constant motion,
Even, and glorious as the sun,
Gratiana steers that noble frame.
Soft as her breast, sweet as her voice
That gave each winding law and poise,
And swifter than the wings of fame.

She beat the happy pavement,
By such a star made firmament,
  Which now no more the roof envies;
But swells up high with Atlas even,
Bearing the brighter, nobler Heaven,
  And in her all the Deities.

Each step trod out a lover's thought
And the ambitious hopes he brought,
  Chained to her brave feet with such arts;
Such sweet command and gentle awe
As when she ceased, we sighing saw
  The floor lay paved with broken hearts.

So did she move; so did she sing
Like the harmonious spheres that bring
  Unto their rounds their music's aid;
Which she performèd such a way
As all the inamoured world will say
  The Graces danced and Apollo played.

Abraham Cowley

On the Death of Mr. William Hervey

It was a dismal and a fearful night:
Scarce could the morn drive on the unwilling light,
When sleep, death's image, left my troubled breast
    By something liker death possest.

My eyes with tears did uncommanded flow,
        And on my soul hung the dull weight
        Of some intolerable fate.
What bell was that? Ah me! too much I know!

My sweet companion and my gentle peer,
Why hast thou left me thus unkindly here,
Thy end for ever and my life to moan?
        O, thou hast left me all alone!
Thy soul and body, when death's agony
        Besieged around thy noble heart,
        Did not with more reluctance part
Than I, my dearest Friend, do part from thee.

My dearest Friend, would I had died for thee!
Life and this world henceforth will tedious be:
Nor shall I know hereafter what to do
        If once my griefs prove tedious too.
Silent and sad I walk about all day,
        As sullen ghosts stalk speechless by
        Where their hid treasures lie;
Alas! my treasure's gone; why do I stay?

Say, for you saw us, ye immortal lights,
How oft unwearied have we spent the nights,
Till the Ledaean stars, so famed for love,
        Wonder'd at us from above!
We spent them not in toys, in lusts, or wine;
        But search of deep philosophy,
        Wit, eloquence, and poetry—
Arts which I loved, for they, my Friend, were thine.

Ye fields of Cambridge, our dear Cambridge, say
Have ye not seen us walking every day?
Was there a tree about which did not know
        The love betwixt us two?

Henceforth, ye gentle trees, for ever fade;
        Or your sad branches thicker join
        And into darksome shades combine,
Dark as the grave wherein my Friend is laid!

Large was his soul: as large a soul as e'er
Submitted to inform a body here;
High as the place 'twas shortly in Heaven to have,
        But low and humble as his grave.
So high that all the virtues there did come,
        As to their chiefest seat
        Conspicuous and great;
So low, that for me too it made a room.

Knowledge he only sought, and so soon caught
As if for him knowledge had rather sought;
Nor did more learning ever crowded lie
        In such a short mortality.
Whene'er the skilful youth discoursed or writ,
        Still did the notions throng
        About his eloquent tongue;
Nor could his ink flow faster than his wit.

His mirth was the pure spirits of various wit,
Yet never did his God or friends forget;
And when deep talk and wisdom came in view,
        Retired, and gave to them their due.
For the rich help of books he always took,
        Though his own searching mind before
        Was so with notions written o'er,
As if wise Nature had made that her book.

With as much zeal, devotion, piety,
He always lived, as other saints do die.
Still with his soul severe accounts he kept,
        Weeping all debts out ere he slept.

Then down in peace and innocence he lay,
Like the sun's laborious light,
Which still in water sets at night,
Unsullied with his journey of the day.

But happy Thou, ta'en from this frantic age,
Where ignorance and hypocrisy does rage!
A fitter time for Heaven no soul e'er chose—
The place now only free from those.
There 'mong the blest thou dost for ever shine
And wheresoe'er thou casts thy view
Upon that white and radiant crew,
See'st not a soul with more light than thine.

Andrew Marvell

The Mower to the Glow-worms

Ye living lamps, by whose dear light
The nightingale does sit so late,
And studying all the summer night,
Her matchless songs does meditate;

Ye country comets, that portend
No war, nor prince's funeral,
Shining unto no higher end
Than to presage the grasses' fall;

Ye glow-worms, whose officious flame
To wandering mowers shows the way,
That in the night have lost their aim,
And after foolish fires do stray;

Your courteous lights in vain you waste,
Since Juliana here is come,
For she my mind hath so displaced
That I shall never find my home.

The Garden

How vainly men themselves amaze
To win the palm the oak, or bays,
And their uncessant labours see
Crown'd from single herb or tree,
Whose short and narrow-vergèd shade
Does prudently their toils upbraid;
While all the flowers and trees do close
To weave the garlands of repose!

Fair Quiet, have I found thee here,
And Innocence thy sister dear?
Mistaken long, I sought you then
In busy companies of men:
You sacred plants, if here below,
Only among the plants will grow:
Society is all but rude
To this delicious solitude.

No white nor red was ever seen
So amorous as this lovely green.
Fond lovers, cruel as their flame,
Cut in these trees their mistress' name:
Little, alas! they know or heed
How far these beauties hers exceed!
Fair trees! wheresoe'er your barks I wound,
No name shall but your own be found.

When we have run our passions' heat
Love hither makes his best retreat:
The gods, that mortal beauty chase,
Still in a tree did end their race;
Apollo haunted Daphne so
Only that she might laurel grow;
And Pan did after Syrinx speed
Not as a nymph, but for a reed.

What wondrous life is this I lead!
Ripe apples drop about my head;
The luscious clusters of the vine
Upon my mouth do crush their wine;
The nectarine and curious[1] peach
Into my hands themselves do reach;
Stumbling on melons, as I pass,
Ensnared with flowers, I fall on grass.

Meanwhile the mind, from pleasure less,
Withdraws into its happiness;
The mind, that ocean where each kind
Does straight its own resemblance find;

[1] choice

Yet it creates, transcending these,
Far other worlds, and other seas;
Annihilating all that's made
To a green thought in a green shade.

Here at the fountain's sliding foot,
Or at some fruit-trees' mossy root,
Casting the body's vest aside,
My soul into the boughs does glide;
There, like a bird, it sits and sings,
Then whets and combs its silver wings,
And, till prepared for longer flight,
Waves in its plumes the various light.

Such was that happy garden-state
While man there walk'd without a mate:
After a place so pure and sweet,
What other help could yet be meet!
But 'twas beyond a mortal's share
To wander solitary there:
Two paradises 'twere in one,
To live in Paradise alone.

How well the skilful gard'ner drew
Of flowers and herbs this dial new!
Where, from above, the milder sun
Does through a fragrant zodiac run:
And, as it works, th' industrious bee
Computes its time as well as we.
How could such sweet and wholesome hours
Be reckon'd, but with herbs and flowers!

To his Coy Mistress

HAD we but world enough, and time,
This coyness, lady, were no crime.
We would sit down, and think which way
To walk, and pass our long love's day.
Thou by the Indian Gange's side
Shouldst rubies find: I by the tide
Of Humber would complain. I would
Love you ten years before the flood,
And you should, if you please, refuse
Till the conversion of the Jews;
My vegetable love should grow
Vaster than empires and more slow;
An hundred years should go to praise
Thine eyes, and on thy forehead gaze;
Two hundred to adore each breast,
But thirty thousand to the rest;
An age at least to every part,
And the last age should show your heart.
For, lady, you deserve this state,
Nor would I love at lower rate.
  But at my back I always hear
Time's wingèd chariot hurrying near,
And yonder all before us lie
Deserts of vast eternity.
Thy beauty shall no more be found,
Nor, in thy marble vault, shall sound
My echoing song; then worms shall try
That long-preserved virginity,
And your quaint honour turn to dust,
And into ashes all my lust:
The grave's a fine and private place,

But none, I think, do there embrace.
  Now therefore, while the youthful hue
Sits on thy skin like morning dew,
And while thy willing soul transpires
At every pore with instant fires,
Now let us sport us while we may,
And now, like amorous birds of prey,
Rather at once our time devour,
Than languish in his slow-chapt power.
Let us roll all our strength and all
Our sweetness up into one ball,
And tear our pleasures with rough strife
Thorough the iron gates of life;
Thus, though we cannot make our sun
Stand still, yet we will make him run.

Henry Vaughan

Man

WEIGHING the stedfastness and state
Of some mean things which here below reside,
  Where birds, like watchful clocks, the noiseless date
And intercourse of times divide,
  Where bees at night get home and hive, and flowers,
Early as well as late,
  Rise with the sun, and set in the same bowers;

I would, said I, my God would give
The staidness of these things to man! for these
To His divine appointments ever cleave,
And no new business breaks their peace;
The birds nor sow nor reap, yet sup and dine,
The flowers without clothes live,
Yet Solomon was never dressed so fine.

Man hath still either toys or care;
He hath no root, nor to one place is tied,
But ever restless and irregular
About this earth doth run and ride.
He knows he hath a home, but scarce knows where;
He says it is so far,
That he hath quite forgot how to go there.

He knocks at all doors, strays and roams;
Nay, hath not so much wit as some stones have,
Which in the darkest nights points to their homes,
By some hid sense their Maker gave;
Man is the shuttle, to whose winding quest
And passage through these looms
God ordered motion, but ordained no rest.

The World of Light

THEY are all gone into the world of light!
And I alone sit ling'ring here;
Their very memory is fair and bright,
And my sad thoughts doth clear.

It glows and glitters in my cloudy breast,
  Like stars upon some gloomy grove,
Or those faint beams in which this hill is drest
  After the sun's remove.

I see them walking in an air of glory,
  Whose light doth trample on my days:
My days, which are at best but dull and hoary,
  Mere glimmering and decays.

O holy Hope! and high Humility,
  High as the heavens above!
These are your walks, and you have show'd them me,
  To kindle my cold love.

Dear, beauteous Death! the jewel of the Just,
  Shining nowhere, but in the dark;
What mysteries do lie beyond thy dust,
  Could man outlook that mark!

He that hath found some fledged bird's nest may know,
  At first sight, if the bird be flown;
But what fair well or grove he sings in now,
  That is to him unknown.

And yet as Angels in some brighter dreams
  Call to the soul, when man doth sleep:
So some strange thoughts transcend our wonted themes,
  And into glory peep.

If a star were confined into a tomb,
  Her captive flames must needs burn there;
But when the hand that lock'd her up gives room,
  She'll shine through all the sphere.

O Father of eternal life, and all
  Created glories under Thee!
Resume Thy spirit from this world of thrall
  Into true liberty.

Either disperse these mists, which blot and fill
  My perspective still as they pass:
Or else remove me hence into that hill
  Where I shall need no glass.

John Hall

A Pastoral Hymn

HAPPY choristers of air,
Who by your nimble flight draw near
    His throne, whose wondrous story
    And unconfinèd glory
Your notes still carol, whom your sound
And whom your plumy pipes rebound.

Yet do the lazy snails no less
The greatness of our Lord confess,
    And those whom weight hath chained
    And to the earth restrained,
Their ruder voices do as well,
Yea and the speechless fishes tell.

Great Lord, from whom each tree receives,
Then pays again as rent, his leaves;
    Thou dost in purple set
    The rose and violet,
And giv'st the sickly lily white,
Yet in them all thy name dost write.

John Dryden

Song for Saint Cecilia's Day

(NOVEMBER 22, 1687)

From harmony, from heavenly harmony
  This universal frame began.
When nature underneath a heap
  Of jarring atoms lay,
  And could not heave her head
The tuneful voice was heard from high,
  Arise, ye more than dead.
Then cold, and hot, and moist, and dry,
In order to their stations leap,
  And Music's power obey.
From harmony, from heavenly harmony
  This universal frame began:
  From harmony to harmony
Through all the compass of the notes it ran,
The diapason closing full in Man.

What passion cannot Music raise and quell?
  When Jubal struck the corded shell,
His listening brethren stood around,
  And, wondering, on their faces fell
  To worship that celestial sound.

Less than a God they thought there could not dwell
  Within the hollow of that shell,
  That spoke so sweetly and so well.
What passion cannot Music raise and quell?

The trumpet's loud clangor
  Excites us to arms,
With shrill notes of anger;
  And mortal alarms.
The double double double beat
  Of the thundering drum
Cries, Hark the foes come;
Charge, charge, 'tis too late to retreat!

  The soft complaining flute
  In dying notes discovers
  The woes of hopeless lovers,
Whose dirge is whisper'd by the warbling lute.

  Sharp violins proclaim
Their jealous pangs and desperation,
Fury, frantic indignation,
Depth of pains, and height of passion,
  For the fair disdainful dame.

  But oh! what art can teach,
  What human voice can reach
The sacred organ's praise?

Notes inspiring holy love,
Notes that wing their heavenly ways
To mend the choirs above.

Orpheus could lead the savage race,
And trees unrooted left their place,
Sequacious of the lyre;
But bright Cecilia rais'd the wonder higher:
When to her organ vocal breath was given.
An angel heard, and straight appear'd,
Mistaking earth for heaven!

Grand Chorus

As from the power of sacred lays
The spheres began to move,
And sung the great Creator's praise
To all the bless'd above;
So, when the last and dreadful hour
This crumbling pageant shall devour,
The trumpet shall be heard on high,
The dead shall live, the living die,
And Music shall untune the sky.

Achitophel

(from *Absalom and Achitophel*)

Of these the false Achitophel was first:
A name to all succeeding ages curst.
For close designs and crooked counsels fit;
Sagacious, bold, and turbulent of wit:

Restless, unfixed in principles and place;
In power unpleas'd, impatient of disgrace.
A fiery soul, which working out its way,
Fretted the pigmy body to decay:
And o'er informed the tenement of clay.
A daring pilot in extremity;
Pleas'd with the danger, when the waves went high
He sought the storms; but, for a calm unfit,
Would steer too nigh the sands, to boast his wit
Great wits are sure to madness near allied;
And thin partitions do their bounds divide:
Else, why should he, with wealth and honour blest,
Refuse his age the needful hours of rest?
Punish a body which he could not please,
Bankrupt of life, yet prodigal of ease?
And all to leave, what with his toil he won,
To that unfeather'd, two-legged thing, a son:
Got, while his soul did huddled notions try;
And born a shapeless lump, like anarchy.
In friendship false, implacable in hate,
Resolv'd to ruin or to rule the State.
To compass this, the triple bond he broke;
The pillars of the public safety shook:
And fitted Israel for a foreign yoke.
Then, seized with fear, yet still affecting fame,
Usurped a patriot's all-atoning name.

Songs from 'The Secular Masque'

(1) *Momus to Mars.*

THY sword within the scabbard keep
  And let mankind agree;
Better the world were fast asleep
    Than kept awake by thee.

The fools are only thinner,
  For all our cost and care;
But neither side a winner,
  For things are as they were.

(2) *Momus to Diana, Mars and Venus.*

All, all of a piece throughout:
  Thy chase had a beast in view;
Thy wars brought nothing about;
  Thy lovers were all untrue.
'Tis well an old age is out,
  And time to begin a new.

Henry Aldrich

A Catch

If all be true that I do think,
There are five good reasons we should drink:
Good wine, a friend, or being dry,
Or lest we should be by and by;
Or any other reason why.

John Wilmot, Earl of Rochester

Love and Life

All my past life is mine no more,
  The flying hours are gone:
Like transitory dreams giv'n o're,
Whose images are kept in store
  By memory alone.

The time that is to come is not,
  How can it then be mine?
The present moment's all my lot,
And that, as fast as it is got,
  Phillis, is only thine.

Then talk not of inconstancy,
False hearts and broken vows;
If I, by miracle can be
This live-long minute true to thee,
'Tis all that Heav'n allows.

Jonathan Swift

Mary the Cook-Maid's Letter to Doctor Sheridan

Well; if ever I saw such another man since my mother bound my head,
You a gentleman! marry come up, I wonder where you were bred?
I am sure such words do not come from a man of your cloth,
I would not give such language to a dog, faith and troth.
Yes; you call'd my master a knave: Fie Mr Sheridan, 'tis shame
For a parson, who should know better things, to come out with such a name.
Knave in your teeth, Mr Sheridan, 'tis both a shame and a sin,
And the Dean my master is an honester man than you and all your kin:
He has more goodness in his little finger, than you have in your whole body,
My master is a parsonable man, and not a spindle-shank'd hoddy doddy.

And now whereby I find you would fain make an excuse,
Because my master one day in anger called you a goose.
Which, and I am sure I have been his servant four years
since October,
And he never call'd me worse than sweet-heart drunk or
sober:
Not that I know his reverence was ever concern'd to my
knowledge,
Though you and your come-rogues keep him out so late in
your College.

You say you will eat grass on his grave: a Christian eat
grass!
Whereby you now confess yourself to be a goose or an
ass:
But that's as much as to say, that my master should die
before ye,
Well, well, that's as God pleases, and I don't believe that's
a true story,
And so say I told you so, and you may go tell my master;
what care I?
And I don't care who knows it, 'tis all one to Mary.
Everybody knows, that I love to tell truth and shame the
Devil,
I am but a poor servant, but I think gentle folks should be
civil.
Besides, you found fault with our victuals one day that
you was here,
I remember it was upon a Tuesday, of all days in the year.
And Saunders the man says, you are always jesting and
mocking,
'Mary' said he, (one day, as I was mending my master's
stocking,)
'My master is so fond of that minister that keeps the
school;

I thought my master a wise man, but that man makes him a
fool.'
'Saunders' said I, 'I would rather than a quart of ale,
He would come into our kitchen, and I would pin a dish-
clout to his tail.'
And now I must go, and get Saunders to direct this letter,
For I write but a sad scrawl, but my sister Marget she
writes better.
Well, but I must run and make the bed before my master
comes from pray'rs,
And see now, it strikes ten, and I hear him coming up
stairs:
Where of I could say more to your verses, if I could write
written hand,
And so I remain in a civil way, your servant to command
Mary.

A Description of a City Shower

Careful observers may foretell the hour
(By sure prognostics) when to dread a show'r:
While rain depends, the pensive cat gives o'er
Her frolicks, and pursues her tail no more.
Returning home at night, you'll find the sink
Strike your offended sense with double stink.
If you be wise, then go not far to dine,
You'll spend in coach-hire more than save in wine.
A coming shower your shooting corns presage,
Old aches throb, your hollow tooth will rage.
Saunt'ring in coffee-house is *Dulman* seen;
He damns the climate, and complains of spleen.

Meanwhile the South rising with dabbled wings,
A sable cloud a-thwart the welkin flings,
That swill'd more liquor than it could contain,
And like a drunkard gives it up again.
Brisk *Susan* whips her linen from the rope,
While the first drizzling shower is born aslope,
Such is that sprinkling which some careless Queen
Flirts on you from her mop, but not so clean.
You fly, invoke the gods; then turning, stop
To rail; she singing, still whirls on her mop.
Not yet, the dust had shunned th'unequal strife,
But aided by the wind, fought yet for life;
And wafted with its foe by violent gust,
'Twas doubtful which was rain, and which was dust.
Ah! where must needy poet seek for aid,
When dust and rain at once his coat invade;
His only coat, where dust confus'd with rain,
Roughen the nap, and leave a mingled stain.

Now in continuous drops the flood comes down,
Threat'ning with deluge this devoted town.
To shops in crowds the daggled females fly,
Pretend to cheapen goods, but nothing buy.
The Templer spruce, while ev'ry spout's a-broach.
Stays till 'tis fair, yet seems to call a coach.
The tuck'd-up Sempstress walks with hasty strides,
Here various kinds by various fortunes led,
Commence acquaintance underneath a shed.
Triumphant Tories, and desponding Whigs,
Forget their feuds, and join to save their wigs,
Box'd in a chair the beau impatient sits,
While spouts run clatt'ring o'er the roof by fits;
And ever and anon with frightful din
The leather sounds, he trembles from within.

When Troy chair-men bore the wooden steed,
Pregnant with Greeks, impatient to be freed,
(Those bully Greeks, who, as the Moderns do,
Instead of paying chair-men, run them through.)
Laoco'n struck the outside with his spear,
And each imprison'd hero quak'd for fear.

Now from all parts the swelling kennels flow,
And bear their trophies with them as they go:
Filth of all hues and odours seem to tell
What street they sail'd from, by their sight and smell,
They, as each torrent drives, with rapid force
From Smithfield, or St. Pulchre's shape their course,
And in huge confluent join at Snow-Hill ridge,
Fall from the conduit prone to Holborn-Bridge.
Sweepings from butchers' stalls, dung, guts and blood,
Drown'd puppies, stinking sprats, all drench'd in mud,
Dead cats and turnip-tops come tumbling down the flood.

Alexander Pope

Where'er You Walk

(from *Summer, the Second Pastoral*)

SEE what delights in sylvan scenes appear!
Descending Gods have found Elisium here.
In woods bright Venus with Adonis strayed,
And chaste Diana haunts the forest shade.

Come, lovely nymph, and bless the silent hours,
When swains from shearing seek their nightly bowers;
When weary reapers quit the sultry field,
And crowned with corn their thanks to Ceres yield.
This harmless grove no lurking vapour hides,
But in my breast the serpent love abides.
Here bees from blossoms sip the rosy dew,
But your Alexis knows no sweets but you.
O deign to visit our forsaken seats,
The mossy fountains and the green retreats!
Where'er you walk, cool gales shall fan the glade
Trees where you sit shall crowd into a shade:
Where'er you tread, the blushing flowers shall rise,
And all things flourish where you turn your eyes.
O how I long with you to pass my days,
Invoke the Muses, and resound your praise!
Your praise the birds shall chant in every grove,
And winds shall waft it to the powers above.
But would you sing, and rival Orpheus' strain,
The wondering forests soon should dance again,
The moving mountains hear the powerful call,
And headlong streams hang listening in their fall!

The Faithless Lover

(from *Autumn, the Third Pastoral*)

Resound, ye hills, resound my mournful strain!
Of perjured Doris, dying I complain:
Here where the mountains, lessening as they rise,
Lose the low vales and steal into the skies;

While labouring oxen, spent with toil and heat,
In their loose traces from the field retreat;
While curling smokes from village-tops are seen,
And the fleet shades glide o'er the dusky green.

Resound, ye hills, resound my mournful lay!
Beneath yon poplar oft we passed the day:
Oft on the rind I carved her amorous vows,
While she with garlands hung the bending boughs:
The garlands fade, the vows are worn away;
So dies her love, and so my hopes decay.

Resound, ye hills, resound my mournful strain!
Now bright Arcturus glads the teeming grain,
Now golden fruits on loaded branches shine,
And grateful clusters swell with floods of wine;
Now blushing berries paint the yellow grove;
Just Gods! shall all things yield returns but love?

Resound, ye hills, resound my mournful lay!
The shepherds cry, 'Thy flocks are left a prey.'—
Ah! what avails it me the flocks to keep,
Who lost my heart while I preserved my sheep?
Pan came, and asked what magic caused my smart,
Or what ill eyes malignant glances dart?
What eyes but hers, alas, have power to move?
And is there magic but what dwells in love?

Resound, ye hills, resound my mournful strains!
I'll fly from shepherds, flocks, and flowery plains.
From shepherds, flocks, and plains, I may remove,
Forsake mankind, and all the world—but love!
I know thee, love! on foreign mountains bred,
Wolves gave thee suck, and savage tigers fed.
Thou wert from Ætna's burning entrails torn,
Got by fierce whirlwinds, and in thunder born!

Resound, ye hills, resound my mournful lay!
Farewell, ye woods, adieu the light of day!
One leap from yonder cliffs shall end my pains;
No more, ye hills, no more resound my strains!
Thus sung the shepherds till the approach of night,
The skies yet blushing with departing light,
When falling dews with spangles decked the glade,
And the low sun had lengthened every shade.

Sporus

(from the *Epistle to Dr. Arbuthnot*)

LET Sporus tremble—'What? that thing of silk,
Sporus, that mere white curd of ass's milk?
Satire or sense, alas! can Sporus feel?
Who breaks a butterfly upon a wheel?'
Yet let me slap this bug with gilded wings,
This painted child of dirt that stinks and stings;
Whose buzz the witty and the fair annoys,
Yet wit ne'er tastes, and beauty ne'er enjoys,
So well-bred spaniels civilly delight
In mumbling of the game they dare not bite.
Eternal smiles his emptiness betray,
As shallow streams run dimpling all the way!
Whether in florid impotence he speaks,
And, as the prompter breathes, the puppet squeaks,
Or at the ear of Eve, familiar toad,
Half froth, half venom, spits himself abroad,
In puns, or politics, or tales, or lies,
Or spite, or smut, or rhymes, or blasphemies,
His wit all see-saw between *that* and *this*,
Now high, now low, now Master up, now Miss,
And he himself one vile antithesis.

Amphibious thing! that acting either part,
The trifling head, or the corrupted heart!
Fop at the toilet, flatt'rer at the board,
Now trips a lady, and now struts a lord.
Eve's tempter thus the Rabbins have expressed,
A cherub's face, a reptile all the rest;
Beauty that shocks you, parts that none will trust,
Wit that can creep, and pride that licks the dust.

Epistle to Miss Blount, on her leaving the Town, after the Coronation

As some fond virgin, whom her mother's care
Drags from the town to wholesome country air,
Just when she learns to roll the melting eye,
And hear a spark, yet think no danger nigh;
From the dear man unwilling she must sever,
Yet take one kiss before she parts for ever:
Thus from the world fair *Zephalinda* flew,
Saw others happy, and with sighs withdrew;
Not that their pleasures caus'd her discontent,
She sigh'd not that They stay'd, but that She went.
    She went, to plain-work, and to purling brooks,
Old-fashion'd halls, dull aunts, and croacking rooks,
She went from Op'ra, park, assembly, play,
To morning walks, and pray'rs three hours a day;
To pass her time 'twixt reading and Bohea,
To muse, and spill her solitary Tea,
Or o'er cold coffee trifle with the spoon,
Count the slow clock, and dine exact at noon;
Divert her eyes with pictures in the fire,
Hum half a tune, tell stories to the squire;

Up to her godly garret after sev'n,
There starve and pray, for that's the way to heav'n.
    Some Squire, perhaps, you take delight to rack;
Whose game is Whisk, whose treat a toast in sack,
Who visits with a gun, presents you birds,
Then gives a smacking buss, and cries—No words!
Or with his hounds comes hollowing from the stable,
Makes love with nods, and knees beneath a table;
Whose laughs are hearty, tho' his jests are coarse,
And loves you best of all things—but his horse.
    In some fair evening, on your elbow laid,
You dream of triumphs in the rural shade;
In pensive thought recall the fancy'd scene,
See Coronations rise on ev'ry green;
Before you pass th' imaginary sights
Of Lords, and Earls, and Dukes, and garter'd Knights;
While the spread Fan o'ershades your closing eyes;
Then give one flirt, and all the vision flies.
Thus vanish sceptres, coronets, and balls,
And leave you in lone woods, or empty walls.
    So when your slave, at some dear, idle time,
(Not plagu'd with headaches, or the want of rhyme)
Stands in the streets, abstracted from the crew,
And while he seems to study, thinks of you:
Just when his fancy points your sprightly eyes,
Or sees the blush of soft *Parthenia* rise,
Gay pats my shoulder, and you vanish quite;
Streets, chairs, and coxcombs rush upon my sight;
Vext to be still in town, I knit my brow,
Look sow'r, and hum a tune—as you may now.

Samuel Johnson

On the Death of Mr. Robert Levet
A Practiser in Physic

Condemn'd to Hope's delusive mine,
  As on we toil from day to day,
By sudden blasts, or slow decline,
  Our social comforts drop away.

Well tried through many a varying year,
  See Levet to the grave descend;
Officious, innocent, sincere,
  Of every friendless name the friend.

Yet still he finds affection's eye,
  Obscurely wise, and coarsely kind;
Nor, letter'd arrogance, deny
  Thy praise to merit unrefin'd.

When fainting nature call'd for aid,
  And hovering death prepar'd the blow,
His vigorous remedy display'd
  The power of art without the show.

In misery's darkest caverns known,
  His useful care was ever nigh,
Where hopeless anguish pour'd his groan,
  And lonely want retir'd to die.

No summons mock'd by chill delay,
  No petty gain disdain'd by pride,
The modest wants of every day
  The toil of every day supplied.

His virtues walk'd their narrow round,
  Nor made a pause, nor left a void;
And sure the Eternal Master found
  The single talent well employ'd.

The busy day, the peaceful night,
  Unfelt, uncounted, glided by;
His frame was firm, his powers were bright,
  Though now his eighteith year was nigh.

Then with no fiery throbbing pain,
  No cold gradations of decay,
Death broke at once the vital chain,
  And freed his soul the nearest way.

Thomas Gray

Elegy Written in a Country Churchyard

THE curfew tolls the knell of parting day,
  The lowing herd wind slowly o'er the lea,
The plowman homeward plods his weary way,
  And leaves the world to darkness and to me.

Now fades the glimmering landscape on the sight,
  And all the air a solemn stillness holds,
Save where the beetle wheels his droning flight,
  And drowsy tinklings lull the distant folds:

Save that from yonder ivy-mantled tower
  The moping owl does to the moon complain
Of such as wand'ring near her secret bower
  Molest her ancient solitary reign.

Beneath those rugged elms, that yew-tree's shade,
  Where heaves the turf in many a mould'ring heap
Each in his narrow cell for ever laid,
  The rude forefathers of the hamlet sleep.

The breezy call of incense-breathing morn,
  The swallow twitt'ring from the straw-built shed,
The cock's shrill clarion, or the echoing horn,
  No more shall rouse them from their lowly bed.

For them no more the blazing hearth shall burn,
  Or busy housewife ply her evening care:
No children run to lisp their sire's return,
  Or climb his knees the envied kiss to share.

Oft did the harvest to their sickle yield,
  Their furrow oft the stubborn glebe has broke;
How jocund did they drive their team afield!
  How bow'd the woods beneath their sturdy stroke!

Let not ambition mock their useful toil,
  Their homely joys, and destiny obscure;
Nor grandeur hear with a disdainful smile
  The short and simple annals of the poor.

The boast of heraldry, the pomp of power,
  And all that beauty, all that wealth e'er gave,
Await alike th' inevitable hour:
  The paths of glory lead but to the grave.

Nor you, ye proud, impute to these the fault,
  If memory o'er their tomb no trophies raise,
Where through the long-drawn aisle and fretted vault
  The pealing anthem swells the note of praise.

Can storied urn or animated bust
  Back to its mansion call the fleeting breath?
Can honour's voice provoke the silent dust,
  Or flattery soothe the dull cold ear of death?

Perhaps in this neglected spot is laid
  Some heart once pregnant with celestial fire;
Hands that the rod of empire might have sway'd,
  Or waked to ecstasy the living lyre:

But knowledge to their eyes her ample page
  Rich with the spoils of time did ne'er unroll;
Chill penury repress'd their noble rage,
  And froze the genial current of the soul.

Full many a gem of purest ray serene
  The dark unfathom'd caves of ocean bear:
Full many a flower is born to blush unseen,
  And waste its sweetness on the desert air.

Some village-Hampden, that with dauntless breast
  The little tyrant of his fields withstood,
Some mute inglorious Milton here may rest,
  Some Cromwell, guiltless of his country's blood.

Th' applause of list'ning senates to command,
  The threats of pain and ruin to despise,
To scatter plenty o'er a smiling land,
  And read their history in a nation's eyes,

Their lot forbad: nor circumscrib'd alone
  Their growing virtues, but their crimes confined;
Forbad to wade through slaughter to a throne,
  And shut the gates of mercy on mankind;

The struggling pangs of conscious truth to hide,
  To quench the blushes of ingenuous shame,
Or heap the shrine of luxury and pride
  With incense kindled at the muse's flame.

Far from the madding crowd's ignoble strife,
  Their sober wishes never learn'd to stray;
Along the cool sequester'd vale of life
  They kept the noiseless tenour of their way.

Yet ev'n these bones from insult to protect
  Some frail memorial still erected nigh,
With uncouth rhymes and shapeless sculpture deck'd,
  Implores the passing tribute of a sigh.

Their name, their years, spelt by th' unletter'd Muse,
  The place of fame and elegy supply:
And many a holy text around she strews
  That teach the rustic moralist to die.

For who, to dumb forgetfulness a prey,
  This pleasing anxious being e'er resign'd,
Left the warm precincts of the cheerful day,
  Nor cast one longing lingering look behind?

On some fond breast the parting soul relies,
  Some pious drops the closing eye requires;
Ev'n from the tomb the voice of nature cries,
  Ev'n in our ashes live their wonted fires.

For thee, who, mindful of th' unhonour'd dead,
  Dost in these lines their artless tale relate;
If chance, by lonely contemplation led,
  Some kindred spirit shall inquire thy fate,—

Haply some hoary-headed swain may say,
  'Oft have we seen him at the peep of dawn
Brushing with hasty steps the dews away
  To meet the sun upon the upland lawn.

'There at the foot of yonder nodding beech
  That wreathes its old fantastic roots so high,
His listless length at noontide would he stretch,
  And pore upon the brook that babbles by.

'Hard by yon wood, now smiling as in scorn,
  Mutt'ring his wayward fancies he would rove,
Now drooping, woeful wan, like one forlorn,
  Or crazed with care, or cross'd in hopeless love.

'One morn I miss'd him on the custom'd hill,
  Along the heath, and near his favourite tree;
Another came; nor yet beside the rill,
  Nor up the lawn, nor at the wood was he;

The next, with dirges due in sad array
  Slow through the church-way path we saw him borne:—
Approach and read (for thou canst read) the lay
  Graved on the stone beneath yon aged thorn.'

The Epitaph

Here rests his head upon the lap of Earth
  A Youth, to Fortune and to Fame unknown;
Fair Science frown'd not on his humble birth,
  And Melancholy mark'd him for her own.

Large was his bounty, and his soul sincere;
  Heaven did a recompense as largely send:
He gave to Misery all he had, a tear,
  He gain'd from Heaven, 'twas all he wish'd, a friend.

No farther seek his merits to disclose,
  Or draw his frailties from their dread abode,
(There they alike in trembling hope repose,)
  The bosom of his Father and his God.

Christopher Smart

My Cat Jeoffry

(from *Jubilate Agno*)

For I will consider my cat Jeoffry.
For he is the servant of the Living God, duly and daily
    serving him.
For at the first glance of the glory of God in the East he
    worships in his way.
For this is done by wreathing his body seven times round
    with elegant quickness.

For then he leaps up to catch the musk, which is the
 blessing of God upon his prayer.
For he rolls upon the prank to work it in.
For having done duty and received blessing he begins to
 consider himself.
For this he performs in ten degrees.
For first he looks upon his fore-paws to see if they are
 clean.
For secondly he kicks up behind to clear away there.
For thirdly he works it upon stretch with the fore-paws
 extended.
For fourthly he sharpens his paws by wood.
For fifthly he washes himself.
For sixthly he rolls upon wash.
For Seventhly he fleas himself, that he may not be
 interrupted upon the beat.
For Eighthly he rubs himself against a post.
For Ninthly he looks up for his instructions.
For Tenthly he goes in quest of food.
For having consider'd God and himself he will consider
 his neighbour.
For if he meets another cat he will kiss her in kindness.
For when he takes his prey he plays with it to give it
 chance.
For one mouse in seven escapes by his dallying.
For when his day's work is done his business more properly
 begins.
For he keeps the Lord's watch in the night against the
 adversary.
For he counteracts the powers of darkness by his electrical
 skin & glaring eyes.
For he counteracts the Devil, who is death, by brisking
 about the life.
For in his morning orisons he loves the sun and the sun
 loves him.

For he is of the tribe of the Tiger.
For the Cherub Cat is a term of the Angel Tiger.
For he has the subtlety and hissing of a serpent, which in
goodness he suppresses.
For he will not do destruction, if he is well-fed, neither
will he spit without provocation.
For he purrs in thankfulness, when God tells him he's a
good Cat.
For he is an instrument for the children to learn benevolence
upon.
For every house is incomplete without him & a blessing is
lacking in the spirit.
For the Lord commanded Moses concerning the cats at the
departure of the children of Israel from Egypt.
For every family had one cat at least in the bag.
For the English Cats are the best in Europe.
For he is the cleanest in the use of his fore-paws of any
quadrupede.
For the dexterity of his defence is an instance of the love of
God to him exceedingly.
For he is the quickest to his mark of any creature.
For he is tenacious of his point.
For he is a mixture of gravity and waggery.
For he knows that God is his Saviour.

William Cowper

The Loss of the 'Royal George'

TOLL for the brave!
  The brave that are no more:
All sunk beneath the wave
  Fast by their native shore!

Eight hundred of the brave,
  Whose courage well was tried,
Had made the vessel heel,
  And laid her on her side.

A land-breeze shook the shrouds,
  And she was overset;
Down went the *Royal George*,
  With all her crew complete.

Toll for the brave!
  Brave Kempenfelt is gone;
His last sea-fight is fought,
  His work of glory done.

It was not in the battle;
  No tempest gave the shock;
She sprang no fatal leak;
  She ran upon no rock.

His sword was in its sheath,
  His fingers held the pen,
When Kempenfelt went down
  With twice four hundred men.

Weigh the vessel up
  Once dreaded by our foes!
And mingle with our cup
  The tear that England owes.

Her timbers yet are sound,
  And she may float again
Full charged with England's thunder.
  And plough the distant main.

But Kempenfelt is gone,
  His victories are o'er;
And he and his eight hundred
  Shall plough the wave no more.

To Mary

The twentieth year is well-nigh past
Since first our sky was overcast;
Ah would that this might be the last!
                My Mary!

Thy spirits have a fainter flow,
I see thee daily weaker grow—
'Twas my distress that brought thee low,
                My Mary!

Thy needles, once a shining store,
For my sake restless heretofore,
Now rust dissus'd, and shine no more,
                My Mary!

For though thou gladly wouldst fulfill
The same kind office for me still,
Thy sight now seconds not thy will,
My Mary!

But well thou play'd'st the housewife's part,
And all thy threads with magic art
Have wound themselves about this heart,
My Mary!

Thy indistinct expressions seem
Like language utter'd in a dream;
Yet me they charm, whate'er the theme,
My Mary!

Thy silver locks, once auburn bright,
Are still more lovely in my sight
Than golden beams of orient light,
My Mary!

For could I view nor them nor thee,
What sight worth seeing could I see?
The sun would rise in vain for me,
My Mary!

Partakers of thy sad decline,
Thy hands their little force resign;
Yet, gently press'd, press gently mine,
My Mary!

And Then I feel that still I hold
A richer store ten thousandfold
Than misers fancy in their gold,
My Mary!

Such feebleness of limbs thou prov'st,
That now at every step thou mov'st
Upheld by two; yet still thou lov'st,
My Mary!

And still to love, though press'd with ill,
In wintry age to feel no chill,
With me is to be lovely still,
My Mary!

But ah! by constant heed I know,
How oft the sadness that I show
Transforms thy smiles to looks of woe,
My Mary!

And should my future lot be cast
With much resemblance of the past,
Thy worn-out heart will break at last,
My Mary!

The Shrubbery

Written in a Time of Affliction

Oh happy shades! to me unblest,
Friendly to peace, but not to me,
How ill the scene that offers rest,
And heart that cannot rest, agree!

This glassy stream, that spreading pine,
Those alders quiv'ring to the breeze,
Might soothe a soul less hurt than mine,
And please, if anything could please.

But fix'd unalterable care
  Forgoes not what she feels within,
Shows the same sadness ev'rywhere,
  And slights the season and the scene.

For all that pleas'd in wood or lawn,
  While peace possess'd these silent bow'rs,
Her animating smile withdrawn,
  Has lost its beauties and its pow'rs.

The saint or moralist should tread
  This moss-grown alley, musing, slow;
They seek, like me, the secret shade,
  But not, like me, to nourish woe.

Me fruitful scenes and prospects waste
  Alike admonish not to roam;
These tell me of enjoyments past,
  And those of sorrows yet to come.

William Blake

Laughing Song

When the green woods laugh with the voice of joy,
And the dimpling stream runs laughing by;
When the air does laugh with our merry wit,
And the green hill laughs with the noise of it;

When the meadows laugh with lively green,
And the grasshopper laughs in the merry scene;
When Mary and Susan and Emily
With their sweet, round mouths sing, 'Ha, Ha, He!'

When the painted birds laugh in the shade,
Where our table with cherries and nuts is spread,
Come live, and be merry, and join with me,
To sing the sweet chorus of 'Ha, Ha, He!'

The Little Black Boy

My mother bore me in the southern wild,
And I am black, but O! my soul is white;
White as an angel is the English child,
But I am black, as if bereaved of light.

My mother taught me underneath a tree,
And sitting down before the heat of day,
She took me on her lap and kissèd me,
And pointing to the east, began to say:

'Look on the rising sun: there God does live,
'And gives his light, and gives his heat away;
'And flowers and trees and beasts and men receive
'Comfort in morning, joy in the noonday.

'And we are put on earth a little space,
'That we may learn to bear the beams of love;
'And these black bodies and this sunburnt face
'Is but a cloud, and like a shady grove.

'For when our souls have learned the heat to bear,
'The cloud will vanish; we shall hear his voice,
'Saying: "Come out from the grove, my love and care,
'And round my golden tent like lambs rejoice."'

Thus did my mother say, and kissèd me;
And thus I say to little English boy:
When I from black and he from white cloud free,
And round the tent of God like lambs we joy,

I'll shade him from the heat, till he can bear
To lean in joy upon our father's knee,
And then I'll stand and stroke his silver hair,
And be like him, and he will then love me.

The Tyger

TYGER! Tyger! burning bright
In the forests of the night,
What immortal hand or eye
Could frame thy fearful symmetry?

In what distant deeps or skies
Burnt the fire of thine eyes?
On what wings dare he aspire?
What the hand dare seize the fire?

And what shoulder, and what art,
Could twist the sinews of thy heart?
And when thy heart began to beat,
What dread hand? and what dread feet?

What the hammer? what the chain?
In what furnace was thy brain?
What the anvil? what dread grasp
Dare its deadly terror clasp?

When the stars threw down their spears,
And watered heaven with their tears,
Did he smile his work to see?
Did he who made the Lamb make thee?

Tyger! Tyger! burning bright
In the forests of the night,
What immortal hand or eye
Dare frame thy fearful symmetry?

A Poison Tree

I WAS angry with my friend:
I told my wrath, my wrath did end.
I was angry with my foe:
I told it not, my wrath did grow.

And I watered it in fears,
Night and morning with my tears;
And I sunnèd it with smiles,
And with soft deceitful wiles.

And it grew both day and night,
Till it bore an apple bright;
And my foe beheld it shine,
And he knew that it was mine,

And into my garden stole
When the night had veiled the pole:
In the morning glad I see
My foe outstretched beneath the tree.

The Sword and the Sickle

The sword sung on the barren heath,
  The sickle in the fruitful field:
The sword he sung a song of death,
  But could not make the sickle yield.

And Did Those Feet in Ancient Time

And did those feet in ancient time
Walk upon England's mountains green?
And was the holy Lamb of God
On England's pleasant pastures seen?

And did the countenance divine
Shine forth upon our clouded hills?
And was Jerusalem builded here
Among these dark Satanic mills?

Bring me my bow of burning gold:
Bring me my arrows of desire:
Bring me my spear: O clouds, unfold!
Bring me my chariot of fire.

I will not cease from mental fight,
Nor shall my sword sleep in my hand
Till we have built Jerusalem
In England's green and pleasant land.

Ah! Sun-flower

Ah! Sun-flower, weary of time,
Who countest the steps of the sun;
Seeking after that sweet golden clime,
Where the traveller's journey is done;

Where the Youth pined away with desire,
And the pale Virgin shrouded in snow,
Arise from their graves, and aspire
Where my Sun-flower wishes to go.

London

I wander through each chartered street,
Near where the chartered Thames does flow,
And mark in every face I meet
Marks of weakness, marks of woe.

In every cry of every man,
In every infant's cry of fear,
In every voice, in every ban
The mind-forged manacles I hear.

How the chimney-sweeper's cry
Every blackening church appals;
And the hapless soldier's sigh
Runs in blood down palace walls.

But most through midnight streets I hear
How the youthful harlot's curse
Blasts the new-born infant's tear,
And blights with plagues the marriage hearse.

Holy Thursday

(from *Songs of Experience*)

Is this a holy thing to see
In a rich and fruitful land,
Babes reduced to misery,
Fed with cold and usurous hand?

Is that trembling cry a song?
Can it be a song of joy?
And so many children poor?
It is a land of poverty!

And their sun does never shine,
And their fields are bleak and bare,
And their ways are filled with thorns:
It is eternal winter there.

For where'er the sun does shine,
And where'er the rain does fall,
Babe can never hunger there,
Nor poverty the mind appal.

Holy Thursday

(from *Songs of Innocence*)

'Twas on a Holy Thursday, their innocent faces clean,
The children walking two and two, in red and blue and
green,
Grey-headed beadles walked before, with wands as white as
snow,
Till into the high dome of Paul's they like Thames's
waters flow.

O what a multitude they seemed, these flowers of London
town!
Seated in companies they sit with radiance all their own.
The hum of multitudes was there, but multitudes of lambs,
Thousands of little boys and girls raising their innocent
hands.

Now like a mighty wind they raise to Heaven the voice of
song,
Or like harmonious thunderings the seats of Heaven among.
Beneath them sit the aged men, wise guardians of the poor;
Then cherish pity, lest you drive an angel from your door.

Robert Burns

A Red, Red Rose

O my love is like a red, red rose
  That's newly sprung in June:
O my love is like the melody,
  That's sweetly played in tune.

As fair thou art, my bonnie lass,
  So deep in love am I;
And I will love thee still, my dear,
  Till a' the seas gang[1] dry.

Till a' the seas gang dry, my dear,
  And the rocks melt wi' the sun;
And I will love thee still, my dear,
  While the sands o' life shall run.

And fare thee weel, my only love!
  And fare thee weel awhile!
And I will come again, my love,
  Tho' it were ten thousand mile.

[1] go

I Murder Hate by Field or Flood

I

I murder hate by field or flood,
    Though Glory's name may screen us.
In wars at hame I'll spend my blood—
    Life-giving wars of Venus.
The deities that I adore
    Are Social Peace and Plenty:
I'm better pleas'd to make one more
    Than be the death of twenty.

II

I would not die like Socrates,
    For all the fuss of Plato;
Nor would I with Leonidas,
    Nor yet would I with Cato;
The zealots of the Church and State
    Shall ne'er my mortal foes be;
But let me have bold Zimri's fate
    Within the arms of Cozbi.

Anna

1

Yestreen I had a pint o' wine,
A place where body saw na;
Yestreen lay on this breast o' mine
The gowden locks of Anna.

2

The hungrey Jew in wilderness
Rejoicing o'er his manna
Has naething to my hiney bliss
Upon the lips of Anna.

3

Ye monarchs take the East and West
Frae Indus to Savannah:
Gie me within my straining grasp
The melting form of Anna!

4

There I'll despise Imperial charms,
An Empress or Sultana,
While dying raptures in her arms
I give and take wi' Anna!

5

Awa, thou flaunting God of Day!
  Awa, thou pale Diana!
Ilk Star, gae hide thy twinkling ray,
  When I'm to meet my Anna!

6

Come, in thy raven plumage, Night
  (Sun, Moon, and Stars, withdrawn a'),
And bring an Angel-pen to write
  My transports with my Anna!

POSTSCRIPT

1

The Kirk an' State may join, and tell
  To do sic things I maunna:
The Kirk an' State may gae to Hell,
  And I'll gae to my Anna.

2

She is the sunshine o' my e'e,
  To live but her I canna:
Had I on earth but wishes three,
  The first should be my Anna.

Anonymous

Waly Waly

Down in the meadows the other day
Gathering flowers both fine and gay,
Gathering flowers both red and blue
I little thought what love could do.

I put my hand into the bush
Thinking the sweetest flower to find.
I pricked my finger to the bone
And left the sweetest flower behind.

I leaned my back up against an oak
Thinking it was a trusty tree.
First he bended and then he broke,
And so did my false love to me.

There is a ship that sails the sea.
It's loaded deep as deep can be,
But not so deep as the love I'm in.
I care not if I sink or swim.

Must I be bound and he go free?
Must I love one that loves not me?
Why should I act such a childish part
To love a man that will break my heart?

O love is handsome and love is fine
And love's a jewel when it is new.
As it grows older, it grows colder
And fades away like the morning dew.

The Seeds of Love

I sowed the seeds of love,
And I sowed them in the spring,
In April and May and in June likewise,
When the small birds they do sing.

My gardener he stood by,
And I asked him to choose for me;
He chose me the violet, the lily and the pink,
But these I refused all three.

The violet I forsook
Because it fades so soon.
The lily and the pink I did overlook
But I vowed I would wait till June.

In June is the red, red rose,
And that's the flower for me,
So I pulled and I plucked at the red rosebud,
Till I gained the willow tree.

O the willow tree will twist,
And the willow tree will twine.
I wish I were in the young man's arms
That first had this heart of mine.

Come all you false young men
That leave me here to complain.
The grass that is now trodden under foot,
In time it will rise again.

The Lowlands of Holland

O yesterday I was married, last night I went to bed.
Up came a bold sea-captain and stood by my bed's head.
'Arise, arise, young married man, and go along with me
To the Lowlands of Holland to face your enemy.'

Said the father to the daughter, 'What makes you so
lament?
There is a lad in our town can give your heart content;
'There's not a lad in our town, neither lord nor duke,'
said she,
'Since the raging sea and stormy winds have parted my
love and me.

'There's not a sash goes round my waist nor comb goes
through my hair,
Neither firelight nor candlelight can ease my heart's
despair,
Nor neither till the day I die shall I ever married be,
Since the low low lands of Holland have parted my love
and me.'

William Wordsworth

Strange Fits of Passion have I Known

STRANGE fits of passion have I known:
And I will dare to tell,
But in the lover's ear alone,
What once to me befell.

When she I loved looked every day
Fresh as a rose in June,
I to her cottage bent my way,
Beneath an evening-moon.

Upon the moon I fixed my eye,
All over the wide lea;
With quickening pace my horse drew nigh
Those paths so dear to me.

And now we reached the orchard-plot;
And, as we climbed the hill,
The sinking moon to Lucy's cot
Came near, and nearer still.

In one of those sweet dreams I slept,
Kind Nature's gentlest boon!
And all the while my eyes I kept
On the descending moon.

My horse moved on; hoof after hoof
He raised, and never stopped:
When down behind the cottage roof,
At once, the bright moon dropped.

What fond and wayward thoughts will slide
Into a Lover's head!
'O mercy!' to myself I cried,
'If Lucy should be dead!'

She Dwelt Among the Untrodden Ways

She dwelt among the untrodden ways
  Beside the springs of Dove,
A maid whom there were none to praise
  And very few to love:

A violet by a mossy stone
  Half hidden from the eye!
—Fair as a star, when only one
  Is shining in the sky.

She lived unknown, and few could know
  When Lucy ceased to be;
But she is in her grave, and, oh,
  The difference to me!

I Travelled Among Unknown Men

I TRAVELLED among unknown men
  In lands beyond the sea;
Nor, England! did I know till then
  What love I bore to thee.

'Tis past, that melancholy dream!
  Nor will I quit thy shore
  A second time; for still I seem
    To love thee more and more.

  Among thy mountains did I feel
    The joy of my desire;
  And she I cherished turned her wheel
    Beside an English fire.

Thy mornings showed, thy nights concealed
  The bowers where Lucy played;
And thine too is the last green field
    That Lucy's eyes surveyed.

Lines Written in Early Spring

I HEARD a thousand blended notes
  While in a grove I sat reclined,
In that sweet mood when pleasant thoughts
  Bring sad thoughts to the mind.

To her fair works did Nature link
  The human soul that through me ran;

And much it grieved my heart to think
  What man has made of man.

Through primrose tufts, in that green bower,
  The periwinkle trailed its wreaths;
And 'tis my faith that every flower
  Enjoys the air it breathes.

The birds around me hopped and played,
  Their thoughts I cannot measure—
But the least motion which they made
  It seemed a thrill of pleasure.

The budding twigs spread out their fan
  To catch the breezy air;
And I must think, do all I can,
  That there was pleasure there.

If this belief from heaven be sent,
  If such be Nature's holy plan,
Have I not reason to lament
  What man has made of man?

To the Cuckoo

O BLITHE new-comer! I have heard,
  I hear thee and rejoice.
O cuckoo! shall I call thee bird,
  Or but a wandering voice?

While I am lying on the grass
  Thy twofold shout I hear;
From hill to hill it seems to pass,
  At once far off, and near.

Though babbling only to the vale
  Of sunshine and of flowers,
Thou bringest unto me a tale
  Of visionary hours.

Thrice welcome, darling of the spring!
  Even yet thou art to me
No bird, but an invisible thing,
  A voice, a mystery;

The same whom in my schoolboy days
  I listened to; that cry
Which made me look a thousand ways
  In bush, and tree, and sky.

To seek thee did I often rove
  Through woods and on the green;
And thou wert still a hope, a love;
  Still longed for, never seen.

And I can listen to thee yet;
  Can lie upon the plain
And listen, till I do beget
  That golden time again.

O blessèd bird! the earth we pace
  Again appears to be
An unsubstantial, faery place,
  That is fit home for thee!

The Solitary Reaper

BEHOLD her, single in the field,
Yon solitary Highland lass!
Reaping and singing by herself;
Stop here, or gently pass!
Alone she cuts and binds the grain,
And sings a melancholy strain;
O listen! for the vale profound
Is overflowing with the sound.

No nightingale did ever chaunt
More welcome notes to weary bands
Of travellers in some shady haunt,
Among Arabian sands:
A voice so thrilling ne'er was heard
In spring-time from the cuckoo-bird,
Breaking the silence of the seas
Among the farthest Hebrides.

Will no one tell me what she sings?—
Perhaps the plaintive numbers flow
For old, unhappy, far-off things,
And battles long ago:
Or is it some more humble lay,
Familiar matter of to-day?
Some natural sorrow, loss, or pain,
That has been, and may be again?

Whate'er the theme, the Maiden sang
As if her song could have no ending;
I saw her singing at her work,
And o'er the sickle bending;

I listen'd, motionless and still;
And, when I mounted up the hill,
The music in my heart I bore,
Long after it was heard no more.

The World Is Too Much With Us

THE world is too much with us; late and soon,
Getting and spending, we lay waste our powers:
Little we see in Nature that is ours;
We have given our hearts away, a sordid boon!
This sea that bares her bosom to the moon;
The winds that will be howling at all hours,
And are up-gathered now like sleeping flowers;
For this, for everything, we are out of tune;
It moves us not.—Great God! I'd rather be
A Pagan suckled in a creed outworn;
So might I, standing on this pleasant lea,
Have glimpses that would make me less forlorn;
Have sight of Proteus rising from the sea;
Or hear old Triton blow his wreathèd horn.

Skating

(from *The Prelude*, Book I)

. . . AND in the frosty season, when the sun
Was set, and visible for many a mile
The cottage windows blazed through twilight gloom,
I heeded not their summons: happy time

It was indeed for all of us—for me
It was a time of rapture! Clear and loud
The village clock tolled six,—I wheeled about,
Proud and exulting like an untired horse
That cares not for his home. All shod with steel,
We hissed along the polished ice in games
Confederates, imitative of the chase
And woodland pleasures,—the resounding horn,
The pack loud chiming, and the hunted hare.
So through the darkness and the cold we flew,
And not a voice was idle; with the din
Smitten, the precipices rang aloud;
The leafless tree and every icy crag
Tinkled like iron; while far distant hills
Into the tumult sent an alien sound
Of melancholy not unnoticed, while the stars
Eastward were sparkling clear, and in the west
The orange sky of evening died away.
Not seldom from the uproar I retired
Into a silent bay, or sportively
Glanced sideway, leaving the tumultuous throng,
To cut across the reflex of a star
That fled, and flying still before me, gleamed
Upon the glassy plain; and oftentimes,
When we had given our bodies to the wind,
And all the shadowy banks on either side
Came sweeping through the darkness spinning still
The rapid line of motion, then at once
Have I, reclining back upon my heels,
Stopped short; yet still the solitary cliffs
Wheeled by me—even as if the earth had rolled
With visible motion her diurnal round!
Behind me did they stretch in solemn train,
Feebler and feebler, and I stood and watched
Till all was tranquil as a dreamless sleep.

Nutting

. . . It seems a day
(I speak of one from many singled out)
One of those heavenly days that cannot die;
When, in the eagerness of boyish hope,
I left our cottage-threshold, sallying forth
With a huge wallet o'er my shoulders slung,
A nutting-crook in hand; and turned my steps
Tow'rd some far-distant wood, a figure quaint,
Tricked out in proud disguise of cast-off weeds
Which for that service had been husbanded,
By exhortation of my frugal dame—
Motley accoutrement, of power to smile
At thorns, and brakes, and brambles,—and in truth
More ragged than need was! O'er pathless rocks,
Through beds of matted fern, and tangled thickets,
Forcing my way, I came to one dear nook
Unvisited, where not a broken bough
Drooped with its withered leaves, ungracious sign
Of devastation; but the hazels rose
Tall and erect, with tempting clusters hung,
A virgin scene!—A little while I stood,
Breathing with such suppression of the heart
As joy delights in; and with wise restraint
Voluptuous, fearless of a rival, eyed
The banquet;—or beneath the trees I sate
Among the flowers, and with the flowers I played;
A temper known to those who, after long
And weary expectation, have been blest
With sudden happiness beyond all hope.
Perhaps it was a bower beneath whose leaves
The violets of five seasons re-appear

And fade, unseen by any human eye;
Where fairy water-breaks do murmur on
For ever; and I saw the sparkling foam,
And—with my cheek on one of those green stones
That, fleeced with moss, under the shady trees,
Lay round me, scattered like a flock of sheep—
I heard the murmur and the murmuring sound,
In that sweet mood when pleasure loves to pay
Tribute to ease; and, of its joy secure,
The heart luxuriates with indifferent things,
Wasting its kindliness on stocks and stones,
And on the vacant air. Then up I rose,
And dragged to earth both branch and bough, with crash
And merciless ravage: and the shady nook
Of hazels, and the green and mossy bower,
Deformed and sullied, patiently gaze up
Their quiet being: and unless I now
Confound my present feelings with the past,
Ere from the mutilated bower I turned
Exulting, rich beyond the wealth of kings,
I felt a sense of pain when I beheld
The silent trees, and saw the intruding sky.—
Then, dearest Maiden, move along these shades
In gentleness of heart; with gentle hand
Touch—for there is a spirit in the woods.

Samuel Taylor Coleridge

Kubla Khan

In Xanadu did Kubla Khan
  A stately pleasure-dome decree:
Where Alph, the sacred river, ran
Through caverns measureless to man
  Down to a sunless sea.
So twice five miles of fertile ground
With walls and towers were girdled round:
And there were gardens bright with sinuous rills,
Where blossomed many an incense-bearing tree;
And here were forests ancient as the hills,
Enfolding sunny spots of greenery.

But oh! that deep romantic chasm which slanted
Down the green hill athwart a cedarn cover!
A savage place! as holy and enchanted
As e'er beneath a waning moon was haunted
By woman wailing for her demon-lover!
And from this chasm, with ceaseless turmoil seething,
As if this earth in fast thick pants were breathing,
A mighty fountain momently was forced:
Amid whose swift half-intermitted burst
Huge fragments vaulted like rebounding hail,
Or chaffy grain beneath the thresher's flail:
And 'mid these dancing rocks at once and ever
It flung up momently the sacred river.
Five miles meandering with a mazy motion

Through wood and dale the sacred river ran,
Then reached the caverns measureless to man,
And sank in tumult to a lifeless ocean:
And 'mid this tumult Kubla heard from far
Ancestral voices prophesying war!

The shadow of the dome of pleasure
Floated midway on the waves;
Where was heard the mingled measure
From the fountain and the caves,
It was a miracle of rare device,
A sunny pleasure-dome with caves of ice!

A damsel with a dulcimer
In a vision once I saw:
It was an Abyssinian maid,
And on her dulcimer she played,
Singing of Mount Abora.
Could I revive within me
Her symphony and song,
To such a deep delight 'twould win me,
That with music loud and long,
I would build that dome in air,
That sunny dome! those caves of ice!
And all who heard should see them there,
And all should cry, Beware! Beware!
His flashing eyes, his floating hair!
Weave a circle round him thrice,
And close your eyes with holy dread.
For he on honey-dew hath fed,
And drunk the milk of Paradise.

The Rime of the Ancient Mariner

Part I

An ancient Mariner meeteth three gallants bidden to a wedding-feast and detaineth one.

It is an ancient Mariner,
And he stoppeth one of three.
'By thy long grey beard and glittering eye,
Now wherefore stopp'st thou me?

The Bridegroom's doors are open'd wide,
And I am next of kin;
The guests are met, the feast is set:
May'st hear the merry din.'

He holds him with his skinny hand,
'There was a ship,' quoth he.
'Hold off! unhand me, grey-beard loon!'
Eftsoons his hand dropt he.

The Wedding-Guest is spellbound by the eye of the old seafaring man, and constrained to hear his tale.

He holds him with his glittering eye—
The Wedding-Guest stood still,
And listens like a three years' child:
The Mariner hath his will.

The Wedding-Guest sat on a stone:
He cannot choose but hear;
And thus spake on that ancient man,
The bright-eyed Mariner:

'The ship was cheer'd, the harbour clear'd,
Merrily did we drop
Below the kirk, below the hill,
Below the lighthouse top.

The Mariner tells how the ship sailed southward with a good wind and fair weather, till it reached the Line.

The Sun came up upon the left,
Out of the sea came he!
And he shone bright, and on the right
Went down into the sea.

Higher and higher every day,
Till over the mast at noon——'
The Wedding-Guest here beat his breast,
For he heard the loud bassoon.

The Wedding-Guest heareth the bridal music; but the Mariner continueth his tale.

The bride hath paced into the hall,
Red as a rose is she;
Nodding their heads before her goes
The merry minstrelsy.

The Wedding-Guest he beat his breast,
Yet he cannot choose but hear;
And thus spake on that ancient man,
The bright-eyed Mariner:

The ship driven by a storm toward the South Pole.

'And now the Storm-blast came, and he
Was tyrannous and strong:
He struck with his o'ertaking wings,
And chased us south along.

With sloping masts and dipping prow,
As who pursued with yell and blow
Still treads the shadow of his foe,
And forward bends his head,
The ship drove fast, loud roar'd the blast,
And southward aye we fled.

And now there came both mist and snow
And it grew wondrous cold:
And ice, mast-high, came floating by,
As green as emerald.

And through the drifts the snowy clifts
Did send a dismal sheen;
Nor shapes of men nor beasts we ken—
The ice was all between.

The land of ice, and of fearful sounds, where no living thing was to be seen.

The ice was here, the ice was there,
The ice was all around:
It crack'd and growl'd, and roar'd and howl'd,
Like noises in a swound!

At length did cross an Albatross,
Thorough the fog it came;
As if it had been a Christian soul,
We hail'd it in God's name.

Till a great sea-bird, called the Albatross, came through the snow-fog, and was received with great joy and hospitality.

It ate the food it ne'er had eat,
And round and round it flew.
The ice did split with a thunder-fit;
The helmsman steer'd us through!

And a good south wind sprung up behind;
The Albatross did follow,
And every day, for food or play,
Came to the mariners' hollo!

And lo! the Albatross proveth a bird of good omen, and followeth the ship as it returned northward through fog and floating ice.

In mist or cloud, on mast or shroud,
It perch'd for vespers nine;
Whiles all the night, through fog-smoke white,
Glimmer'd the white moonshine.'

'God save thee, ancient Mariner,
From the fiends, that plague thee thus!—
Why look'st thou so?'—'With my crossbow
I shot the Albatross.

The ancient Mariner inhospitably killeth the pious bird of good omen.

Part II

'The Sun now rose upon the right:
Out of the sea came he,
Still hid in mist, and on the left
Went down into the sea.

His shipmates cry out against the ancient Mariner for killing the bird of good luck.

And the good south wind still blew behind,
But no sweet bird did follow,
Nor any day for food or play
Came to the mariners' hollo!

And I had done a hellish thing,
And it would work 'em woe:
For all averr'd I had kill'd the bird
That made the breeze to blow.
Ah wretch! said they, the bird to slay
That made the breeze to blow!

But when the fog cleared off, they justify the same, and thus make themselves accomplices in the crime.

Nor dim nor red, like God's own head,
The glorious Sun uprist:
Then all averr'd I had kill'd the bird
That brought the fog and mist.
'Twas right, said they, such birds to slay,
That bring the fog and mist.

The fair breeze continues; the ship enters the Pacific Ocean, and sails northward, even till it reaches the Line.

The fair breeze blew, the white foam flew,
The furrow follow'd free;
We were the first that ever burst
Into that silent sea.

The ship hath been suddenly becalmed.

Down dropt the breeze, the sails dropt down,
'Twas sad as sad could be;
And we did speak only to break
The silence of the sea!

All in a hot and copper sky,
The bloody Sun, at noon,
Right up above the mast did stand,
No bigger than the Moon.

Day after day, day after day,
We stuck, nor breath nor motion;
As idle as a painted ship
Upon a painted ocean.

Water, water, everywhere,
And all the boards did shrink;
Water, water, everywhere,
Nor any drop to drink.

And the Albatross begins to be avenged.

The very deep did rot: O Christ!
That ever this should be!
Yea, slimy things did crawl with legs
Upon the slimy sea.

About, about, in reel and rout
The death-fires danced at night;
The water, like a witch's oils,
Burnt green, and blue, and white.

And some in dreams assurèd were
Of the Spirit that plagued us so;
Nine fathom deep he had follow'd us
From the land of mist and snow.

A Spirit had followed them: one of the invisible inhabitants of this planet, neither departed souls nor angels; concerning whom the learned Jew, Josephus, and the Platonic Constantinopolitan, Michael Psellus, may be consulted. They are very numerous, and there is no climate or element without one or more.

And every tongue, through utter drought,
Was wither'd at the root;
We could not speak, no more than if
We had been chok'd with soot.

The ship-mates in their sore distress, would fain throw the whole guilt on the ancient Mariner: in sign whereof they hang the dead sea-bird round his neck.

Ah! well-a-day! what evil looks
Had I from old and young!
Instead of the cross, the Albatross
About my neck was hung.

Part III

'There passed a weary time. Each throat
Was parch'd, and glazed each eye.
A weary time! a weary time!
How glazed each weary eye!
When looking westward, I beheld
A something in the sky.

The ancient Mariner beholdeth a sign in the element afar off.

At first it seem'd a little speck,
And then it seem'd a mist;
It mov'd and mov'd, and took at last
A certain shape, I wist.

A speck, a mist, a shape, I wist!
And still it near'd and near'd:
As if it dodg'd a water-sprite,
It plung'd, and tack'd, and veer'd.

At its nearer approach, it seemeth him to be a ship; and at a dear ransom he freeth his speech from the bonds of thirst.

With throats unslak'd, with black lips bak'd,
We could nor laugh nor wail;
Through utter drought all dumb we stood!
I bit my arm, I suck'd the blood,
And cried, "A sail! a sail!"

With throats unslak'd, with black lips bak'd,
Agape they heard me call:

A flash of joy!

Gramercy! they for joy did grin,
And all at once their breath drew in,
As they were drinking all.

See! see! (I cried) she tacks no more
Hither to work us weal—
Without a breeze, without a tide,
She steadies with upright keel!

And horror follows. For can it be a ship that comes onward without wind or tide?

The western wave was all aflame,
The day was wellnigh done!
Almost upon the western wave
Rested the broad, bright Sun;
When that strange shape drove suddenly
Betwixt us and the Sun.

And straight the Sun was fleck'd with bars
(Heaven's Mother send us grace!)
As if through a dungeon-grate he peer'd
With broad and burning face.

It seemeth him but the skeleton of a ship.

Alas! (thought I, and my heart beat loud)
How fast she nears and nears!
Are those her sails that glance in the sun,
Like restless gossameres?

Are those her ribs through which the Sun
Did peer, as through a grate?
And is that Woman all her crew?
Is that a Death? and are there two?
Is Death that Woman's mate?

And its ribs are seen as bars on the face of the setting Sun. The Spectre-Woman and her Death-mate, and no other, on board the skeleton ship. Like vessel, like crew!

Her lips were red, her looks were free,
Her locks were yellow as gold:
Her skin was as white as leprosy,
The Nightmare Life-in-Death was she,
Who thicks man's blood with cold.

Death and Life-in-Death have diced for the ship's crew, and she (the latter) winneth the ancient Mariner.

The naked hulk alongside came,
And the twain were casting dice;
'The game is done! I've won! I've won!'
Quoth she, and whistles thrice.

No twilight within the courts of the Sun.

The Sun's rim dips; the stars rush out:
At one stride comes the dark;
With far-heard whisper, o'er the sea,
Off shot the spectre-bark.

We listen'd and look'd sideways up!
Fear at my heart, as at a cup,
My life-blood seem'd to sip!
The stars were dim, and thick the night,
The steersman's face by his lamp gleam'd white;

From the sails the dew did drip—
Till clomb above the eastern bar
The hornèd Moon, with one bright star
Within the nether tip.

At the rising of the Moon.

One after one, by the star-dogg'd Moon,
Too quick for groan or sigh,
Each turn'd his face with a ghastly pang,
And cursed me with his eye.

One after another.

Four times fifty living men
(And I heard nor sigh nor groan),
With heavy thump, a lifeless lump,
They dropp'd down one by one.

His shipmates drop down dead.

The souls did from their bodies fly—
They fled to bliss or woe!
And every soul, it pass'd me by
Like the whizz of my crossbow!'

But Life-in-Death begins her work on the ancient Mariner.

Part IV

'I fear thee, ancient Mariner!
'I fear thy skinny hand!
And thou art long, and lank, and brown,
As is the ribb'd sea-sand.

The Wedding-Guest feareth that a spirit is talking to him.

I fear thee and thy glittering eye,
And thy skinny hand so brown.'—
'Fear not, fear not, thou wedding guest!
This body dropt not down.

But the ancient Mariner assureth him of his bodily life, and proceedeth to relate his horrible penance.

Alone, alone, all, all alone,
Alone on a wide, wide sea!
And never a saint took pity on
My soul in agony.

The many men, so beautiful!
And they all dead did lie:
And a thousand thousand slimy things
Liv'd on; and so did I.

He despiseth the creatures of the calm.

I look'd upon the rotting sea,
And drew my eyes away;
I look'd upon the rotting deck,
And there the dead men lay.

And envieth that they should live, and so many lie dead.

I look'd to heaven, and tried to pray;
But or ever a prayer had gusht,
A wicked whisper came, and made
My heart as dry as dust.

I clos'd my lids, and kept them close,
And the balls like pulses beat;
For the sky and the sea, and the sea and the sky
Lay like a load on my weary eye,
And the dead were at my feet.

But the curse liveth for him in the eye of the dead men.

The cold sweat melted from their limbs,
Nor rot nor reed did they:
The look with which they look'd on me
Had never pass'd away.

An orphan's curse would drag to hell
A spirit from on high;
But oh! more horrible than that
Is the curse in a dead man's eye!
Seven days, seven nights, I saw that curse,
And yet I could not die.

In his loneliness and fixedness he yearneth towards the journeying Moon, and the stars that still sojourn, yet still move onward; and everywhere the blue sky belongs to them, and is their appointed rest and their native country and their own natural homes, which they enter unannounced, as lords that are certainly expected, and yet there is a silent joy at their arrival.

The moving Moon went up the sky,
And nowhere did abide;
Softly she was going up,
And a star or two beside—

Her beams bemock'd the sultry main,
Like April hoar-frost spread;
But where the ship's huge shadow lay,
The charmèd water burnt alway
A still and awful red.

By the light of the Moon he beholdeth God's creatures of the great calm.

Beyond the shadow of the ship,
I watch'd the water-snakes:
They moved in tracks of shining white,
And when they rear'd, the elfish light
Fell off in hoary flakes.

Within the shadow of the ship
I watch'd their rich attire:
Blue, glossy green, and velvet black,
They coil'd and swam; and every track
Was a flash of golden fire.

O happy living things! no tongue
Their beauty might declare:
A spring of love gush'd from my heart,
And I bless'd them unaware:
Sure my kind saint took pity on me,
And I bless'd them unaware.

Their beauty and their happiness.

He blesseth them in his heart.

The self-same moment I could pray;
And from my neck so free
The Albatross fell off, and sank
Like lead into the sea.

The Spell begins to break.

Part V

'O sleep! it is a gentle thing,
Belov'd from pole to pole!
To Mary Queen the praise be given!
She sent the gentle sleep from Heaven,
That slid into my soul.

The silly[1] buckets on the deck,
That had so long remain'd,
I dreamt that they were fill'd with dew;
And when I awoke, it rain'd.

By grace of the holy Mother, the ancient Mariner is refreshed with rain.

My lips were wet, my throat was cold,
My garments all were dank,
Sure I had drunken in my dreams,
And still my body drank.

I mov'd, and could not feel my limbs:
I was so light—almost
I thought that I had died in sleep,
And was a blessèd ghost.

[1] useless

He heareth sounds and seeth strange sights and commotions in the sky and the element.

And soon I heard a roaring wind:
It did not come anear;
But with its sound it shook the sails,
That were so thin and sere.

The upper air burst into life!
And a hundred fire-flags sheen,
To and fro they were hurried about!
And to and fro, and in and out,
The wan stars danc'd between.

And the coming wind did roar more loud,
And the sails did sigh like sedge;
And the rain pour'd down from one black cloud;
The Moon was at its edge.

The thick black cloud was cleft, and still
The Moon was at its side;
Like waters shot from some high crag,
The lightning fell with never a jag,
A river steep and wide.

The bodies of the ship's crew are inspired, and the ship moves on.

The loud wind never reach'd the ship,
Yet now the ship mov'd on!
Beneath the lightning and the Moon
The dead men gave a groan.

They groan'd, they stirr'd, they all uprose,
Nor spake, nor mov'd their eyes;
It had been strange, even in a dream,
To have seen those dead men rise.

The helmsman steer'd, the ship mov'd on;
Yet never a breeze up-blew;
The mariners all 'gan work the ropes,

Where they were wont to do;
They rais'd their limbs like lifeless tools—
We were a ghastly crew.

The body of my brother's son
Stood by me, knee to knee:
The body and I pull'd at one rope,
But he said naught to me.'

'I fear thee, ancient Mariner!'
'Be calm, thou Wedding-Guest:
'Twas not those souls that fled in pain,
Which to their corses came again,
But a troop of spirits blest:

But not by the souls of the men, nor by demons of earth or middle air, but by a blessed troop of angelic spirits, sent down by the invocation of the guardian saint.

For when it dawn'd—they dropp'd their arms,
And cluster'd round the mast;
Sweet sounds rose slowly through their mouths,
And from their bodies pass'd.

Around, around, flew each sweet sound,
Then darted to the Sun;
Slowly the sounds came back again,
Now mix'd, now one by one.

Sometimes a-dropping from the sky
I heard the skylark sing;
Sometimes all little birds that are,
How they seem'd to fill the sea and air
With their sweet jargoning!

And now 'twas like all instruments,
Now like a lonely flute;
And now it is an angel's song,
That makes the Heavens be mute.

It ceas'd; yet still the sails made on
A pleasant noise till noon,
A noise like of a hidden brook
In the leafy month of June,
That to the sleeping woods all night
Singeth a quiet tune.

Till noon we quietly sail'd on,
Yet never a breeze did breathe:
Slowly and smoothly went the ship,
Mov'd onward from beneath.

The lonesome Spirit from the South Pole carries on the ship as far as the Line, in obedience to the angelic troop, but still requireth vengeance.

Under the keel nine fathom deep,
From the land of mist and snow,
The Spirit slid: and it was he
That made the ship to go.
The sails at noon left off their tune,
And the ship stood still also.

The Sun, right up above the mast,
Had fix'd her to the ocean;
But in a minute she 'gan stir,
With a short uneasy motion—
Backwards and forwards half her length
With a short uneasy motion.

Then like a pawing horse let go,
She made a sudden bound:
It flung the blood into my head,
And I fell down in a swound.

The Polar Spirit's fellow-demons, the invisible inhabitants of the element, take part in his wrong; and two of them relate,

How long in that same fit I lay,
I have not to declare;
But ere my living life return'd,
I heard, and in my soul discern'd
Two voices in the air.

"Is it he?" quoth one, "is this the man?
By Him who died on cross,
With his cruel bow he laid full low
The harmless Albatross.

one to the other, that penance long and heavy for the ancient Mariner hath been accorded to the Polar Spirit, who returneth southward.

The Spirit who bideth by himself
In the land of mist and snow,
He lov'd the bird that lov'd the man
Who shot him with his bow."

The other was a softer voice,
As soft as honey-dew:
Quoth he, "The man hath penance done,
And penance more will do."

Part VI

First Voice:

'"But tell me, tell me! speak again,
Thy soft response renewing—
What makes that ship drive on so fast?
What is the Ocean doing?"

Second Voice:

"Still as a slave before his lord,
The Ocean hath no blast;
His great bright eye most silently
Up to the Moon is cast—

If he may know which way to go;
For she guides him smooth or grim.
See, brother, see! how graciously
She looketh down on him."

First Voice:

The Mariner hath been cast into a trance; for the angelic power causeth the vessel to drive northward faster than human life could endure.

"But why drives on that ship so fast,
Without or wave or wind?"

Second Voice:

"The air is cut away before,
And closes from behind.

Fly, brother, fly! more high, more high!
Or we shall be belated:
For slow and slow that ship will go,
When the Mariner's trance is abated."

The supernatural motion is retarded; the Mariner awakes, and his penance begins anew.

I woke, and we were sailing on
As in a gentle weather:
'Twas night, calm night, the Moon was high;
The dead men stood together.

All stood together on the deck,
For a charnel-dungeon fitter:
All fix'd on me their stony eyes,
That in the Moon did glitter.

The pang, the curse, with which they died,
Had never pass'd away:
I could not draw my eyes from theirs,
Nor turn them up to pray.

The curse is finally expiated.

And now this spell was snapt: once more
I viewed the ocean green,
And look'd far forth, yet little saw
Of what had else been seen—

Like one that on a lonesome road
Doth walk in fear and dread,
And having once turn'd round, walks on,
And turns no more his head;
Because he knows a frightful fiend
Doth close behind him tread.

But soon there breath'd a wind on me,
Nor sound nor motion made:
Its path was not upon the sea,
In ripple or in shade.

It rais'd my hair, it fann'd my cheek
Like a meadow-gale of spring—
It mingled strangely with my fears,
Yet it felt like a welcoming.

Swiftly, swiftly flew the ship,
Yet she sail'd softly too:
Sweetly, sweetly blew the breeze—
On me alone it blew.

And the ancient Mariner beholdeth his native country.

O dream of joy! is this indeed
The lighthouse top I see?
Is this the hill? is this the kirk?
Is this mine own countree?

We drifted o'er the harbour-bar,
And I with sobs did pray—
O let me be awake, my God!
Or let me sleep alway.

The harbour-bay was clear as glass,
So smoothly it was strewn!
And on the bay the moonlight lay,
And the shadow of the Moon.

The rock shone bright, the kirk no less
That stands above the rock:
The moonlight steep'd in silentness
The steady weathercock.

The angelic spirits leave the dead bodies.

And the bay was white with silent light,
Till rising from the same,
Full many shapes, that shadows were,
In crimson colours came.

And appear in their own form of light.

A little distance from the prow
Those crimson shadows were:
I turn'd my eyes upon the deck—
O Christ! what saw I there!

Each corse lay flat, lifeless and flat,
And, by the holy rood!
A man all light, a seraph-man,
On every corse there stood.

This seraph-band, each wav'd his hand:
It was a heavenly sight!
They stood as signals to the land,
Each one a lovely light;

This seraph-band, each wav'd his hand,
No voice did they impart—
No voice; but O, the silence sank
Like music on my heart.

But soon I heard the dash of oars,
I heard the Pilot's cheer;
My head was turn'd perforce away,
And I saw a boat appear.

The Pilot and the Pilot's boy,
I heard them coming fast:
Dear Lord in Heaven! it was a joy
The dead men could not blast.

I saw a third—I heard his voice:
It is the Hermit good!
He singeth loud his godly hymns
That he makes in the wood.
He'll shrieve my soul, he'll wash away
The Albatross's blood.

Part VII

'This Hermit good lives in that wood
Which slopes down to the sea.
How loudly his sweet voice he rears!
He loves to talk with marineres
That come from a far countree.

The Hermit of the Wood.

He kneels at morn, and noon, and eve—
He hath a cushion plump:
It is the moss that wholly hides
The rotted old oak-stump.

The skiff-boat near'd: I heard them talk,
"Why, this is strange, I trow!
Where are those lights so many and fair,
That signal made but now?"

"Strange, by my faith!" the Hermit said—
"And they answer'd not our cheer!
The planks look warp'd! and see those sails,
How thin they are and sere!
I never saw aught like to them,
Unless perchance it were

Approacheth the ship with wonder.

Brown skeletons of leaves that lag
My forest-brook along;
When the ivy-tod is heavy with snow,
And the owlet whoops to the wolf below,
That eats the she-wolf's young."

"Dear Lord! it hath a fiendish look—
(The Pilot made reply)
I am a-fear'd."—"Push on, push on!"
Said the Hermit cheerily.

The boat came closer to the ship,
But I nor spake nor stirr'd;
The boat came close beneath the ship,
And straight a sound was heard.

The ship suddenly sinketh.

Under the water it rumbled on,
Still louder and more dread:
It reach'd the ship, it split the bay;
The ship went down like lead.

The ancient Mariner is saved in the Pilot's boat.

Stunn'd by that loud and dreadful sound,
Which sky and ocean smote,
Like one that hath been seven days drown'd
My body lay afloat;
But swift as dreams, myself I found
Within the Pilot's boat.

Upon the whirl, where sank the ship
The boat spun round and round;
And all was still, save that the hill
Was telling of the sound.

I mov'd my lips—the Pilot shriek'd
And fell down in a fit;
The holy Hermit rais'd his eyes,
And pray'd where he did sit.

I took the oars: the Pilot's boy,
Who now doth crazy go,
Laugh'd loud and long, and all the while
His eyes went to and fro.
"Ha! ha!" quoth he, "full plain I see
The Devil knows how to row."

And now, all in my own countree,
I stood on the firm land!
The Hermit stepp'd forth from the boat,
And scarcely could he stand.

"O shrieve me, shrieve me, holy man!"
The Hermit cross'd his brow.
"Say quick," quoth he, "I bid thee say—
What manner of man art thou?"

The ancient Mariner earnestly entreateth the Hermit to shrieve him; and the penance of life falls on him.

Forthwith this frame of mine was wrench'd
With a woeful agony,
Which forc'd me to begin my tale;
And then it left me free.

Since then, at an uncertain hour,
That agony returns:
And till my ghastly tale is told,
This heart within me burns.

And ever and anon throughout his future life an agony constraineth him to travel from land to land.

I pass, like night, from land to land;
I have strange power of speech;
That moment that his face I see,
I know the man that must hear me:
To him my tale I teach.

What loud uproar bursts from that door!
The wedding-guests are there:
But in the garden-bower the bride
And bride-maids singing are:
And hark the little vesper bell,
Which biddeth me to prayer!

O Wedding-Guest! this soul hath been
Alone on a wide, wide sea:
So lonely 'twas, that God himself
Scarce seemèd there to be.

O sweeter than the marriage-feast,
'Tis sweeter far to me,
To walk together to the kirk
With a goodly company!—

To walk together to the kirk,
And all together pray,
While each to his great Father bends,
Old men, and babes, and loving friends,
And youths and maidens gay!

And to teach, by his own example, love and reverence to all things that God made and loveth.

Farewell, farewell! but this I tell
To thee, thou Wedding-Guest!
He prayeth well, who loveth well
Both man and bird and beast.

He prayeth best, who loveth best
All things both great and small;
For the dear God who loveth us,
He made and loveth all.'

The Mariner, whose eye is bright,
Whose beard with age is hoar,
Is gone: and now the Wedding-Guest
Turn'd from the bridegroom's door.

He went like one that hath been stunn'd,
And is of sense forlorn:
A sadder and a wiser man
He rose the morrow morn.

Walter Savage Landor

Well I Remember How You Smiled

Well I remember how you smiled
To see me write your name upon
The soft sea-sand . . . '*O! what a child!*
You think you're writing upon stone!'
I have since written what no tide
Shall ever wash away, what men
Unborn shall read o'er ocean wide
And find Ianthe's name again.

Percy Bysshe Shelley

A Widow Bird Sate Mourning for Her Love

A WIDOW bird sate mourning for her love
Upon a wintry bough;
The frozen wind crept on above,
The freezing stream below.

There was no leaf upon the forest bare,
No flower upon the ground,
And little motion in the air
Except the mill-wheel's sound.

Ozymandias

I MET a traveller from an antique land
Who said: Two vast and trunkless legs of stone
Stand in the desert. . . . Near them, on the sand,
Half sunk, a shattered visage lies, whose frown,
And wrinkled lip, and sneer of cold command,
Tell that its sculptor well those passions read
Which yet survive, stamped on these lifeless things,
The hand that mocked them, and the heart that fed:
And on the pedestal these words appear:
'My name is Ozymandias, king of kings:

Look on my works, ye Mighty, and despair!'
Nothing beside remains. Round the decay
Of that colossal wreck, boundless and bare
The lone and level sands stretch far away.

Ode to the West Wind

I

O WILD West Wind, thou breath of Autumn's being,
Thou, from whose unseen presence the leaves dead
Are driven, like ghosts from an enchanter fleeing,

Yellow, and black, and pale, and hectic red,
Pestilence-stricken multitudes: O thou,
Who chariotest to their dark wintry bed

The wingèd seeds, where they lie cold and low,
Each like a corpse within its grave, until
Thine azure sister of the Sring shall blow

Her clarion o'er the dreaming earth, and fill
(Driving sweet buds like flocks to feed in air)
With living hues and odours plain and hill:

Wild Spirit, which art moving everywhere;
Destroyer and preserver; hear, O hear!

II

Thou on whose stream, mid the step sky'd commotion,
Loose clouds like earth's decaying leaves are shed,
Shook from the tangled boughs of Heaven and Ocean,

Angels of rain and lightning: there are spread
On the blue surface of thine aëry surge,
Like the bright hair uplifted from the head

Of some fierce Mænad, even from the dim verge
Of the horizon to the zenith's height,
The locks of the approaching storm. Thou dirge

Of the dying year, to which this closing night
Will be the dome of a vast sepulchre,
Vaulted with all thy congregated might

Of vapours, from whose solid atmosphere
Black rain, and fire, and hail will burst: O hear!

III

Thou who didst waken from his summer dreams
The blue Mediterranean, where he lay,
Lull'd by the coil of his crystàlline streams,

Beside a pumice isle in Baieæ's bay,
And saw in sleep old palaces and towers
Quivering within the wave's intenser day,

All overgrown with azure moss and flowers
So sweet, the sense faints picturing them! Thou
For whose path the Atlantic's level powers

Cleave themselves into chasms, while far below
The sea-blooms and the oozy woods which wear
The sapless foliage of the ocean, know

Thy voice, and suddenly grow gray with fear,
And tremble and despoil themselves: O hear!

IV

If I were a dead leaf thou mightest bear;
If I were a swift cloud to fly with thee;
A wave to pant beneath thy power, and share

The impulse of thy strength, only less free
Than thou, O uncontrollable! If even
I were as in my boyhood, and could be

The comrade of thy wanderings over Heaven,
As then, when to outstrip thy skiey speed
Scarce seem'd a vision; I would ne'er have striven

As thus with thee in prayer in my sore need.
O lift me as a wave, a leaf, a cloud!
I fall upon the thorns of life! I bleed!

A heavy weight of hours has chain'd and bow'd
One too like thee: tameless, and swift, and proud.

V

Make me thy lyre, even as the forest is:
What if my leaves are falling like its own!
The tumult of thy mighty harmonies

Will take from both a deep, autumnal tone,
Sweet though in sadness. Be thou, Spirit fierce,
My spirit! Be thou me, impetuous one!

Drive my dead thoughts over the universe
Like wither'd leaves to quicken a new birth!
And, by the incantation of this verse,

Scatter, as from an unextinguish'd hearth
Ashes and sparks, my words among mankind!
Be through my lips to unawaken'd earth

The trumpet of a prophecy! O Wind,
If Winter comes, can Spring be far behind?

John Clare

Pleasant Sounds

THE rustling of leaves under the feet in woods and under hedges;
The crumping of cat-ice and snow down woodrides, narrow lanes and every street causeway;
Rustling through a wood or rather rushing, while the wind halloos in the oak-top like thunder;
The rustle of birds' wings startled from their nests or flying unseen into the bushes;
The whizzing of larger birds overhead in a wood, such as crows, paddocks,[1] buzzards;
The trample of robins and woodlarks on the brown leaves, and the patter of squirrels on the green moss;

[1] kites

The fall of an acorn on the ground, the pattering of nuts on the hazel branches as they fall from ripeness;
The flirt of the ground-lark's wings from the stubbles—how sweet such pictures on dewy mornings, when the dew flashes from its brown feathers!

Autumn

THE thistle down's flying, though the winds are all still,
On the green grass now lying, now mounting the hill,
The spring from the fountain now boils like a pot;
Through stones past the counting it bubbles red-hot.

The ground parched and cracked is like overbaked bread,
The greensward all wracked is, bents dried up and dead.
The fallow fields glitter like water indeed,
And gossamers twitter, flung from weed unto weed.

Hill tops like hot iron glitter bright in the sun,
And the rivers we're eyeing burn to gold as they run;
Burning hot is the ground, liquid gold is the air;
Whoever looks round sees Eternity there.

Badger

WHEN midnight comes a host of dogs and men
Go out and track the badger to his den,
And put a sack within the hole, and lie
Till the old grunting badger passes by.

He comes and hears—they let the strongest loose.
The old fox hears the noise and drops the goose.
The poacher shoots and hurries from the cry,
And the old hare half wounded buzzes by.
They get a forkèd stick to bear him down
And clap the dogs and take him to the town,
And bait him all the day with many dogs,
And laugh and shout and fright the scampering hogs.
He runs along and bites at all he meets:
They shout and hollo down the noisy streets.

He turns about to face the loud uproar
And drives the rebels to their very door.
The frequent stone is hurled where'er they go;
When badgers fight, then every one's a foe.
The dogs are clapt and urged to join the fray;
The badger turns and drives them all away.
Though scarcely half as big, demure and small,
He fights with dogs for hours and beats them all.
The heavy mastiff, savage in the fray,
Lies down and licks his feet and turns away.
The bulldog knows his match and waxes cold,
The badger grins and never leaves his hold.
He drives the crowd and follows at their heels
And bites them through—the drunkard swears and reels.

The frighted women take the boys away,
The blackguard laughs and hurries on the fray.
He tries to reach the woods, an awkward race,
But sticks and cudgels quickly stop the chase.
He turns agen and drives the noisy crowd
And beats the many dogs in noises loud.
He drives away and beats them every one,
And then they loose them all and set them on.

He falls as dead and kicked by boys and men,
Then starts and grins and drives the crowd agen;
Till kicked and torn and beaten out he lies
And leaves his hold and cackles, groans, and dies.

Country Letter

DEAR brother Robin, this comes from us all
With our kind love, and could Gip write and all,
Though but a dog he'd have his love to spare,
For still he knows, and by your corner chair
The moment he comes in he lies him down
And seems to fancy you are in the town.
This leaves us well in health, thank God for that!
For old acquaintance Sue has kept your hat
Which mother brushes ere she lays it by
And every Sunday goes upstairs to cry.
Jane is still yours till you come back agen
And ne'er so much as dances with the men;
And Ned the woodman every week comes in
And asks about you kindly as our kin;
And he with this and Goody Thompson sends
Remembrances with those of all our friends.
Father with us sends love until he hears
And mother she has nothing but her tears,
Yet wishes you like us in health the same
And longs to see a letter with your name,
So, loving brother, don't forget to write.
Old Gip lies on the hearthstone every night;
Mother can't bear to turn him out of doors
And never noises now of dirty floors;

Father will laugh but lets her have her way,
And Gip for kindness gets a double pay.
So Robin write and let us quickly see
You don't forget old friends no more than we,
Nor let my mother have so much to blame
To go three journeys ere your letter came.

I Am

I AM: yet what I am none cares or knows,
  My friends forsake me like a memory lost;
I am the self-consumer of my woes,
  They rise and vanish in oblivious host,
Like shades in love and death's oblivion lost;
And yet I am, and live with shadows tost

Into the nothingness of scorn and noise,
  Into the living sea of waking dreams,
Where there is neither sense of life nor joys,
  But the vast shipwreck of my life's esteems;
And e'en the dearest—that I loved the best—
Are strange—nay, rather stranger than the rest.

I long for scenes where man has never trod,
  A place where woman neither smiled or wept;
There to abide with my Creator, God,
  And sleep as I in childhood sweetly slept:
Untroubling and untroubled where I lie,
The grass below—above the vaulted sky.

John Keats

Ode to Autumn

SEASON of mists and mellow fruitfulness,
  Close bosom-friend of the maturing sun;
Conspiring with him how to load and bless
  With fruit the vines that round the thatch-eaves run;
To bend with apples the moss'd cottage-trees,
  And fill all fruit with ripeness to the core;
    To swell the gourd, and plump the hazel shells
With a sweet kernel; to set budding more,
And still more, later flowers for the bees,
Until they think warm days will never cease,
    For Summer has o'er-brimm'd their clammy cells.

II

Who hath not seen thee oft amid thy store?
  Sometimes whoever seeks abroad may find
Thee sitting careless on a granary floor,
  Thy hair soft-lifted by the winnowing wind;
Or on a half-reap'd furrow sound asleep,
  Drowsed with the fume of poppies, while thy hook
    Spares the next swath and all its twinèd flowers:
And sometime like a gleaner thou dost keep
  Steady thy laden head across a brook;
  Or by a cider-press, with patient look,
    Thou watchest the last oozings hours by hours.

III

Where are the songs of Spring? Ay, where are they?
Think not of them, thou hast thy music too,—
While barrèd clouds bloom the soft-dying day,
And touch the stubble-plains with rosy hue;
Then in a wailful choir the small gnats mourn
Among the river sallows, borne aloft
Or sinking as the light wind lives or dies;
And full-grown lambs loud bleat from hilly bourn;
Hedge-crickets sing; and now with treble soft
The redbreast whistles from a garden-croft;
And gathering swallows twitter in the skies.

La Belle Dame sans Merci

'O WHAT can ail thee, knight-at-arms,
Alone and palely loitering?
The sedge has withered from the lake,
And no birds sing.

'O what can ail thee, knight-at-arms,
So haggard and so woe-begone?
The squirrel's granary is full,
And the harvest's done.

'I see a lily on thy brow
With anguish moist and fever dew,
And on thy cheeks a fading rose
Fast withereth too.'

'I met a lady in the meads,
Full beautiful—a faery's child:
Her hair was long, her foot was light,
And her eyes were wild.

'I made a garland for her head,
And bracelets too, and fragrant zone;
She look'd at me as she did love,
And made sweet moan.

'I set her on my pacing steed,
And nothing else saw all day long,
For sidelong would she bend, and sing
A faery's song.

'She found me roots of relish sweet,
And honey wild and manna dew;
And sure in language strange she said,
"I love thee true."

'She took me to her elfin grot,
And there she wept, and sigh'd full sore,
And there I shut her wild, wild eyes
With kisses four.

'And there she lullèd me asleep,
And there I dream'd—ah! woe betide!—
The latest dream I ever dreamed
On the cold hill's side.

'I saw pale kings, and princes too,
Pale warriors, death pale were they all;
They cried—"La belle Dame sans Merci
Hath thee in thrall!"

'I saw their starv'd lips in the gloam
With horrid warning gapèd wide,
And I awoke, and found me here,
On the cold hill's side.

'And this is why I sojourn here
Alone and palely loitering,
Though the sedge is withered from the lake,
And no birds sing.'

In a Drear-nighted December

In a drear-nighted December,
Too happy, happy tree,
Thy branches ne'er remember
Their green felicity:
The north cannot undo them
With a sleety whistle through them,
Nor frozen thawings glue them
From budding at the prime.

In a drear-nighted December,
Too happy, happy brook,
Thy bubblings ne'er remember
Apollo's summer look;
But with a sweet forgetting
They stay their crystal fretting,
Never, never petting
About the frozen time.

Ah, would 'twere so with many
  A gentle girl and boy!
But were there ever any
  Writhed not at passèd joy?
To know the change and feel it,
When there is none to heal it
Nor numbèd sense to steel it—
  Was never said in rhyme.

Written on a Blank Page in Shakespeare's Poems, facing 'A Lover's Complaint'

BRIGHT Star, would I were stedfast as thou art—
Not in lone splendour hung aloft the night,
And watching, with eternal lids apart,
Like nature's patient, sleepless eremite,
The moving waters at their priestlike task
Of pure ablution round earth's human shores,
Or gazing on the new soft-fallen mask
Of snow upon the mountains and the moors—
No—yet still stedfast, still unchangeable,
Pillow'd upon my fair love's ripening breast,
To feel for ever its soft fall and swell,
Awake for ever in a sweet unrest,
Still, still to hear her tender-taken breath,
And so live ever—or else swoon to death.

Hartley Coleridge

To a Friend

When we were idlers with the loitering rills,
The need of human love we little noted:
Our love was nature; and the peace that floated
On the white mist, and dwelt upon the hills,
To sweet accord subdued our wayward wills:
One soul was ours, one mind, one heart devoted,
That, wisely doting, ask'd not why it doted,
And ours the unknown joy, which knowing kills.
But now I find, how dear thou wert to me;
That man is more than half of nature's treasure,
Of that fair Beauty which no eye can see,
Of that sweet music which no ear can measure;
And now the streams may sing for others' pleasure,
The hills sleep on in their eternity.

'Tis strange to me...

'Tis strange to me, who long have seen no face
That was not like a book whose every page
I knew by heart, a kindly common-place—
And faithful record of progressive age—
To wander forth, and view an unknown race;
Of all that I have been, to find no trace,

No footstep of my by-gone pilgrimage.
Thousands I pass, and no one stays his pace
To tell me that the day is fair, or rainy—
Each one his object seeks with anxious chase,
And I have not a common hope with any—
Thus like one drop of oil upon a flood,
In uncommunicating solitude—
Single am I amid the countless many.

Alfred, Lord Tennyson

The Splendour Falls on Castle Walls

THE splendour falls on castle walls
And snowy summits old in story:
The long light shakes across the lakes,
And the wild cataract leaps in glory.
Blow, bugle, blow, set the wild echoes flying,
Blow, bugle; answer, echoes, dying, dying, dying.

O hark, O hear! how thin and clear,
And thinner, clearer, farther going!
O sweet and far from cliff and scar
The horns of Elfland faintly blowing!
Blow, let us hear the purple glens replying:
Blow, bugle; answer, echoes, dying, dying, dying.

O love, they die in yon rich sky,
    They faint on hill or field or river:
O our echoes roll from soul to soul,
    And grow for ever and for ever.
Blow, bugle, blow, set the wild echoes flying,
And answer, echoes, answer, dying, dying, dying.

Now Fades the Last Long Streak of Snow

(from *In Memoriam*)

Now fades the last long streak of snow,
    Now burgeons every maze of quick
    About the flowering squares, and thick
By ashen roots the violets blow.

Now rings the woodland loud and long,
    The distance takes a lovelier hue,
    And drown'd in yonder living blue
The lark becomes a sightless song.

Now dance the lights on lawn and lea,
    The flocks are whiter down the vale,
    And milkier every milky sail
On winding stream or distant sea;

Where now the seamew pipes, or dives
    In yonder greening gleam, and fly
    The happy birds, that change their sky
To build and brood; that live their lives

From land to land; and in my breast
    Spring wakens too; and my regret
    Becomes an April violet,
And buds and blossoms like the rest.

Tithonus

The woods decay, the woods decay and fall,
The vapours weep their burthen to the ground,
Man comes and tills the field and lies beneath,
And after many a summer dies the swan
Me only cruel immortality
Consumes: I wither slowly in thine arms,
Here at the quiet limit of the world,
A white-hair'd shadow roaming like a dream
The ever silent spaces of the East,
Far-folded mists, and gleaming halls of morn.
    Alas! for this grey shadow, once a man—
So glorious in his beauty and thy choice,
Who madest him thy chosen, that he seem'd
To his great heart none other than a God!
I ask'd thee, 'Give me immortality.'

    Then didst thou grant mine asking with a smile,
Like wealthy men who care not how they give.
But thy strong Hours indignant work'd their wills,
And beat me down and marr'd and wasted me,
And tho' they could not end me, left me maim'd
To dwell in presence of immortal youth,
Immortal age beside immortal youth,
And all I was, in ashes. Can thy love,
Thy beauty, make amends, tho' even now,

Close over us, the silver star, thy guide,
Shines in those tremulous eyes that fill with tears
To hear me? Let me go: take back thy gift:
Why should a man desire in any way
To vary from the kindly race of men,
Or pass beyond the goal of ordinance
Where all should pause, as is most meet for all?

A soft air fans the cloud apart; there comes
A glimpse of that dark world where I was born.
Once more the old mysterious glimmer steals
From thy pure brows, and from thy shoulders pure,
And bosom beating with a heart renew'd.
Thy cheek begins to redden thro' the gloom,
Thy sweet eyes brighten slowly close to mine,
Ere yet they blind the stars, and the wild team
Which love thee, yearning for thy yoke, arise,
And shake the darkness from their loosen'd manes,
And beat the twilight into flakes of fire.
Lo! ever thus thou growest beautiful
In silence, then before thine answer given
Departest, and thy tears are on my cheek.

Why wilt thou ever scare me with thy tears,
And make me tremble lest a saying learnt,
In days far-off, on that dark earth, be true?
'The Gods themselves cannot recall their gifts.'

Ay me! ay me! with what another heart
In days far-off, and with what other eyes
I us'd to watch—if I be he that watch'd
The lucid outline forming round thee; saw
The dim curls kindle into sunny rings;
Chang'd with thy mystic change, and felt my blood

Glow with the glow, that slowly crimson'd all
Thy presence and thy portals, while I lay,
Mouth, forehead, eyelids, growing dewy-warm
With kisses balmier than half-opening buds
Of April, and could hear the lips that kiss'd
Whispering I knew not what of wild and sweet,
Like that strange song I heard Apollo sing,
While Ilion like a mist rose into towers.

Yet hold me not for ever in thine East;
How can my nature longer mix with thine?
Coldly thy rosy shadows bathe me, cold
Are all thy lights, and cold my wrinkled feet
Upon thy glimmering thresholds, when the steam
Floats up from those dim fields about the homes
Of happy men that have the power to die,
And grassy barrows of the happier dead.
Release me, and restore me to the ground;
Thou seest all things, thou wilt see my grave:
Thou wilt renew thy beauty morn by morn;
I earth in earth forget these empty courts,
And thee returning on thy silver wheels.

Ulysses

It little profits that an idle king,
By this still hearth, among these barren crags,
Match'd with an aged wife, I mete and dole
Unequal laws unto a savage race,
That hoard, and sleep, and feed, and know not me.
I cannot rest from travel: I will drink
Life to the lees: all times I have enjoy'd
Greatly, have suffer'd greatly, both with those

That loved me, and alone; on shore, and when
Thro' scudding drifts the rainy Hyades
Vext the dim sea: I am become a name;
For always roaming with a hungry heart
Much have I seen and known; cities of men
And manners, climates, councils, governments,
Myself not least, but honour'd of them all;
And drunk delight of battle with my peers,
Far on the ringing plains of windy Troy.
I am a part of all that I have met;
Yet all experience is an arch wherethro'
Gleams that untravell'd world, whose margin fades
For ever and for ever when I move.
How dull it is to pause, to make an end,
To rust unburnish'd, not to shine in use!
As tho' to breathe were life. Life piled on life
Were all too little, and of one to me
Little remains: but every hour is sav'd
From that eternal silence, something more,
A bringer of new things; and vile it were
For some three suns to store and hoard myself,
And this gray spirit yearning in desire
To follow knowledge, like a sinking star,
Beyond the utmost bound of human thought.
  This is my son, mine own Telemachus,
To whom I leave the sceptre and the isle—
Well-lov'd of me, discerning to fulfil
This labour, by slow prudence to make mild
A rugged people, and thro' soft degrees
Subdue them to the useful and the good.
Most blameless is he, centred in the sphere
Of common duties, decent not to fail
In offices of tenderness, and pay
Meet adoration to my household gods,
When I am gone. He works his work, I mine.

There lies the port: the vessel puffs her sail:
There gloom the dark broad seas. My mariners,
Souls that have toil'd, and wrought, and thought with me—
That ever with a frolic welcome took
The thunder and the sunshine, and oppos'd
Free hearts, free foreheads—you and I are old;
Old age hath yet his honour and his toil;
Death closes all: but something ere the end,
Some work of noble note, may yet be done,
Not unbecoming men that strove with Gods.
The lights begin to twinkle from the rocks:
The long day wanes: the slow moon climbs: the deep
Moans round with many voices. Come, my friends,
'Tis not too late to seek a newer world.
Push off, and sitting well in order smite
The sounding furrows; for my purpose holds
To sail beyond the sunset, and the baths
Of all the western stars, until I die.
It may be that the gulfs will wash us down:
It may be we shall touch the Happy Isles,
And see the great Achilles, whom we knew.
Tho' much is taken, much abides; and tho'
We are not now that strength which in old days
Mov'd earth and heaven; that which we are, we are;
One equal temper of heroic hearts,
Made weak by time and fate, but strong in will
To strive, to seek, to find, and not to yield.

Robert Browning

A Toccata of Galuppi's

Oh, Galuppi, Baldassaro, this is very sad to find!
I can hardly misconceive you; it would prove me deaf
and blind;
But although I give you credit, 'tis with such a heavy mind!

Here you come with your old music, and here's all the good
it brings.
What, they lived once thus at Venice, where the merchants
were the kings,
Where St. Mark's is, where the Doges used to wed the sea
with rings?

Ay, because the sea's the street there; and 'tis arched by . . .
what you call
. . . Shylock's bridge with houses on it, where they kept the
carnival!
I was never out of England—it's as if I saw it all!

Did young people take their pleasure when the sea was
warm in May?
Balls and masks begun at midnight, burning ever to mid-
day,
When they made up fresh adventures for the morrow, do
you say?

Was a lady such a lady, cheeks so round and lips so red,—
On her neck the small face buoyant, like a bell-flower on
 its bed,
O'er the breast's superb abundance where a man might base
 his head?

Well (and it was graceful of them) they'd break talk off and
 afford
—She, to bite her mask's black velvet, he to finger on his
 sword,
While you sat and played Toccatas, stately at the
 clavichord?

What? Those lesser thirds so plaintive, sixths diminished
 sigh on sigh,
Told them something? Those suspensions, those solutions—
 'Must we die?'
Those commiserating sevenths—'Life might last! we can
 but try!'

'Were you happy?'—'Yes.'—'And are you still as happy?'
 —'Yes—and you?'
—'Then more kisses'—'Did I stop them, when a million
 seemed so few?'
Hark—the dominant's persistence, till it must be answered
 to!

So an octave struck the answer. Oh, they praised you, I dare
 say!
'Brave Galuppi! that was music! good alike at grave and
 gay!
I can always leave off talking, when I hear a master play.'

Then they left you for their pleasure: till in due time, one
by one,
Some with lives that came to nothing, some with deeds as
well undone,
Death came tacitly and took them where they never see the
sun.

But when I sit down to reason,—think to take my stand nor
swerve
Till I triumph o'er a secret wrung from nature's close reserve,
In you come with your cold music, till I creep thro' every
nerve.

Yes, you, like a ghostly cricket, creaking where a house was
burned—
'Dust and ashes, dead and done with, Venice spent what
Venice earned!
The soul doubtless, is immortal—where a soul can be dis-
cerned.

'Yours for instance, you know physics, something of
geology,
Mathematics are your pastime; souls shall rise in their degree;
Butterflies may dread extinction,—you'll not die, it cannot be!

'As for Venice and its people, merely born to bloom and drop,
Here on earth they bore their fruitage, mirth and folly
were the crop.
What of soul was left, I wonder, when the kissing had to stop?

'Dust and ashes!' So you creak it, and I want the heart to
scold.
Dear dead women with such hair, too—what's become of all
the gold
Used to hang and brush their bosoms? I feel chilly and
grown old.

My Last Duchess

That's my last Duchess painted on the wall,
Looking as if she were alive. I call
That piece a wonder, now: Frà Pandolf's hands
Worked busily a day, and there she stands.
Will't please you sit and look at her? I said
'Frà Pandolf' by design, for never read
Strangers like you that pictured countenance,
The depth and passion of its earnest glance,
But to myself they turned (since none puts by
The curtain I have drawn for you, but I)
And seemed if they would ask me, if they durst,
How such a glance came there; so, not the first
Are you to turn and ask thus. Sir, 'twas not
Her husband's presence only, called that spot
Of joy into the Duchess' cheek: perhaps
Frà Pandolf chanced to say 'Her mantle laps
'Over my lady's wrist too much,' or 'Paint
'Must never hope to reproduce the faint
'Half-flush that dies along her throat:' such stuff
Was courtesy, she thought, and cause enough
For calling up that spot of joy. She had
A heart—how shall I say?—too soon made glad,
Too easily impressed; she liked whate'er
She looked on, and her looks went everywhere.
Sir, 'twas all one! My favour at her breast,
The dropping of the daylight in the West,
The bough of cherries some officious fool
Broke in the orchard for her, the white mule
She rode with round the terrace—all and each
Would draw from her alike the approving speech,
Or blush, at least. She thanked men,—good! but thanked

Somehow—I know not how—as if she ranked
My gift of a nine-hundred-years-old name
With anybody's gift. Who'd stoop to blame
This sort of trifling? Even had you skill
In speech—(which I have not)—to make your will
Quite clear to such a one, and say, 'Just this
'Or that in you disgusts me; here you miss,
'Or there exceed the mark'—and if she let
Herself be lessoned so, nor plainly set
Her wits to yours, forsooth, and made excuse,
—E'en then would be some stooping; and I choose
Never to stoop. Oh sir, she smiled, no doubt,
Whene'er I passed her; but who passed without
Much the same smile? This grew; I gave commands;
Then all smiles stopped together. There she stands
As if alive. Will't please you rise? We'll meet
The company below, then. I repeat,
The Count your master's known munificence
Is ample warrant that no just pretence
Of mine for dowry will be disallowed;
Though his fair daughter's self, as I avowed
At starting, is my object. Nay, we'll go
Together down, sir. Notice Neptune, though,
Taming a sea-horse, thought a rarity,
Which Claus of Innsbruck cast in bronze for me.

Emily Brontë

I am the only being whose doom. . .

I am the only being whose doom
No tongue would ask, no eye would mourn;
I never caused a thought of gloom,
A smile of joy, since I was born.

In secret pleasure, secret tears,
This changeful life has slipped away,
As friendless after eighteen years,
As lone as on my natal day.

There have been times I cannot hide,
There have been times when this was drear,
When my sad soul forgot its pride
And longed for one to love me here.

But those were in the early glow
Of feelings since subdued by care;
And they have died so long ago,
I hardly now believe they were.

First melted off the hope of youth,
Then fancy's rainbow fast withdrew;
And then experience told me truth
In mortal bosoms never grew.

'Twas grief enough to think mankind
All hollow, servile, insincere;
But worse to trust to my own mind
And find the same corruption there.

Walt Whitman

Beginning My Studies

BEGINNING my studies the first step pleas'd me so much,
The mere fact consciousness, these forms, the power of
motion,
The least insect or animal, the senses, eyesight, love,
The first step I say aw'd me and pleas'd me so much,
I have hardly gone and hardly wish'd to go any farther,
But stop and loiter all the time to sing it in ecstatic songs.

After the Sea-ship

AFTER the sea-ship, after the whistling winds,
After the white-grey sails taut to their spars and ropes,
Below, a myriad myriad waves hastening, lifting up their
necks,
Tending in ceaseless flow toward the track of the ship,
Waves of the ocean bubbling and gurgling, blithely prying,
Waves, undulating waves, liquid, uneven, emulous waves,

Toward that whirling current, laughing and buoyant, with
curves,
Where the great vessel sailing and tacking displaced the
surface,
Larger and smaller waves in the spread of the ocean
yearnfully flowing,
The wake of the sea-ship after she passes, flashing and
frolicsome under the sun,
A motley procession with many a fleck of foam and many
fragments,
Following the stately and rapid ship, in the wake following.

Animals

(from *Song of Myself*)

I THINK I could turn and live with animals, they are so
placid and self-contain'd,
I stand and look at them long and long.

They do not sweat and whine about their condition,
They do not lie awake in the dark and weep for their sins,
They do not make me sick discussing their duty to God,
Not one is dissatisfied, not one is demented with the mania
of owning things,
Not one kneels to another, nor to his kind that lived
thousands of years ago,
Not one is respectable or unhappy over the whole earth.

Native Moments

Native moments—when you come upon me—ah you are here now,
Give me now libidinous joys only,
Give me the drench of my passions, give me life coarse and rank,
To-day I go consort with Nature's darlings, to-night too,
I am for those who believe in loose delights, I share the midnight orgies of young men,
I dance with the dancers and drink with the drinkers,
The echoes ring with our indecent calls, I pick out some low person for my dearest friend,
He shall be lawless, rude, illiterate, he shall be one condemned by others for deeds done,
I will play a part no longer, why should I exile myself from my companions?
O you shunn'd persons, I at least do not shun you,
I come forthwith in your midst, I will be your poet,
I will be more to you than to any of the rest.

When I Heard the Learn'd Astronomer

When I heard the learn'd astronomer,
When the proofs, the figures, were ranged in columns before me,
When I was shown the charts and diagrams, to add, divide, and measure them,
When I sitting heard the astronomer where he lectured with much applause in the lecture-room,

How soon unaccountably I became tired and sick,
Till rising and gliding out I wander'd off by myself,
In the mystical moist night-air, and from time to time,
Look'd up in perfect silence at the stars.

A Sight in Camp in the Daybreak Gray and Dim

A sight in camp in the daybreak gray and dim,
As from my tent I emerge so early sleepless,
As slow I walk in the cool fresh air the path near by the hospital tent,
Three forms I see on stretchers lying, brought out there untended lying,
Over each the blanket spread, ample brownish woollen blanket,
Gray and heavy blanket, folding, covering all.

Curious I halt and silent stand,
Then with light fingers I from the face of the nearest the first just lift the blanket;
Who are you elderly man so gaunt and grim, with well-gray'd hair, and flesh all sunken about the eyes?
Who are you my dear comrade?
Then to the second I step—and who are you my child and darling?
Who are you sweet boy with cheeks yet blooming?
Then to the third—a face nor child nor old, very calm, as of beautiful yellow-white ivory;
Young man I think I know you—I think this face is the face of the Christ himself,
Dead and divine and brother of all, and here again he lies.

By the Bivouac's Fitful Flame

By the bivouac's fitful flame,
A procession winding around me, solemn and sweet and
slow—but first I note,
The tents of the sleeping army, the fields' and woods' dim
outline,
The darkness lit by spots of kindled fire, the silence,
Like a phantom far or near an occasional figure moving,
The shrubs and trees, (as I lift my eyes they seem to be
stealthily watching me,)
While wind in procession thoughts, O tender and wondrous
thoughts,
Of life and death, of home and the past and loved, and of
those that are far away;
A solemn and slow procession there as I sit on the ground,
By the bivouac's fitful flame.

Arthur Hugh Clough

There is no God

'There is no God,' the wicked saith,
'And truly it's a blessing,
For what he might have done with us
It's better only guessing.'

'There is no God,' a youngster thinks,
'Or really, if there may be,
He surely didn't mean a man
Always to be a baby.'

'There is no God, or if there is,'
The tradesman thinks, ''twere funny
If He should take it ill in me
To make a little money.'

'Whether there be,' the rich man says,
'It matters very little,
For I and mine, thank somebody,
Are not in want of victual.'

Some others, also, to themselves,
Who scarce so much as doubt it,
Think there is none, when they are well,
And do not think about it.

But the country folks who live beneath
The shadow of the steeple;
The parson and the parson's wife,
And mostly married people;

Youths green and happy in first love,
So thankful for illusion,
And men caught out in what the world
Calls guilt, in first confusion;

And almost everyone when age,
Disease, or sorrows strike him,
Inclines to think there is a God,
Or something very like Him.

Herman Melville

The Maldive Shark

About the shark, phlegmatical one,
Pale sot of the Maldive sea,
The sleek little pilot-fish, azure and slim,
How alert in attendance be.
From his saw-pit of mouth, from his charnel of maw
They have nothing of harm to dread,
But liquidly glide on his ghastly flank
Or before his Gorgonian head;
Or lurk in the port of serrated teeth
In white triple tiers of glittering gates,
And there find a haven when peril's abroad,
An asylum in jaws of the Fates!
They are friends; and friendly they guide him to prey,
Yet never partake of the treat—
Eyes and brains to the dotard lethargic and dull,
Pale ravener of horrible meat.

Matthew Arnold

The Gods are Happy

(from *The Strayed Reveller*)

THE Gods are happy.
They turn on all sides
Their shining eyes:
And see, below them,
The Earth and men.

They see Tiresias
Sitting, staff in hand,
On the warm, grassy
Asopus' bank:
His robe drawn over
His old, sightless head:
Revolving inly
The doom of Thebes.

They see the Centaurs
In the upper glens
Of Pelion, in the streams,
Where red-berried ashes fringe
The clear-brown shallow pools;
With streaming flanks, and heads
Rear'd proudly, snuffing
The mountain wind.

They see the Indian
Drifting, knife in hand,
His frail boat moor'd to
A floating isle thick matted
With large-leav'd, low-creeping melon-plants
And the dark cucumber.
He reaps, and stows them,
Drifting—drifting:—round him,
Round his green harvest-plot,
Flow the cool lake-waves:
The mountains ring them.

They see the Scythian
On the wide Stepp, unharnessing
His wheel'd house at noon.
He tethers his beast down, and makes his meal,
Mares' milk, and bread
Bak'd on the embers:—all around
The boundless waving grass-plains stretch,
thick-starr'd
With saffron and the yellow hollyhock
And flag-leav'd iris flowers.
Sitting in his cart
He makes his meal: before him, for long miles,
Alive with bright green lizards,
And the springing bustard fowl,
The track, a straight black line,
Furrows the rich soil: here and there
Clusters of lonely mounds
Topp'd with rough-hewn,
Grey, rain-blear'd statues, overpeer
The sunny Waste.

They see the Ferry
On the broad, clay-laden
Lone Chorasmian stream: thereon

With snort and strain,
Two horses, strongly swimming, tow
The ferry-boat, with woven ropes
To either bow
Firm-harness'd by the mane:—a Chief,
With shout and shaken spear
Stands at the prow, and guides them:
        but astern,
The cowering Merchants, in long robes,
Sit pale beside their wealth
Of silk-bales and of balsam-drops,
Of gold and ivory,
Of turquoise-earth and amethyst,
Jasper and chalcedony,
And milk-barr'd onyx stones.
The loaded boat swings groaning
In the yellow eddies.
The Gods behold them.

They see the Heroes
Sitting in the dark ship
On the foamless, long-heaving,
Violet sea,
At sunset nearing
The Happy Islands.

The Forsaken Merman

COME, dear children, let us away;
  Down and away below.
Now my brothers call from the bay;
  Now the great winds shorewards blow;
  Now the salt tides seawards flow;

Now the wild white horses play,
Champ and chafe and toss in the spray.
Children dear, let us away.
  This way, this way.

Call her once before you go.
  Call once yet.
In a voice that she will know:
  'Margaret! Margaret!'
Children's voices should be dear
(Call once more) to a mother's ear:
Children's voices, wild with pain.
Surely she will come again.
Call her once and come away,
  This way, this way.
'Mother dear, we cannot stay.'
The wild white horses foam and fret.
  Margaret! Margaret!

Come, dear children, come away down.
  Call no more.
One last look at the white-walled town,
And the little grey church on the windy shore.
  Then come down.
She will not come though you call all day.
  Come away, come away.

Children dear, was it yesterday
We heard the sweet bells over the bay?
In the caverns where we lay,
Through the surf and through the swell,
The far-off sound of a silver bell?
Sand-strewn caverns, cool and deep,
Where the winds are all asleep;

Where the spent lights quiver and gleam;
Where the salt weed sways in the stream;
Where the sea-beasts ranged all round
Feed in the ooze of their pasture-ground;
Where the sea-snakes coil and twine,
Dry their mail and bask in the brine;
Where great whales come sailing by,
Sail and sail, with unshut eye,
Round the world for ever and aye?
When did music come this way?
Children dear, was it yesterday?

Children dear, was it yesterday
(Call yet once) that she went away?
Once she sate with you and me,
On a red gold throne in the heart of the sea,
And the youngest sate on her knee.
She combed its bright hair, and she tended it well,
When down swung the sound of the far-off bell.
She sighed, she looked up through the clear green sea.
She said, 'I must go, for my kinsfolk pray
In the little grey church on the shore to-day.
'Twill be Easter-time in the world—ah me!
And I lose my poor soul, Merman, here with thee.'
I said, 'Go up, dear heart, through the waves;
Say thy prayer, and come back to the kind sea-caves.'
She smiled, she went up through the surf in the bay.
Children dear, was it yesterday?

Children dear, were we long alone?
'The sea grows stormy, the little ones moan.
Long prayers,' I said, 'in the world they say.
Come!' I said, and we rose through the surf in the bay.
We went up the beach, by the sandy down
Where the sea-stocks bloom, to the white-walled town.

Through the narrow paved streets, where all was still,
To the little grey church on the windy hill.
From the church came a murmer of folk at their prayers,
But we stood without in the cold-blowing airs.
We climbed on the graves, on the stones worn with rains,
And we gazed up the aisle through the small-leaded panes.
She sate by the pillar; we saw her clear:
'Margaret, hist! come quick, we are here.
Dear heart,' I said, 'we are long alone.
The sea grows stormy, the little ones moan.'
But ah, she gave me never a look,
For her eyes were sealed to the holy book.
Loud prays the priest; shut stands the door.
Come away, children, call no more!
Come away, come down, call no more!

Down, down, down.
Down to the depths of the sea,
She sits at her wheel in the humming town,
Singing most joyfully.
Hark what she sings: 'O joy, O joy,
For the humming street, and the child with its toy,
For the priest, and the bell, and the holy well.
For the wheel where I spun,
And the blessed light of the sun.'
And so she sings her fill,
Singing most joyfully,
Till the shuttle falls from her hand,
And the whizzing wheel stands still.

She steals to the window, and looks at the sand,
And over the sand at the sea;
And her eyes are set in a stare;
And anon there breaks a sigh,
And anon there drops a tear,
From a sorrow-clouded eye,

And a heart sorrow-laden,
A long, long sigh;
For the cold, strange eyes of a little Mermaiden,
And the gleam of her golden hair.

Come away, away, children!
Come, children, come down!
The hoarse wind blows colder;
Lights shine in the town.
She will start from her slumber
When gusts shake the door;
She will hear the winds howling,
Will hear the waves roar.
We shall see, while above us
The waves roar and whirl,
A ceiling of amber,
A pavement of pearl.
Singing: 'Here came a mortal,
But faithless was she.
And alone dwell for ever
The kings of the sea.'

But, children, at midnight,
When soft the winds blow,
When clear falls the moonlight,
When spring-tides are low;
When sweet airs come seaward
From heaths starred with broom,
And high rocks throw mildly
On the blanched sands a gloom;
Up the still, glistening beaches,
Up the creeks we will hie,
Over banks of bright seaweed
The ebb-tide leaves dry.

We will gaze, from the sand-hills,
At the white, sleeping town;
At the church on the hillside—
  And then come back down.
  Singing: 'There dwells a loved one,
  But cruel is she!
She left lonely for ever
  The kings of the sea.'

Dante Gabriel Rossetti

Lovesight

When do I see thee most, beloved one?
  When in the light the spirits of mine eyes
  Before thy face, their altar, solemnize
The worship of that Love through thee made known?
Or when in the dusk hours, (we two alone,)
  Close-kissed and eloquent of still replies
  Thy twilight-hidden glimmering visage lies,
And my soul only sees thy soul its own?

O love, my love! if I no more should see
Thyself, nor on the earth the shadow of thee,
  Nor image of thine eyes in any spring,—
How then should sound upon Life's darkening slope
The ground-whirl of the perished leaves of Hope,
  The wind of Death's imperishable wing?

On the Site of a Mulberry-Tree; Planted by Wm. Shakespeare; felled by the Rev. F. Gastrell

THIS tree, here fall'n, no common birth or death
Shared with its kind. The world's enfranchised son,
Who found the trees of Life and Knowledge one,
Here set it, frailer than his laurel-wreath.
Shall not the wretch whose hand it fell beneath
Rank also singly—the supreme unhung?
Lo! Sheppard, Turpin, pleading with black tongue
This viler thief's unsuffocated breath!

We'll search thy glossary, Shakespeare! whence almost,
And whence alone, some name shall be reveal'd
For this deaf drudge, to whom no length of ears
Sufficed to catch the music of the spheres;
Whose soul is carrion now,—too mean to yield
Some Starveling's ninth allotment of a ghost.

Emily Dickinson

Success is counted sweetest

SUCCESS is counted sweetest
By those who ne'er succeed.
To comprehend a nectar
Requires sorest need.

Not one of all the purple host
Who took the flag today
Can tell the definition
So clear of victory

As he defeated, dying,
On whose forbidden ear
The distant strains of triumph
Burst agonised and clear.

I know some lonely houses. . .

I know some lonely houses off the road
A robber'd like the look of—
Wooden barred,
And windows hanging low,
Inviting to
A portico,

Where two could creep;
One hand the tools,
The other peep
To make sure all's asleep—
Old fashioned eyes
Not easy to surprise!

How orderly the kitchen'd look by night,
With just a clock,
But they could gag the tick,
And mice won't bark;
And so the walls don't tell,
None will.

A pair of spectacles ajar just stir;
An almanac's aware.
Was it the mat winked,
Or a nervous star?
The moon slides down the stair
To see who's there.

There's plunder, where
Tankard or spoon,
Earring or stone,
A watch, some ancient brooch
To match the grandmama
Staid sleeping there.

Day rattles too;
Stealth's slow.
The sun has got as far
As the third sycamore.
Screams Chanticleer
'Who's there?'

And echoes, trains away,
Sneer 'Where?'
While the old couple, just astir,
Fancy the sunrise left the door ajar.

I like to see it lap the miles

I LIKE to see it lap the miles
And lick the valleys up,
And stop to feed itself at tanks
And then prodigious step

Around a pile of mountains,
And supercilious peer
In shanties by the sides of roads,
And then a quarry pare

To fit its sides
And crawl between
Complaining all the while
In horrid, hooting stanza,
Then chase itself down hill

And neigh like Boanergesf
Then prompter than a star,
Stop, docile and omnipotent,
At its own stable door.

It dropped so low in my regard

It dropped so low in my regard
I heard it hit the ground
And go to pieces on the stones
At bottom of my mind;

Yet blamed the fate that fractured less
Than I reviled myself
For entertaining plated wares
Upon my silver shelf.

A narrow fellow in the grass

A narrow fellow in the grass
Occasionally rides.
You may have met him—did you not?
His notice sudden is.

The grass divides as with a comb,
A spotted shaft is seen,
And then it closes at your feet
And opens further on.

He likes a boggy acre,
A floor too cool for corn;
Yet when a boy and barefoot,
I more than once at noon

Have passed, I thought, a whiplash
Unbraiding in the sun;
When, stooping to secure it,
It wrinkled and was gone.

Several of nature's people
I know, and they know me;
I them feel for a transport
Of cordiality,

But never met this fellow,
Attended or alone,
Without a tighter breathing,
And zero at the bone.

Christina Rossetti

Summer

WINTER is cold-hearted,
  Spring is yea and nay,
Autumn is a weathercock
  Blown every way:
Summer days for me
When every leaf is on its tree;

When Robin's not a beggar,
  And Jenny Wren's a bride,
And larks hang singing, singing, singing,
  Over the wheat-fields wide,
  And anchored lilies ride,
And the pendulum spider
  Swings from side to side,

And blue-black beetles transact business,
  And gnats fly in a host,
And furry caterpillars hasten
  That no time be lost,
And moths grow fat and thrive,
And ladybirds arrive.

Before green apples blush,
  Before green nuts embrown,
Why, one day in the country
  Is worth a month in town;
  Is worth a day and a year
Of the dusty, musty, lag-last fashion
  That days drone elsewhere.

Lewis Carroll

Jabberwocky

'Twas brillig, and the slithy toves
  Did gyre and gimble in the wabe;
All mimsy were the borogoves,
  And the mome raths outgrabe.

'Beware the Jabberwock, my son!
  The jaws that bite, the claws that catch!
Beware the Jubjub bird, and shun
  The frumious Bandersnatch!'

He took his vorpal sword in hand:
  Long time the manxome foe he sought—
So rested he by the Tumtum tree,
  And stood awhile in thought.

And as in uffish thought he stood,
  The Jabberwock, with eyes of flame,
Came whiffling through the tulgey wood,
  And burbled as it came!

One, two! One, two! And through and through
  The vorpal blade went snicker-snack!
He left it dead, and with its head
  He went galumphing back.

'And hast thou slain the Jabberwock?
  Come to my arms, my beamish boy!
O frabjous day! Callooh! Callay!'
  He chortled in his joy.

'Twas brillig, and the slithy toves
  Did gyre and gimble in the wabe;
All mimsy were the borogoves,
  And the mome raths outgrabe.

William Morris

The Burghers' Battle

THICK rise the spear-shafts o'er the land
That erst the harvest bore;
The sword is heavy in the hand,
And we return no more.

The light wind waves the Ruddy Fox,
Our banner of the war,
And ripples in the Running Ox,
And we return no more.

Across our stubble acres now
The teams go four and four;
But out-worn elders guide the plough,
And we return no more.

And now the women heavy-eyed
Turn through the open door
From gazing down the highway wide,
Where we return no more.

The shadows of the fruited close
Dapple the feast-hall floor;
There lie our dogs and dream and doze,
And we return no more.

Down from the minster tower to-day
Fall the soft chimes of yore
Amidst the chattering jackdaws' play:
And we return no more.

But underneath the streets are still;
Noon, and the market's o'er!
Back go the goodwives o'er the hill;
For we return no more.

What merchant to our gates shall come?
What wise man bring us lore?
What abbot ride away to Rome,
Now we return no more?

What mayor shall rule the hall we built?
Whose scarlet sweep the floor?
What judge shall doom the robber's guilt,
Now we return no more?

New houses in the street shall rise
Where builded we before,
Of other stone wrought otherwise;
For we return no more.

And crops shall cover field and hill
Unlike what once they bore,
And all be done without our will,
Now we return no more.

Look up! the arrows streak the sky,
The horns of battle roar;
The long spears lower and draw nigh,
And we return no more.

Remember how beside the wain,
We spoke the word of war,
And sowed this harvest of the plain,
And we return no more.

Lay spears about the Ruddy Fox!
The days of old are o'er;
Heave sword about the Running Ox!
For we return no more.

In Prison

WEARILY, drearily,
Half the day long,
Flap the great banners
High over the stone:

Strangely and eerily
Sounds the wind's song,
Bending the banner-poles.
While, all alone,
Watching the loophole's spark,
Lie I, with life all dark,
Feet tether'd, hands fetter'd
Fast to the stone,
The grim walls, square letter'd
With prison'd men's groan.
Still strain the banner-poles
Through the wind's song,
Westward the banner rolls
Over my wrong.

Thomas Hardy

Great Things

Sweet cyder is a great thing,
    A great thing to me,
Spinning down to Weymouth town
    By Ridgway thirstily,
And maid and mistress summoning
    Who tend the hostelry:
O cyder is a great thing,
    A great thing to me!

The dance it is a great thing,
    A great thing to me,
With candles lit and partners fit
    For night-long revelry;
And going home when day-dawning
    Peeps pale upon the lea:
O dancing is a great thing,
    A great thing to me!

Love is, yea, a great thing,
    A great thing to me,
When, having drawn across the lawn
    In darkness silently,
A figure flits like one a-wing
    Out from the nearest tree:
O love is, yes, a great thing,
    A great thing to me!

Will these be always great things,
    Great things to me? . . .
Let it befall that One will call,
    'Soul, I have need of these':
What then? Joy-jaunts, impassioned flings,
    Love, and its ecstasy,
Will always have been great things,
    Great things to me!

Old Furniture

I KNOW not how it may be with others
    Who sit amid relics of householdry
That date from the days of their mothers' mothers,
    But well I know how it is with me
        Continually.

I see the hands of the generations
That owned each shiny familiar thing
In play on its knobs and indentations,
And with its ancient fashioning
Still dallying:

Hands behind hands, growing paler and paler,
As in a mirror a candle-flame
Shows images of itself, each frailer
As it recedes, though the eye may frame
Its shape the same.

On the clock's dull dial a foggy finger,
Moving to set the minutes right
With tentative touches that lift and linger
In the wont of a moth on a summer night,
Creeps to my sight.

On this old viol, too, fingers are dancing—
As whilom—just over the strings by the nut,
The tip of a bow receding, advancing
In airy quivers, as if it would cut
The plaintive gut.

And I see a face by that box for tinder,
Glowing forth in fits from the dark,
And fading again, as the linten cinder
Kindles to red at the flinty spark,
Or goes out stark.

Well, well. It is best to be up and doing,
The world has no use for one to-day
Who eyes things thus—no aim pursuing!
He should not continue in this stay,
But sink away.

Friends Beyond

WILLIAM Dewy, Tranter Reuben, Farmer Ledlow late at plough,
Robert's kin, and John's, and Ned's,
And the Squire, and Lady Susan, lie in Mellstock churchyard now!
'Gone,' I call them, gone for good, that group of local hearts and heads;
Yet at mothy curfew-tide,
And at midnight when the noon-heat breathes it back from walls and leads,

They've a way of whispering to me—fellow-wight who yet abide—
In the muted, measured note
Of a ripple under archways, or a lone cave's stillicide:

'We have triumphed: this achievement turns the bane to antidote,
Unsuccesses to success,
Many thought-worn eyes and morrows to a morrow free of thought.

'No more need we corn and clothing, feel of old terrestrial stress;
Chill detraction stirs no sigh;
Fear of death has even bygone us: death gave all that we possess.'

W.D.—'Ye mid burn the old bass-viol that I set such value by.'
Squire.—'You may hold the manse in fee,
You may wed my spouse, may let my children's memory of me die.'

Lady S.—'You may have my rich brocades, my laces; take each household key;
Ransack coffer, desk, bureau;
Quiz the few poor treasures hid there, con the letters kept by me.'
Far.—'Ye mid zell my favourite heifer, ye mid let the charlock grow,
Foul the grinterns, give up thrift.'
Far. Wife.—'If ye break my best blue china, children, I shan't care or ho.'

All.—'We've no wish to hear the tidings, how the people's fortunes shift;
What your daily doings are;
Who are wedded, born, divided; if your lives beat slow or swift.

'Curious not the least are we if our intents you make or mar
If you quire to our old tune,
If the City stage still passes, if the weirs still roar afar.'

—Thus, with very gods' composure, freed those crosses late and soon
Which, in life, the Trine allow
(Why, none witteth), and ignoring all that haps beneath the moon,

William Dewy, Tranter Reuben, Farmer Ledlow late at plough,
Robert's kin, and John's, and Ned's,
And the Squire, and Lady Susan, murmur mildly to me now.

Afterwards

WHEN the Present has latched its postern behind my
tremulous stay,
And the May month flaps its glad green leaves like
wings,
Delicate-filmed as new-spun silk, will the neighbours say,
'He was a man who used to notice such things'?

If it be in the dusk when, like an eyelid's soundless blink,
The dewfall-hawk comes crossing the shades to alight
Upon the wind-warped upland thorn, a gazer may think,
'To him this must have been a familiar sight.'

If I pass during some nocturnal blackness, mothy and warm,
When the hedgehog travels furtively over the lawn,
One may say, 'He strove that such innocent creatures
should come to no harm,
But he could do little for them; and now he is gone.'

If, when hearing that I have been stilled at last, they stand
at the door,
Watching the full-starred heavens that winter sees,
Will this thought rise on those who will meet my face no
more,
'He was one who had an eye for such mysteries'?

And will any say when my bell of quittance is heard in the
gloom,
And a crossing breeze cuts a pause in its outrollings,
Till they rise again, as they were a new bell's boom,
'He hears it not now, but used to notice such things'?

Regret Not Me

Regret not me;
Beneath the sunny tree
I lie uncaring, slumbering peacefully.

Swift as the light
I flew my faery flight;
Ecstatically I moved, and feared no night.

I did not know
That heydays fade and go,
But deemed that what was would be always so.

I skipped at morn
Between the yellowing corn,
Thinking it good and glorious to be born.

I ran at eves
Among the piled-up sheaves,
Dreaming, 'I grieve not, therefore nothing grieves.'

Now soon will come
The apple, pear and plum,
And hinds will sing, and autumn insects hum.

Again you will fare
To cider-makings rare,
And junketings; but I shall not be there.

Yet gaily sing
Until the pewter ring
Those songs we sang when we went gipsying.

And lightly dance
Some triple-timed romance
In coupled figures, and forget mischance;

And mourn not me
Beneath the yellowing tree;
For I shall mind not, slumbering peacefully.

Gerard Manley Hopkins

Hurrahing in Harvest

SUMMER ends now; now, barbarous in beauty, the stooks
arise
Around; up above, what wind-walks! what lovely
behaviour
Of silk-sack clouds! has wilder, wilful-wavier
Meal-drift moulded ever and melted across skies?

I walk, I lift up, I lift up heart, eyes,
Down all that glory in the heavens to glean our
Saviour;
And, eyes, heart, what looks, what lips yet—gave you a
Rapturous love's greeting of realer, of rounder replies?

And the azurous hung hills are his world-wielding shoulder
Majestic—as a stallion stalwart, very-violet-sweet!—
These things, these things were here and but the beholder
Wanting; which two when they once meet,
The heart rears wings bold and bolder
And hurls for him, O half hurls earth for him off under
his feet.

The Sea and the Skylark

On ear and ear two noises too old to end
Trench—right, the tide that ramps against the shore;
With a flood or a fall, low lull-off or all roar,
Frequenting there while moon shall wear and wend.

Left hand, off land, I hear the lark ascend,
His rash-fresh re-winded new-skeined score
In crisps of curl off wild winch whirl, and pour
And pelt music, till none's to spill nor spend.

How these two shame this shallow and frail town!
How ring right out our sordid turbid time,
Being pure! We, life's pride and cared-for crown,

Have lost that cheer and charm of earth's past prime:
Our make and making break, are breaking, down
To man's last dust, drain fast towards man's first slime.

Felix Randal

Felix Randal, the farrier, O he is dead then? my duty all
        ended,
Who have watched his mould of man, big-boned and
        hardy-handsome
Pining, pining, till time when reason rambled in it and some
Fatal four disorders, fleshed there, all contended?

Sickness broke him. Impatient he cursed at first, but mended
Being anointed and all; though a heavenlier heart began
        some
Months earlier, since I had our sweet reprieve and ransom
Tendered to him. Ah well, God rest him all road ever he
        offended!

This seeing the sick endears them to us, us too it endears.
My tongue had taught thee comfort, touch had quenched
        thy tears,
Thy tears that touched my heart, child, Felix, poor Felix
        Randal;

How far from then forethought of, all thy more boisterous
        years,
When thou at the random grim forge, powerful amidst
        peers,
Didst fettle for the great grey drayhorse his bright and
        battering sandal!

Thou Art Indeed Just, Lord

THOU art indeed just, Lord, if I contend
With thee; but, sir, so what I plead is just.
Why do sinners' ways prosper? and why must
Disappointment all I endeavour end?
  Wert thou my enemy, O thou my friend,
How wouldst thou worse, I wonder, than thou dost
Defeat, thwart me? Oh, the sots and thralls of lust
Do in spare hours more thrive than I that spend,
Sir, life upon thy cause. See, banks and brakes
Now, leavèd how thick! lacèd they are again
With fretty chervil, look, and fresh wind shakes
Them; birds build—but not I build; no, but strain,
Time's eunuch, and not breed one work that wakes.
Mine, O thou lord of life, send my roots rain.

In honour of
ST. ALPHONSUS RODRIGUEZ
Laybrother of the Society of Jesus

Honour is flashed off exploit, so we say;
And those strokes once that gashed flesh or galled shield
Should tongue that time now, trumpet now that field,
And, on the fighter, forge his glorious day.

On Christ they do and on the martyr may;
But be the war within, the brand we wield
Unseen, the heroic breast not outward-steeled,
Earth hears no hurtle then from fiercest fray.

Yet God (that hews mountain and continent,
Earth, all, out; who, with trickling increment,
Veins violets and tall trees makes more and more)
Could crowd career with conquest while there went
Those years and years by of world without event
That in Majorca Alfonso watched the door.

Spring and Fall
To a young child

MARGARET, are you grieving
Over Goldengrove unleaving?
Leaves, like the things of man, you
With your fresh thoughts care for, can you?
Ah! as the heart grows older
It will come to such sights colder
By and by, nor spare a sigh
Though worlds of wanwood leafmeal lie;
And yet you will weep and know why.
Now no matter, child, the name:
Sorrow's springs are the same.
Nor mouth had, no nor mind, expressed
What heart heard of, ghost guessed:
It is the blight man was born for,
It is Margaret you mourn for.

Alfred Edward Housman

In Valleys Green and Still

In valleys green and still
  Where lovers wander maying
They hear from over hill
  A music playing.

Behind the drum and fife,
  Past hawthorn wood and hollow,
Through earth and out of life
  The soldiers follow.

The soldier's is the trade:
  In any wind or weather
He steals the heart of maid
  And man together.

The lover and his lass
  Beneath the hawthorn lying
Have heard the soldiers pass,
  And both are sighing.

And down the distance they
  With dying note and swelling
Walk the resounding way
  To the still dwelling.

On Wenlock Edge

ON Wenlock Edge the wood's in trouble;
His forest fleece the Wrekin heaves;
The gale, it plies the saplings double,
And thick on Severn snow the leaves.

'Twould blow like this through holt and hanger
When Uricon the city stood:
'Tis the old wind in the old anger,
But then it threshed another wood.

Then, 'twas before my time, the Roman
At yonder heaving hill would stare:
The blood that warms an English yeoman,
The thoughts that hurt him, they were there.

There, like the wind through woods in riot,
Through him the gale of life blew high;
The tree of man was never quiet:
Then 'twas the Roman, now 'tis I.

The gale, it plies the saplings double,
It blows so hard, 'twill soon be gone.
To-day the Roman and his trouble
Are ashes under Uricon.

The chestnut casts his flambeaux, and the flowers

The chestnut casts his flambeaux, and the flowers
Stream from the hawthorn on the wind away,
The doors clap to, the pane is blind with showers.
Pass me the can, lad; there's an end of May.

There's one spoilt spring to scant our mortal lot,
One season ruined of our little store.
May will be fine next year as like as not:
Oh ay, but then we shall be twenty-four.

We for a certainty are not the first
Have sat in taverns while the tempest hurled
Their hopeful plans to emptiness, and cursed
Whatever brute and blackguard made the world.

It is in truth iniquity on high
To cheat our sentenced souls of aught they crave,
And mar the merriment as you and I
Fare on our long fool's-errand to the grave.

Iniquity it is; but pass the can.
My lad, no pair of kings our mothers bore;
Our only portion is the estate of man:
We want the moon, but we shall get no more.

If here to-day the cloud of thunder lours
To-morrow it will hie on far behests;
The flesh will grieve on other bones than ours
Soon, and the soul will mourn in other breasts.

The troubles of our proud and angry dust
Are from eternity, and shall not fail.
Bear them we can, and if we can we must.
Shoulder the sky, my lad, and drink your ale.

Others, I am not the first

Others, I am not the first,
Have willed more mischief than they durst:
If in the breathless night I too
Shiver now, 'tis nothing new.

More than I, if truth were told,
Have stood and sweated hot and cold,
And through their reins in ice and fire
Fear contended with desire.

Agued once like me were they,
But I like them shall win my way
Lastly to the bed of mould
Where there's neither heat nor cold.

But from my grave across my brow
Plays no wind of healing now,
And fire and ice within me fight
Beneath the suffocating night.

The laws of God, the laws of man

THE laws of God, the laws of man,
He may keep that will and can;
Not I: let God and man decree
Laws for themselves and not for me;
And if my ways are not as theirs
Let them mind their own affairs.
Their deeds I judge and much condemn,
Yet when did I make laws for them?
Please yourselves, say I, and they
Need only look the other way.
But no, they will not; they must still
Wrest their neighbour to their will,
And made me dance as they desire
With jail and gallows and hell-fire,
And how am I to face the odds
Of man's bedevilment and God's?
I, a stranger and afraid
In a world I never made.
They will be master, right or wrong;
Though both are foolish, both are strong.
And since, my soul, we cannot fly
To Saturn nor to Mercury,
Keep we must, if keep we can,
These foreign laws of God and man.

William Butler Yeats

The Hour Before Dawn

A ONE-LEGGED, one-armed, one-eyed man,
A bundle of rags upon a crutch,
Stumbled on windy Cruachan
Cursing the wind. It was as much
As the one sturdy leg could do
To keep him upright while he cursed.
He had counted, where long years ago
Queen Maeve's nine Maines had been nursed,
A pair of lapwings, one old sheep
And not a house to the plain's edge,
When close to his right hand a heap
Of grey stones and a rocky ledge
Reminded him that he could make,
If he but shifted a few stones,
A shelter till the daylight broke.
But while he fumbled with the stones
They toppled over; 'Were it not
I have a lucky wooden shin
I had been hurt'; and toppling brought
Before his eyes, where stones had been,
A dark deep hole in the rock's face.
He gave a gasp and thought to run,
Being certain it was no right place
But the Hell Mouth at Cruachan
That's stuffed with all that's old and bad,
And yet stood still, because inside

He had seen a red-haired jolly lad
In some outlandish coat beside
A ladle and a tub of beer,
Plainly no phantom by his look.
So with a laugh at his own fear
He crawled into that pleasant nook.
Young Red-head stretched himself to yawn
And murmured, 'May God curse the night
That's grown uneasy near the dawn
So that it seems even I sleep light;
And who are you that wakens me?
Has one of Maeve's nine brawling sons
Grown tired of his own company?
But let him keep his grave for once
I have to find the sleep I have lost.'
And then at last being wide awake,
'I took you for a brawling ghost,
Say what you please, but from daybreak
I'll sleep another century.'
The beggar deaf to all but hope
Went down upon a hand and knee
And took the wooden ladle up
And would have dipped it in the beer
But the other pushed his hand aside,
'Before you have dipped it in the beer
That sacred Goban brewed,' he cried,
'I'd have assurance that you are able
To value beer—I will have no fool
Dipping his nose into my ladle
Because he has stumbled on this hole
In the bad hour before the dawn.
If you but drink that beer and say
I will sleep until the winter's gone,
Or maybe, to Midsummer Day
You will sleep that length; and at the first

I waited so for that or this—
Because the weather was a-cursed
Or I had no woman there to kiss,
And slept for half a year or so;
But year by year I found that less
Gave me such pleasure I'd forgo
Even a half hour's nothingness,
And when at one year's end I found
I had not waked a single minute,
I chose this burrow under ground.
I will sleep away all Time within it:
My sleep were now nine centuries
But for those mornings when I find
The lapwing at their foolish cries
And the sheep bleating at the wind
As when I also played the fool.'
The beggar in a rage began
Upon his hunkers in the hole,
'It's plain that you are no right man
To mock at everything I love
As if it were not worth the doing.
I'd have a merry life enough
If a good Easter wind were blowing,
And though the winter wind is bad
I should not be too down in the mouth
For anything you did or said
If but this wind were in the south.'
But the other cried, 'You long for spring
Or that the wind would shift a point
And do not know that you would bring,
If time were suppler in the joint,
Neither the spring nor the south wind
But the hour when you shall pass away
And leave no smoking wick behind,
For all life longs for the Last Day

And there's no man but cocks his ear
To know when Michael's trumpet cries
That flesh and bone may disappear,
And souls as if they were but sighs,
And there be nothing but God left;
But I alone being blessed keep
Like some old rabbit to my cleft
And wait Him in a drunken sleep.'

He dipped his ladle in the tub
And drank and yawned and stretched him out.
The other shouted, 'You would rob
My life of every pleasant thought
And every comfortable thing
And so take that and that.' Thereon
He gave him a great pummelling,
But might have pummelled at a stone
For all the sleeper knew or cared;
And after heaped the stones again
And cursed and prayed, and prayed and cursed:
'Oh God if he got loose!' And then
In fury and in panic fled
From the Hell Mouth at Cruachan
And gave God thanks that overhead
The clouds were brightening with the dawn.

An Irish Airman Foresees his Death

I KNOW that I shall meet my fate
Somewhere among the clouds above;
Those that I fight I do not hate,
Those that I guard I do not love;

My country is Kiltartan Cross,
My countrymen Kiltartan's poor,
No likely end could bring them loss
Or leave them happier than before.
Nor law, nor duty bade me fight,
Nor public men, nor cheering crowds,
A lonely impulse of delight
Drove to this tumult in the clouds;
I balanced all, brought all to mind,
The years to come seemed waste of breath,
A waste of breath the years behind
In balance with this life, this death.

The Three Monuments

THEY hold their public meetings where
Our most renowned patriots stand,
One among the birds of the air,
A stumpier on either hand;
And all the popular statesmen say
That purity built up the state
And after kept it from decay;
Admonish us to cling to that
And let all base ambition be,
For intellect would make us proud
And pride bring in impurity:
The three old rascals laugh aloud.

William Henry Davies

In the Country

THIS life is sweetest; in this wood
I hear no children cry for food;
I see no woman, white with care;
No man, with muscles wasting here.

No doubt it is a selfish thing
To fly from human suffering;
No doubt he is a selfish man,
Who shuns poor creatures sad and wan.

But 'tis a wretched life to face
Hunger in almost every place;
Cursed with a hand that's empty, when
The heart is full to help all men.

Can I admire the statue great,
When living men starve at its feet?
Can I admire the park's green tree,
A roof for homeless misery?

When I can see few men in need,
I then have power to help by deed,
Nor lose my cheerfulness in pity—
Which I must do in every city.

For when I am in those great places,
I see ten thousand suffering faces;
Before me stares a wolfish eye,
Behind me creeps a groan or sigh.

The Heap of Rags

ONE night when I went down
Thames' side, in London Town,
A heap of rags saw I,
And sat me down close by.
That thing could shout and bawl,
But showed no face at all;
When any steamer passed
And blew a loud shrill blast,
That heap of rags would sit
And make a sound like it;
When struck the clock's deep bell,
It made those peals as well.
When winds did moan around,
It mocked them with that sound;
When all was quiet, it
Fell into a strange fit;
Would sigh, and moan and roar,
It laughed, and blessed, and swore.
Yet that poor thing, I know,
Had neither friend nor foe;
Its blessing or its curse
Made no one better or worse.
I left it in that place—

The thing that showed no face.
Was it a man that had
Suffered till he went mad?
So many showers and not
One rainbow in the lot;
Too many bitter fears
To make a pearl from tears?

The Villain

WHILE joy gave clouds the light of stars,
  That beamed where'er they looked;
And calves and lambs had tottering knees,
  Excited, while they sucked;
While every bird enjoyed his song,
  Without one thought of harm or wrong—
I turned my head and saw the wind,
  Not far from where I stood,
Dragging the corn by her golden hair,
  Into a dark and lonely wood.

Walter De La Mare

Farewell

WHEN I lie where shades of darkness
Shall no more assail mine eyes,
Nor the rain make lamentation
    When the wind sighs;
How will fare the world whose wonder
Was the very proof of me?
Memory fades, must the remembered
    Perishing be?

Oh, when this my dust surrenders
Hand, foot, lip, to dust again,
May these loved and loving faces
    Please other men!
May the rusting harvest hedgerow
Still the Traveller's Joy entwine,
And as happy children gather
    Posies once mine.

Look thy last on all things lovely,
Every hour. Let no night
Seal thy sense in deathly slumber
    Till to delight
Thou have paid thy utmost blessing;
Since that all things thou wouldst praise
Beauty took from those who loved them
    In other days.

By Order!

SLANT sunshine and these naked fields once more;
Evening: the wayfarer now nearing home.
Once it was 'Surely, I've been here before!'
Now, 'Why has all so strange to me become?'

Through crowds I wander, isolate and alone,
As if they were mere phantasmata of my mind;
As do the autumnal birds—a *whirr*; they are gone;

A listening solitude—dark fields, a gate;
Dusk, and a baffling signboard—'By Order, Fate.'

Dry August Burned

DRY August burned. A harvest hare
Limp on the kitchen table lay,
Its fur blood-blubbered, eyes astare,
While a small child that stood near by
Wept out her heart to see it there.
Sharp came the *clop* of hoofs, the clang
Of dangling chain, voices that rang.
Out like a leveret she ran,
To feast her glistening bird-clear eyes
On a team of field artillery,
Gay, to manoeuvres, thudding by.
Spur and gun and limber plate
Flashed in the sun. Alert, elate,
Noble horses, foam at lip,
Harness, stirrup, holster, whip,
She watched the sun-tanned soldiery,

Till dust-white hedge had hidden away—
Its din into a rumour thinned—
The laughing, jolting, wild array:
And then—the wonder and tumult gone—
Stood nibbling a green leaf, alone,
Her dark eyes, dreaming. . . . She turned, and ran,
Elf-like, in to the house again.
The hare had vanished. . . . 'Mother,' she said,
Her tear-stained cheek now flushed with red,
'Please, may I go and see it skinned?'

Drugged

INERT in his chair,
In a candle's guttering glow;
His bottle empty,
His fire sunk low;
With drug-sealed lids shut fast,
Unsated mouth ajar,
This darkened phantasm walks
Where nightmares are:
In a frenzy of life and light,
Crisscross—a menacing throng—
They gibe, they squeal at the stranger,
Jostling along,
Their faces cadaverous grey:
While on high from an attic stare
Horrors, in beauty apparelled,
Down the dark air.

A stream gurgles over its stones,
The chambers within are afire.
Stumble his shadowy feet
Through shine, through mire;
And the flames leap higher.
In vain yelps the wainscot mouse;
In vain beats the hour;
Vacant his body must drowse
Until daybreak flower—
Staining these walls with its rose,
And the draughts of the morning shall stir
Cold on cold brow, cold hands.
And the wanderer
Back to flesh house must return.
Lone soul—in horror to see,
Than dream more meagre and awful,
Reality.

Robert Frost

The Rabbit Hunter

CARELESS and still
The hunter lurks
With gun depressed,
Facing alone
The alder swamps
Ghastly snow-white.
And his hound works

In the offing there
Like one possessed,
And yelps delight
And sings and romps,
Bringing him on
The shadowy hare
For him to rend
And deal a death
That he nor it
(Nor I) have wit
To comprehend.

The Road Not Taken

Two roads diverged in a yellow wood,
And sorry I could not travel both
And be one traveler, long I stood
And looked down one as far as I could
To where it bent in the undergrowth;

Then took the other, as just as fair,
And having perhaps the better claim,
Because it was grassy and wanted wear;
Though as for that the passing there
Had worn them really about the same,

And both that morning equally lay
In leaves no step had trodden black.
Oh, I kept the first for another day!
Yet knowing how way leads on to way,
I doubted if I should ever come back.

I shall be telling this with a sigh
Somewhere ages and ages hence:
Two roads diverged in a wood, and I—
I took the one less traveled by,
And that has made all the difference.

Not to Keep

THEY sent him back to her. The letter came
Saying . . . And she could have him. And before
She could be sure there was no hidden ill
Under the formal writing, he was there,
Living. They gave him back to her alive—
How else? They are not known to send the dead—
And not disfigured visibly. His face?
His hands? She had to look, to look and ask,
'What is it, dear?' And she had given all
And still she had all—*they* had—they the lucky!
Wasn't she glad now? Everything seemed won,
And all the rest for them permissible ease.
She had to ask, 'What was it, dear?'
'Enough,
Yet not enough. A bullet through and through,
High in the breast. Nothing but what good care
And medicine and rest, and you a week,
Can cure me of to go again.' The same
Grim giving to do over for them both.
She dared no more than ask him with her eyes
How was it with him for a second trial.
And with his eyes he asked her not to ask.
They had given him back to her, but not to keep.

An Importer

Mrs. Someone's been to Asia.
What she brought back would amaze ye.
Bamboos, ivories, jades, and lacquers,
Devil-scaring firecrackers,
Recipes for tea with butter,
Sacred rigmaroles to mutter,
Subterfuge for saving faces,
A developed taste in vases,
Arguments too stale to mention
'Gainst American invention;
Most of all the mass production
Destined to prove our destruction.
What are telephones, skyscrapers,
Safety razors, Sunday papers,
But the silliest evasion
Of the truths we owe an Asian?
But the best of her exhibit
Was a prayer machine from Tibet
That by brook power in the garden
Kept repeating Pardon, pardon;
And as picturesque machinery
Beat a sundial in the scenery—
The most primitive of engines
Mass producing with a vengeance.
Teach those Asians mass production?
Teach your grandmother egg suction.

Desert Places

SNOW falling and night falling fast, oh, fast
In a field I looked into going past,
And the ground almost covered smooth in snow,
But a few weeds and stubble showing last.

The woods around it have it—it is theirs.
All animals are smothered in their lairs.
I am too absent-spirited to count;
The loneliness includes me unawares.

And lonely as it is that loneliness
Will be more lonely ere it will be less—
A blanker whiteness of benighted snow
With no expression, nothing to express.

They cannot scare me with their empty spaces
Between stars—on stars where no human race is.
I have it in me so much nearer home
To scare myself with my own desert places.

John Masefield

The Blowing of the Horn

(from *The Song of Roland*)

ROLAND gripped his horn with might and main,
Put it to his mouth and blew a great strain.
The hills were high and the sound was very plain,
Thirty leagues thence they heard the strain,
Charles heard it, and all his train.
'Our men are fighting,' said Charlemain.
And the Count Guenes answered him again,
'If another said that, we should think him insane.'
Ahoy.

Roland was broken by pain and outworn,
In great anguish he blew his horn;
Out of his mouth the bright blood did fall,
The temples of his brain were now all torn:
He blew a great noise as he held the horn.
Charles heard it in the pass forlorn,
Naimes heard it, the Franks listened all.
Then the King said, 'I hear Roland's horn;
He would never blow it if he were not overborne.'
Guenes answered, 'You are old and outworn,
Such words are worthy of a child new-born,
There is no battle at all, neither won nor lorn.
Ahoy.

'Moreover, you know of Roland's great pride,
It is a marvel that God lets him bide.
Without your command and knowing you would chide,
He took Noples, and killed the men inside,
With his sword Durendal he smote them hip and side,
Then with water washed the fields where the blood had
dried,
So that his killings might never be spied.
All day long he will horn a hare and ride,
Gabbing before his peers, showing his pride,
No man would dare attack him in all the world wide.
Press on your horse now. Why do you abide?
France is still far from us over the divide.'

Ahoy.

Count Roland's mouth bled from a vein,
Broken were the temples that held his brain,
He blew his horn with grief and in pain,
The Franks heard it and Charlemain.
The King said, 'That horn blows a long strain.'
Duke Naimes answered, 'Roland is in pain.
There is a battle, by my hope of gain,
He here has betrayed him who did so feign;
Put on your war-gear, cry your war-cry again,
Go and succour your noble train,
You hear clearly how Roland does complain.'

Ahoy.

The Emperor made his trumpets blow clear,
The Franks dismounted to put on their gear.
Hawberks and helmets and swords with gold gear,
Men had shields and many a strong spear,
And banners scarlet, white and blue in the air to rear.
On his war-horse mounted each peer,

And spurred right through the pass among the rocks sheer:
Each man said to his comrade dear,
'If we reach Roland ere he be dead on bier,
We will strike good blows with him and make pagans fear.
But they had stayed too long, and they were nowhere near.
Ahoy.

Edward Thomas

The Owl

DOWNHILL I came, hungry, and yet not starved;
Cold, yet had heat within me that was proof
Against the North wind; tired, yet so that rest
Had seemed the sweetest thing under a roof.

Then at the inn I had food, fire, and rest,
Knowing how hungry, cold, and tired was I.
All of the night was quite barred out except
An owl's cry, a most melancholy cry

Shaken out long and clear upon the hill,
No merry note, nor cause of merriment,
But one telling me plain what I escaped
And others could not, that night, as in I went.

And salted was my food, and my repose,
Salted and sobered, too, by the bird's voice
Speaking for all who lay under the stars,
Soldiers and poor, unable to rejoice.

The New House

Now first, as I shut the door,
  I was alone
In the new house; and the wind
  Began to moan.

Old at once was the house,
  And I was old;
My ears were teased with the dread
  Of what was foretold,

Nights of storm, days of mist, without end;
  Sad days when the sun
Shone in vain: old griefs and griefs
  Not yet begun.

All was foretold me; naught
  Could I foresee;
But I learned how the wind would sound
  After these things should be.

Cock-Crow

Out of the wood of thoughts that grow by night
To be cut down by the sharp axe of light,—
Out of the night, two cocks together crow,
  Cleaving the darkness with a silver blow.
  And bright before my eyes twin trumpeters stand,

Heralds of splendour, one at either hand,
Each facing each as in a coat of arms:
The milkers lace their boots up at the farms.

Nicholas Vachel Lindsay

The Daniel Jazz

DARIUS the Mede was a king and a wonder.
His eye was proud, and his voice was thunder.
He kept bad lions in a monstrous den.
He fed up the lions on Christian men.

Daniel was the chief hired man of the land.
He stirred up the jazz in the palace band.
He whitewashed the cellar. He shovelled in the coal.
And Daniel kept a-praying: 'Lord, save my soul.'
Daniel kept a-praying: 'Lord save my soul.'
Daniel kept a-praying: 'Lord, save my soul.'

Daniel was the butler, swagger and swell.
He ran upstairs. He answered the bell.
And *he* would let in whoever came a-calling:
Saints so holy, scamps so appalling.
'Old man Ahab leaves his card.
Elisha and the bears are a-waiting in the yard.
Here comes Pharaoh and his snakes a-calling.
Here comes Cain and his wife a-calling.
Shadrach, Meshach and Abednego for tea.

Here comes Jonah and the whale,
And the *Sea*!
Here comes St. Peter and his fishing-pole.
Here comes Judas and his silver a-calling.
Here comes old Beelzebub a-calling.'
And Daniel kept a-praying: 'Lord, save my soul.'
Daniel kept a-praying: 'Lord, save my soul.'
Daniel kept a-praying: 'Lord, save my soul.'

His sweetheart and his mother were Christian and meek.
They washed and ironed for Darius every week.
One Thursday he met them at the door:
Paid them as usual, but acted sore.
He said: 'Your Daniel is a dead little pigeon.
He's a good hard worker, but he talks religion.'
And he showed them Daniel in the lion's cage.
Daniel standing quietly, the lions in a rage.

His good old mother cried:—
'Lord, save him.'
And Daniel's tender sweetheart cried:—
'Lord, save him.'

And she was a golden lily in the dew.
And she was as sweet as an apple on the tree.
And she was as fine as a melon in the corn-field.
Gliding and lovely as a ship on the sea,
Gliding and lovely as a ship on the sea.
And she prayed to the Lord:—
'*Send* Gabriel. *Send* Gabriel.'

King Darius said to the lions:—
'Bite Daniel. Bite Daniel.

Bite him. Bite him. Bite him!'
Thus roared the lions:—
'We want Daniel, Daniel, Daniel,
We want Daniel, Daniel, Daniel.
Grrrrrrrrrrrrrrrrrrrrrrrr.
Grrrrrrrrrrrrrrrrrrrrrrrr.'
And Daniel did not frown,
Daniel did not cry.
He kept on looking at the sky.
And the Lord said to Gabriel:—
'Go chain the lions down,
Go chain the lions down.
Go chain the lions down.
Go chain the lions down.'
And *Gabriel* chained the lions,
And *Gabriel* chained the lions,
And *Gabriel* chained the lions,
And Daniel got out of the den,
And Daniel got out of the den,
And Daniel got out of the den.
And Darius said: 'You're a Christian child,'
Darius said: 'You're a Christian child,'
Darius said: 'You're a Christian child,'
And gave him his job again,
And gave him his job again,
And gave him his job again.

Wallace Stevens

Disillusionment of Ten O'Clock

THE houses are haunted
By white night-gowns.
None are green,
Or purple with green rings,
Or green with yellow rings,
Or yellow with blue rings.
None of them are strange,
With socks of lace
And beaded ceintures.
People are not going
To dream of baboons and periwinkles.
Only, here and there, an old sailor,
Drunk and asleep in his boots,
Catches tigers
In red weather.

Thomas Ernest Hulme

Autumn

A TOUCH of cold in the Autumn night—
I walked abroad,
And saw the ruddy moon lean over a hedge,
Like a red-faced farmer.
I did not stop to speak, but nodded,
And round about were the wistful stars
With white faces like town children.

Above the Dock

ABOVE the quiet dock in midnight,
Tangled in the tall mast's corded height,
Hangs the moon. What seemed so far away
Is but a child's balloon, forgotten after play.

Ezra Pound

Salutation

O GENERATION of the thoroughly smug and thoroughly
uncomfortable,
I have seen fishermen picnicking in the sun,
I have seen them with untidy families,
I have seen their smiles full of teeth and heard ungainly
laughter.
And I am happier than you are,
And they were happier than I am;
And the fish swim in the lake and do not even own clothing.

David Herbert Lawrence

Spray

IT is a wonder foam is so beautiful.
A wave bursts in anger on a rock, broken up
in wild white sibilant spray
and fall back, drawing in its breath with rage,
with frustration how beautiful!

Talk

I WISH people, when you sit near them,
wouldn't think it necessary to make conversation
and send thin draughts of words
blowing down your neck and your ears
and giving you a cold in your inside.

Poverty

THE only people I ever heard talk about My Lady Poverty
were rich people, or people who imagined themselves
rich.
Saint Francis himself was a rich and spoiled young man.
Being born among the working people
I know that poverty is a hard old hag,
and a monster, when you're pinched for actual necessities.
And whoever says she isn't is a liar.

I don't want to be poor, it means I am pinched.
But neither do I want to be rich.
When I look at this pine-tree near the sea,
that grows out of rock, and plumes forth, plumes forth,
I see it has a natural abundance.

With its roots it has a grand grip on its daily bread,
and its plumes look like green cups held up to the sun and air
and full of wine.

I want to be like that, to have a natural abundance
and plume forth, and be splendid.

Bat

At evening, sitting on this terrace,
When the sun from the west, beyond Pisa, beyond the mountains of Carrara
Departs, and the world is taken by surprise . . .

When the tired flower of Florence is in gloom beneath the glowing
Brown hills surrounding . . .

When under the arches of the Ponte Vecchio
A green light enters against stream, flush from the west,
Against the current of obscure Arno . . .

Look up, and you see things flying
Between the day and the night;
Swallows with spools of dark thread sewing the shadows together.

A circle swoop, and a quick parabola under the bridge arches
Where light pushes through;
A sudden turning upon itself of a thing in the air.
A dip to the water.

And you think:
'The swallows are flying so late!'

Swallows?

Dark air-life looping
Yet missing the pure loop . . .
A twitch, a twitter, an elastic shudder in flight

And serrated wings against the sky,
Like a glove, a black glove thrown up at the light,
And falling back.

Never swallows!
Bats!
The swallows are gone.

At a wavering instant the swallows give way to bats
By the Ponte Vecchio . . .
Changing guard.

Bats, and an uneasy creeping in one's scalp
As the bats swoop overhead!
Flying madly.

Pipistrello!
Blackon piper an infinitesimal pipe.
Little lumps that fly in air and have voices indefinite, wildly
 vindictive;

Wings like bits of umbrella.

Bats!

Creatures that hang themselves up like an old rag, to sleep
And disgustingly upside down.
Hanging upside down like rows of disgusting old rags
And grinning in their sleep.
Bats!

In China the bat is symbol of happiness.

Not for me!

Piano

Softly, in the dusk, a woman is singing to me;
Taking me back down the vista of years, till I see
A child sitting under the piano, in the boom of the tingling strings
And pressing the small, poised feet of a mother who smiles as she sings.

In spite of myself the insidious mastery of song
Betrays me back, till the heart of me weeps to belong
To the old Sunday evenings at home, with winter outside
And hymns in the cosy parlour, the tinkling piano our guide.
So now it is vain for the singer to burst into clamour
With the great black piano appassionato. The glamour
Of childish days is upon me, my manhood is cast
Down in the flood of remembrance, I weep like a child for the past.

Andrew Young

Last Snow

Although the snow still lingers,
Heaped on the ivy's blunt webbed fingers
And painting tree-trunks on one side,
Here in this sunlit ride

The fresh unchristened things appear,
Leaf, spathe and stem,
With crumbs of earth clinging to them
To show the way they came
But no flower yet to tell their name,
And one green spear,
Stabbing a dead leaf from below
Kills winter at a blow.

Siegfried Sassoon

The Dug-Out

Why do you lie with your legs ungainly huddled,
And one arm bent across your sullen, cold,
Exhausted face? It hurts my heart to watch you,
Deep-shadow'd from the candle's guttering gold;
And you wonder why I shake you by the shoulder;
Drowsy, you mumble and sigh and turn your head . . .
You are too young to fall asleep for ever;
And when you sleep you remind me of the dead.

To Any Dead Officer

Well, how are things in heaven? I wish you'd say,
  Because I'd like to know that you're all right.
Tell me, have you found everlasting day,
  Or been sucked in by everlasting night?
For when I shut my eyes your face shows plain;
  I hear you make some cheery old remark—
I can rebuild you in my brain,
  Though you've gone out patrolling in the dark.

You hated tours of trenches; you were proud
  Of nothing more than having good years to spend;
Longed to get home and join the careless crowd
  Of chaps who work in peace with Time for friend.
That's all washed out now. You're beyond the wire:
  No earthly chance can send you crawling back;
You've finished with machine-gun fire—
  Knocked over in a hopeless dud-attack.

Somehow I always thought you'd get done in,
  Because you were so desperate keen to live:
You were all out to save your skin,
  Well knowing how much the world had to give.
You joked at shells and talked the usual 'shop,'
  Stuck to your dirty job and did it fine:
With 'Jesus Christ! when will it stop?
  Three years . . . It's hell unless we break their line.'

So when they told me you'd been left for dead
  I wouldn't believe them, feeling it *must* be true.
Next weak the bloody Roll of Honour said
  'Wounded and missing'—(That's the thing to do

When lads are left in shell-holes,
  With nothing but blank sky and wounds that ache,
Moaning for water till they know
  It's night, and then it's not worth while to wake!)

. . . .

Good-bye, old lad! Remember me to God,
  And tell Him that our Politicians swear
They won't give in till Prussian Rule's been trod
  Under the Heel of England. . . Are you there, . . .
Yes . . . And the War won't end for at least two years;
But we've got stacks of men . . . I'm blind with tears,
  Staring into the dark. Cheerio!
I wish they'd killed you in a decent show.

Edwin Muir

The Return

THE doors flapped open in Ulysses' house,
The lolling latches gave to every hand,
Let traitor, babbler, tout and bargainer in.
The rooms and passages resounded
With ease and chaos of a public market,
The walls mere walls to lean on as you talked,
Spat on the floor, surveyed some newcomer
With an absent eye. There you could be yourself.
Dust in the nooks, weeds nodding in the yard,

The thick walls crumbling. Even the cattle came
About the doors with mild familiar stare
As if this were their place.
All round the island stretched the clean blue sea.

Sole at the house's heart Penelope
Sat at her chosen task, endless undoing
Of endless doing, endless weaving, unweaving,
In the clean chamber. Still her loom ran empty
Day after day. She thought: 'Here I do nothing
Or less than nothing, making an emptiness
Amid disorder, weaving, unweaving the lie
The day demands. Ulysses, this is duty,
To do and undo, to keep a vacant gate
Where order and right and hope and peace can enter.
Or will you ever return? Or are you dead,
And this wrought emptiness my ultimate emptiness?'

She wove and unwove and wove and did not know
That even then Ulysses on the long
And winding road of the world was on his way.

Thomas Stearns Eliot

Prelude

The winter evening settles down
With smell of steaks in passageways.
Six o'clock.

The burnt-out ends of smoky days.
And now a gusty shower wraps
The grimy scraps
Of withered leaves about your feet
And newspapers from vacant lots;
The showers beat
On broken blinds and chimney-pots,
And at the corner of the street
A lonely cab-horse steams and stamps.
And then the lighting of the lamps.

Rannoch, by Glencoe

HERE the crow starves, here the patient stag
Breeds for the rifle. Between the soft moor
And the soft sky, scarcely room
To leap or soar. Substance crumbles, in the thin air
Moon cold or moon hot. The road winds in
Listlessness of ancient war,
Languor of broken steel,
Clamour of confused wrong, apt
In silence. Memory is strong
Beyond the bone. Pride snapped,
Shadow of pride is long, in the long pass
No concurrence of bone.

The Journey of the Magi

'A COLD coming we had of it,
Just the worst time of the year
For a journey, and such a long journey:
The ways deep and the weather sharp,
The very dead of winter.'
And the camels galled, sore-footed, refractory,
Lying down in the melting snow.
There were times we regretted
The summer palaces on slopes, the terraces,
And the silken girls bringing sherbet.
Then the camel men cursing and grumbling
And running away, and wanting their liquor and women,
And the night-fires going out, and the lack of shelters,
And the cities hostile and the towns unfriendly
And the villages dirty and charging high prices:
A hard time we had of it.
At the end we preferred to travel all night,
Sleeping in snatches,
With the voices singing in our ears, saying
That this was all folly.

Then at dawn we came down to a temperate valley,
Wet, below the snow line, smelling of vegetation;
With a running stream and a water-mill beating the darkness,
And three trees on the low sky,
And an old white horse galloped away in the meadow.
Then we came to a tavern with vine-leaves over the lintel,
Six hands at an open door dicing for pieces of silver,
And feet kicking the empty wine-skins.
But there was no information, and so we continued
And arrived at evening, not a moment too soon
Finding the place; it was (you may say) satisfactory.

All this was a long time ago, I remember,
And I would do it again, but set down
This set down
This: were we led all that way for
Birth or Death? There was a Birth, certainly,
We had evidence and no doubt. I had seen birth and death,
But had thought they were different; this Birth was
Hard and bitter agony for us, like Death, our death.
We returned to our places, these Kingdoms,
But no longer at ease here, in the old dispensation,
With an alien people clutching their gods.
I should be glad of another death.

Rhapsody on a Windy Night

TWELVE o'clock.
Along the reaches of the street
Held in a lunar synthesis,
Whispering lunar incantations
Dissolve the floors of memory
And all its clear relations,
Its divisions and precisions,
Every street lamp that I pass
Beats like a fatalistic drum,
And through the spaces of the dark
Midnight shakes the memory
As a madman shakes a dead geranium.

Half-past one,
The street-lamp sputtered,
The street-lamp muttered,
The street-lamp said, 'Regard that woman

Who hesitates toward you in the light of the door
Which opens on her like a grin.
You see the border of her dress
Is torn and stained with sand,
And you see the corner of her eye
Twists like a crooked pin.'

The memory throws up high and dry
A crowd of twisted things;
A twisted branch upon the beach
Eaten smooth, and polished
As if the world gave up
The secret of its skeleton,
Stiff and white.
A broken spring in a factory yard,
Rust that clings to the form that the strength has left
Hard and curled and ready to snap.

Half-past two,
The street-lamp said,
'Remark the cat which flattens itself in the gutter,
Slips out its tongue
And devours a morsel of rancid butter.'
So the hand of the child, automatic,
Slipped out and pocketed a toy that was running along the quay.
I could see nothing behind that child's eye.
I have seen eyes in the street
Trying to peer through lighted shutters,
And a crab one afternoon in a pool,
An old crab with barnacles on his back,
Gripped the end of a stick which I held him.
Half-past three,
The lamp sputtered,

The lamp muttered in the dark.
The lamp hummed:
'Regard the moon,
La lune ne garde aucune rancune,
She winks a feeble eye,
She smiles into corners.
She smooths the hair of the grass.
The moon has lost her memory.
A washed-out smallpox cracks her face,
Her hand twists a paper rose,
That smells of dust and eau de Cologne,
She is alone
With all the old nocturnal smells
That cross and cross across her brain.'

The reminiscence comes
Of sunless dry geraniums
And dust in crevices,
Smells of chestnuts in the streets,
And female smells in shuttered rooms,
And cigarettes in corridors
And cocktail smells in bars.

The lamp said,
'Four o'clock,
Here is the number on the door.
Memory!
You have the key,
The little lamp spreads a ring on the stair,
Mount.
The bed is open; the tooth-brush hangs on the wall,
Put your shoes at the door, sleep, prepare for life.'

The last twist of the knife.

John Crowe Ransom

Old Man Playing With Children

A DISCREET householder exclaims on the grandsire
In warpaint and feathers, with fierce grandsons and axes
Dancing round a backyard fire of boxes:
'Watch grandfather, he'll set the house on fire.'

But I will unriddle for you the thought of his mind,
An old one you cannot open with conversation.
What animates the thin legs in risky motion?
Mixes the snow on the head with snow on the wind?

'Grandson, grandsire. We are equally boy and boy.
Do not offer your reclining-chair and slippers
With tedious old women talking in wrappers.
This life is not good but in danger and in joy.

'It is you the elder to these and junior to me
Who are penned as slaves by properties and causes
And never walk from your insupportable houses.
Shamefully, when boys shout, you turn and flee.

'May God forgive me, I know your middling ways,
Having taken care and performed ignominies unreckoned
Between the first brief childhood and brief second,
But I will be more honourable in these days.'

Piazza Piece

—I AM a gentleman in a dustcoat trying
To make you hear. Your ears are soft and small
And listen to an old man not at all,
They want the young men's whispering and sighing.
But see the roses on your trellis dying
And hear the spectral singing of the moon;
For I must have my lovely lady soon,
I am a gentleman in a dustcoat trying.

—I am a lady young in beauty waiting
Until my truelove comes, and then we kiss.
But what grey man among the vines is this
Whose words are dry and faint as in a dream?
Back from my trellis, Sir, before I scream!
I am a lady young in beauty waiting.

Blue Girls

TWIRLING your blue skirts, travelling the sward
Under the towers of your seminary,
Go listen to your teachers old and contrary
Without believing a word.

Tie the white fillets then about your hair
And think no more of what will come to pass
Than bluebirds that go walking on the grass
And chattering on the air.

Practice your beauty, blue girls, before it fail;
And I will cry with my loud lips and publish
Beauty which all our power shall never establish,
It is so frail.

For I could tell you a story which is true;
I know a woman with a terrible tongue,
Blear eyes fallen from blue,
All her perfections tarnished—yet it is not long
Since she was lovelier than you.

Arthur Waley

Fighting South of the Castle

THEY fought south of the Castle,
They died north of the wall.
They died in the moors and were not buried.
Their flesh was the food of crows.
'Tell the crows we are not afraid;
We have died in the moors and cannot be buried.
Crows, how can our bodies escape you?'
The waters flowed deep
And the rushes in the pool were dark.
The riders fought and were slain:
Their horses wander neighing.

By the bridge there was a house.
Was it south, was it north?
The harvest was never gathered.
How can we give you your offerings?
You served your Prince faithfully,
Though all in vain.
I think of you, faithful soldiers;
Your service shall not be forgotten.
For in the morning you went out to battle
And at night you did not return.

Burial Songs 1 *and* 2

"*The dew on the garlic-leaf,*" *sung at the burial of kings and princes*

How swiftly it dries,
The dew on the garlic-leaf,
The dew that dries so fast
To-morrow will fall again.
But he whom we carry to the grave
Will never more return.

"*The Graveyard,*" *sung at the burial of common men*

WHAT man's land is the graveyard?
It is the crowded home of ghosts,—
Wise and foolish shoulder to shoulder.
The King of the Dead claims them all;
Man's fate knows no tarrying.

On the Birth of His Son

Families, when a child is born,
Want it to be intelligent,
I, through intelligence,
Having wrecked my whole life,
Only hope the baby will prove
Ignorant and stupid,
Then he will crown a tranquil life
By becoming a Cabinet Minister.

The Hat Given to the Poet by Li Chien

Long ago to a white-haired gentleman
You made the present of a black gauze hat.
The gauze hat still sits on my head;
But you already are gone to the Nether Springs.
The thing is old, but still fit to wear;
The man is gone and will never be seen again.
Out on the hill the moon is shining to-night
And the trees on your tomb are swayed by the autumn wind.

A Love Song

I heard my love was going to Yang-chou
And went with him as far as Ch'u-shan.
For a moment when you held me fast in your outstretched
arms
I thought the river stood still and did not flow.

Plucking the Rushes

(A boy and girl are sent to gather rushes for thatching)

GREEN rushes with red shoots,
Long leaves bending to the wind—
You and I in the same boat
Plucking rushes at the Five Lakes.
We started at dawn from the orchid-island:
We rested under the elms till noon.
You and I plucking rushes
Had not plucked a handful when night came!

Wilfred Owen

Futility

MOVE him into the sun—.
Gently its touch awoke him once,
At home, whispering of fields unsown.
Always it woke him, even in France,
Until this morning and this snow.
If anything might rouse him now
The kind old sun will know.

Think how it wakes the seeds,—
Woke, once, the clays of a cold star.
Are limbs, so dear-achieved, are sides,
Full-nerved—still warm—too hard to stir?
Was it for this the clay grew tall?
—O what made fatuous sunbeams toil
To break earth's sleep at all?

Arms and the Boy

LET the boy try along this bayonet-blade
How cold steel is, and keen with hunger of blood;
Blue with all malice, like a madman's flash;
And thinly drawn with famishing for flesh.

Lend him to stroke these blind, blunt bullet-heads
Which long to nuzzle in the hearts of lads,
Or give him cartridges of fine zinc teeth,
Sharp with the sharpness of grief and death.

For his teeth seem for laughing round an apple.
There lurk no claws behind his fingers supple;
And God will grow no talons at his heels,
Nor antlers through the thickness of his curls.

The Parable of the Old Man and the Young

So Abram rose, and clave the wood, and went,
And took the fire with him, and a knife.
And as they sojourned both of them together,

Isaac the first-born spake and said, My Father,
Behold the preparations, fire and iron,
But where the lamb for this burnt-offering?
Then Abram bound the youth with belts and straps,
And builded parapets and trenches there,
And stretchèd forth the knife to slay his son.
When lo! an angel called him out of heaven,
Saying, Lay not thy hand upon the lad,
Neither do anything to him. Behold,
A ram, caught in a thicket by its horns;
Offer the Ram of Pride instead of him.
But the old man would not so, but slew his son,
And half the seed of Europe, one by one.

Anthem for Doomed Youth

WHAT passing bells for these who die as cattle?
  Only the monstrous anger of the guns.
  Only the stuttering rifles' rapid rattle
Can patter out their hasty orisons.
No mockeries now for them; no prayers nor bells,
  Nor any voice of mourning save the choirs,—
The shrill, demented choirs of wailing shells;
  And bugles calling for them from sad shires.

What candles may be held to speed them all?
  Not in the hands of boys, but in their eyes
Shall shine the holy glimmers of good-byes.
  The pallor of girls' brows shall be their pall;
Their flowers the tenderness of patient minds,
And each slow dusk a drawing-down of blinds.

Robert Graves

1805

At Viscount Nelson's lavish funeral,
While the mob milled and yelled about St. Paul's,
A General chatted with an Admiral:

'One of your Colleagues, Sir, remarked to-day
That Nelson's *exit*, though to be lamented,
Falls not inopportunely, in its way.'

'He was a thorn in our flesh,' came the reply—
'The most bird-witted, unaccountable,
Odd little runt that ever I did spy.

'One arm, one peeper, vain as Pretty Poll,
A meddler, too, in foreign politics
And gave his heart in pawn to a plain moll.

'He would dare lecture us Sea Lords, and then
Would treat his ratings as though men of honour
And play at leap-frog with his midshipmen!

'We tried to box him down, but up he popped,
And when he'd banged Napoleon at the Nile
Became too much the hero to be dropped.

'You've heard that Copenhagen "blind eye" story?
We'd tied him to Nurse Parker's apron-strings—
By G-d, he snipped them through and snatched the glory!'

'Yet,' cried the General, 'six-and-twenty sail
Captured or sunk by him off Trafalgar—
That writes a handsome *finis* to the tale.'

'Handsome enough. The seas are England's now.
That fellow's foibles need no longer plague us.
He died most creditably, I'll allow.'

'And, Sir, the secret of his victories?'
'By his unServicelike, familiar ways, Sir,
He made the whole Fleet love him, damn his eyes!'

To Lucia at Birth

THOUGH the moon beaming matronly and bland
Greets you, among the crowd of the new-born,
With 'welcome to the world' yet understand
That still her pale, lascivious unicorn
And bloody lion are loose on either hand:
With din of bones and tantarará of horn
Their fanciful cortege parades the land—
Pest on the high road, wild-fire in the corn.

Outrageous company to be born into,
Lunatics of the Royal age long dead.
Then reckon time by what you are or do,
Not by the epochs of the war they spread.
Hark how they roar; but never turn your head,
Nothing will change them, let them not change you.

Edmund Blunden

The Ballast-Hole

CAN malice live in natural forms,
As tree, or stone, or winding lane?
Beside this winding lane of ours
The fangy roots of trees contain
A pond that seems to feed the powers
Of ugly passion. Thunder-storms
No blacker look. If forth it shook
Blue snarling flashes lightning-like,
I scarce should marvel; may it strike
When I'm not by its sullen dyke!

Report on Experience

I HAVE been young, and now am not too old;
And I have seen the righteous forsaken,
His health, his honour and his quality taken.
This is not what we were formerly told.

I have seen a green country, useful to the race,
Knocked silly with guns and mines, its villages vanished,
Even the last rat and last kestrel banished—
God bless us all, this was peculiar grace.

I knew Seraphina; Nature gave her hue,
Glance, sympathy, note, like one from Eden.
I saw her smile warp, heard her lyric deaden;
    She turned to harlotry;—this I took to be new.

Say what you will, our God sees how they run.
These disillusions are His curious proving
That he loves humanity and will go on loving;
    Over there are faith, life, virtue in the sun.

Cecil Day Lewis

It Would Be Strange

It would be strange
If at a crucial question, in wild-beast dens
Or cellars sweating with pain the stammerers
Should find their confidence.

It would be strange
If the haphazard starling learned a neat
Construction from the goldcrest, and the blackcap's
Seamless song in a night.

It would be strange
If from the consternation of the ant-hill
Arose some order angelic, ranked for loving,
Equal to good or ill.

It would be more than strange
If the devil we raised to avenge our envy, grief,
Weakness, should take our hand like a prince and raise us
And say, 'I forgive'.

Norman Cameron

The Compassionate Fool

My enemy had bidden me as guest.
His table all set out with wine and cake,
His ordered chairs, he to beguile me dressed
So neatly, moved my pity for his sake.

I knew it was an ambush, but could not
Leave him to eat his cake up by himself
And put his unused glasses on the shelf,
I made pretence of falling in his plot,

And trembled when in his anxiety
He bared it too absurdly to my view.
And even as he stabbed me through and through
I pitied him for his small strategy.

James Reeves

Thoughts and Memories

Do others waking in the morning hear
  Dog bark or cuckoo call
And suddenly not know for certain whether
  Dog or bird was there at all?
Perhaps a poacher or a country boy
  Is never taken unawares
    But active with his snares
Is not so caught up in the past as I.

Do you too wonder if the finest thing
  A promising flower can do
Is but to imitate with all its art
  All other flowers that ever grew?
You looking from your window see the spring
  Each year perform its leisurely
    Long act of memory,
All nature gone into remembering.

Perhaps a cow's large inward-dreaming eyes
  See nature that way too,
Confounding all to-morrows and to-days
  In one perpetual grassy view.

I more resemble that same thoughtful cow
  Than any poacher or his prey;
    Less purposive than they,
We ruminants absorb old things with new.

Do you too lying sleepless think of things
  That you have said or done,
Communicate with ghosts and fantasies
  As if you feared to be alone?
You start to fall asleep, and one by one
  Thoughts and memories go their ways;
    You sleep and no ghost stays—
And oh, the horror if you waken then!

Dylan Thomas

The Force That Through The Green Fuse Drives The Flower

THE force that through the green fuse drives the
  flower
Drives my green age; that blasts the roots of trees
Is my destroyer.
And I am dumb to tell the crooked rose
My youth is bent by the same wintry fever.

The force that drives the water through the rocks
Drives my red blood; that dries the mouthing streams
Turns mine to wax.
And I am dumb to mouth unto my veins
How at the mountain spring the same mouth sucks.

The hand that whirls the water in the pool
Stirs the quicksand; that ropes the blowing wind
Hauls my shroud sail.
And I am dumb to tell the hanging man
How of my clay is made the hangman's lime.

The lips of time leech to the fountain head;
Love drips and gathers, but the fallen blood
Shall calm her sores.
And I am dumb to tell a weather's wind
How time has ticked a heaven round the stars.

And I am dumb to tell the lover's tomb
How at my sheet goes the same crooked worm.

Notes

1. A LYKE-WAGE DIRGE (Anonymous).

This dirge (probably incomplete) used to be sung at the family gathering (*wake*) held each night round the corpse (lyke) of a dead relative until the day of the funeral. This practice was common until fairly modern times in Scotland and the north of England, and this dirge, though heard as late as the seventeenth century, is very much older. It is based on the ancient and widespread belief that after death the soul went on a journey to Heaven or Hell by way of the fires of Purgatory, in which it was tested for goodness or evil. It had to pass over, first, Whinny Moor (a moor covered with furze or gorse), protection against which could be secured by giving away a new pair of shoes during life to some poor person; then, the Bridge of Death, a narrow bridge across a dark water into which the traveller might slip and lose his soul.

v. 1—*fire and fleet and candle-lighte*: several explanations of this line have been given, none altogether convincing. For *fleet*, some editors read *sleet*, a corruption of *selte* meaning *salt*. Salt and earth were placed separately on the breast of the corpse, the salt being a symbol of the immortal soul, the earth a symbol of the body. On the other hand, there are three possible meanings for *fleet*: (1) water, (2) burning embers, and (3) house-room, *fire and fleet* being an alliterative expression like *hearth and home*. The fire and the house-room would be for the entertainment of the mourners, and a candle was kept burning near the corpse, probably to frighten away evil spirits.

v. 3—*hosen*, stockings.

2. THE WIFE OF USHER'S WELL (Anonymous).

v. 11—*channerin' worm*, fretting serpent or dragon, that guards the entrance to Paradise.

4. EDWARD (Anonymous).

See *Introduction* (p. xxxiii) *l.* 3.

(p. 5) *v.* 3—*some other dule ye dree*, you have some other cause for grief.

6. THE TWA CORBIES (Anonymous).

corbies, crows.

v. 2—*fail-dyke*, wall built of turves.

15. The Old Cloak (Anonymous).

v. 1—*Boreas*, the north wind.

v. 3—*go so fine*, be so well dressed.

v. 8—*first give o'er the play*, is prepared to let her have the last word.

20. An Old Soldier of the Queen's (Anonymous: slightly abridged).

Compare this poem with Peele's *His Golden Locks* (p. 51).

v. 1—*Maumsie*, red from drinking Malmsey wine.

21. Boney Was a Warrior (Anonymous).

An early nineteenth century sea-shanty.

v. 1—*John Fran-swah*, Jean François, the typical Frenchman.

v. 5—*Elbow*, the isle of Elba, where Napoleon was first sent and whence he escaped.

v. 7—*Billy Ruffian*, British seaman's corruption of the ship's name *Bellerophon*.

24. The Big Rock Candy Mountains (Anonymous).

An American tramp's ballad; composed towards the end of the nineteenth century.

v. 2—*handouts*, charity given to beggars; *boxcars*, covered goods wagons.

v. 4—*brakemen*, guards; *bulls*, police.

26. Alexander the Great (Anonymous).

Compare Shirley's *The Glories of our Blood and State* (p. 104) and Shelley's *Ozymandias* (p. 202). Alexander the Great (356–323 B.C.) was the son of Philip of Macedonia.

27. The Whale (Anglo-Saxon, trans. Gavin Bone).

A translation by a modern scholar of an anonymous Anglo-Saxon poem. The resemblance to Milton's famous simile in *Paradise Lost*, Book I, is striking.

Him, haply slumbering on the Norway foam,
The pilot of some small night-foundered skiff,
Deeming some island, oft, as seamen tell,
With fixèd anchor in his scaly rind,
Moors by his side under the lee, while night
Invests the sea, and wishèd morn delays.

30. Now Welcome Summer (Geoffrey Chaucer).

This is a rondeau (or rondel), a poetic form in which only two rhymes are used and the opening lines are repeated as a refrain.

v. 2—*Seynt Valentyn*. St. Valentine's day is February 14, when birds were supposed to choose their mates.

31. A Garden in a Dream (Geoffrey Chaucer).

An ideal description of the 'garden' in which the birds meet to decide which of three eagles shall marry a beautiful female eagle. Compare the idealised scenes in Marvell's *The Garden* (p. 115) and Coleridge's *Kubla Khan* (p. 177). The verse-form in this poem is known as rhyme royal.

32. The Squire (Geoffrey Chaucer).

Chaucer's Squire, described in the Prologue to *The Canterbury Tales*, was the son of the Knight. He was a 'bachelor', i.e. a young man aspiring to become a knight. Notice that the medieval ideal of knighthood, embodied even as late as the Elizabethan period in such a man as Sir Philip Sidney, embraced not only athletic and military prowess, but also a practical knowledge of the arts—writing poems, composing songs, singing and playing music.

l. 3—*as they were leyd in presse*, as if they had been pressed.

l. 9–10—*and born him wel*, etc., and had made good progress, considering his brief experience, in the hope of standing high in his lady's favour.

33. The Chase (Geoffrey Chaucer, *Nun's Priest's Tale*).

An extract from one of the liveliest of the Canterbury Tales, in which a poor widow's cock is stolen by a fox by means of flattery.

l. 1—*sely widwe*, simple widow; *eek*, also.

l. 3—*anoon*, at once.

l. 6—And cried, 'Help, help! alas!'

l. 9—Traditional names for dogs.

l. 12—*fered*, frightened.

l. 14—They ran so fast that they thought their hearts would burst.

l. 16—The ducks squawked as if they were being struck.

l. 19—*benedicite*, Lord bless us!

l. 20–23—Indeed, Jack Straw (a leader in the Peasants Revolt of 1381) and his mob never shouted half so shrilly when they attacked the Flemings (immigrant competitive labour) as the shouts made that day after the fox.

l. 24—They brought trumpets made of brass and of boxwood.

l. 25—*pouped*, puffed.

34. Truth: Ballade de Bon Conseyl (Geoffrey Chaucer).

This 'ballade of good advice' is a moral exhortation against worldliness. The form of the poem derives from French models, its chief feature being the repetition of the final lines of each stanza.

l. 1—*prees*, press, crowd; *sothfastnesse*, adherence to truth.

l. 2—*Suffyce unto thy good*, Be content with what you have.

l. 3—For avarice breeds hatred, and ambition is unsure.

l. 4—The world is full of envy, and prosperity is everywhere cheated.

l. 5—Have a taste for no more than what becomes you.

l. 6—*that other folk canst rede*, who can advise others.

l. 7—And truth shall make you free, there is no doubt.

l. 8—Do not put yourself into a passion to set right all crookedness.

l. 9—*hir*, her, i.e. Fortune.

l. 10—Much repose consists in abstaining from fussiness.

l. 11—Equivalent to 'Do not strive to kick against the pricks'.

l. 12—*crokke*, earthenware pitcher—the reference is to the fable in Aesop where the pitcher is broken against the wall and the brass vessel is not.

l. 13—*Daunte*, Subdue *otheres dede*, the actions of others.

l. 15—Receive with due submission whatever is sent you.

l. 17—*Her his non hoom*, Here (on earth) is no home.

l. 19—*thy contree*, i.e. Heaven.

l. 20—Keep to the spiritual road and let your spirit be your guide.

l. 22—*vache*, literally 'cow' (a reference back to 'beste' in line 18).

l. 23—*leve now to be thral*, leave off being a slave.

l. 24—*Crye him*, Beg for his (i.e. God's).

l. 26—*Draw unto*, Approach.

l. 27—*hevenlich made*: the reward of Heaven.

35. LAMENT FOR THE MAKERS (William Dunbar).

v. 1—*Timor Mortis*, etc., the fear of death troubles me.

v. 5—*all Estatis*, people of all degrees.

v. 13—*the Monk of Bury*, John Lydgate, 1370?–1451?

v. 14–23—Scottish poets of whom little is now known, Robert Henryson (1430?–1506) was the most famous.

v. 19—*He has reft Mersier*, etc. He (Death) has bereft Mercer of his power of writing, who wrote such lively love-poems in brief, clear lines full of noble thoughts.

39. POVERTY (John Skelton).

A self-portrait of a character in the play *Magnificence*. Compare D. H. Lawrence's *Poverty* (p. 299), where it is called 'a hard old hag'. Compare also W. H. Davies' *The Heap of Rags* (p. 279).

40. THOUGH YE SUPPOSE (John Skelton).

See *Introduction* (p. xliv). *l.* 3–4—The precise meaning is not clear:

the general idea is that of a game of chance in which Fortune keeps, as we should say, 'an ace up her sleeve'.

41. TO MISTRESS MARGARET HUSSEY (John Skelton).

l. 22—*Isiphil,* Hypsipile, Queen of Lemnos, a heroine of Greek legend.

l. 23—*coliander,* or coriander, a scented fruit.

l. 24—*pomander,* a perfume.

l. 25—*Cassander,* Cassandra, a prophetess, daughter of Priam, King of Troy.

43. THE HIND (Sir Thomas Wyatt).

Wyatt, who introduced the sonnet form into English poetry from Italy, was also a diplomat at the court of Henry VIII. He is said to have been in love with Anne Boleyn before her marriage to the King. There is no good reason for rejecting the supposition that this poem refers allegorically to his pursuit of Anne and to his giving up the chase when she married the King.

l. 1—*Whoso list,* Whoever likes.

l. 2—*helas,* alas.

l. 3—*travail,* labour.

l. 8—A metaphor for any futile action.

l. 11—i.e. on an engraved neckband or collar.

l. 12—Touch me not: I belong to the King.

43. TO HIS LADY (Sir Thomas Wyatt).

The poet is urging his lady to make up her mind whether she wants him or not and to stop alternately encouraging and discouraging him.

l. 3—*the,* thou; *bourds,* flirtatious tricks.

l. 6—*one that burneth,* one that is on fire with love, i.e. the poet himself.

l. 9—*fain,* willing (to be your lover).

l. 12—*mine own,* i.e. man—he will belong to himself and no one else.

44. HONESTY (Sir Thomas Wyatt).

A reflection on Wyatt's experience of court and diplomatic life.

l. 5–6—But to speak fair (or promise well) and mean what you say—such sweet agreement is uncommon.

45. YOUTH AND AGE (Henry Howard, Earl of Surrey).

Surrey, as he is usually called, was a courtier-poet who, like Wyatt, was highly influential in the development of Tudor lyric poetry, as well as being the first to use blank verse. Much of his material was translated from foreign sources; his chief originality was in the field of metrical innovation. This poem is written in an unusual combination of alternate hexameters (six-stress iambics) and fourteeners (seven-foot iambics).

l. 6—Did wish to God that he might escape the (schoolmaster's) rod by growing up.

l. 7—*eke*, also.

l. 12—*degree*, age.

l. 14—That a man should wish to give up the status of the wealthy old man he once wanted to be in favour of the youthful status he once thought woeful.

l. 16—*dinted*, dented, hollow.

l. 17—*chaps*, jaws.

l. 19—*hoarish*, hoary, fristy.

l. 20—The white hairs appear like that belief in truth which makes life tolerable.

l. 23—Give up the practices of wanton youth, like one who gives up hunting.

l. 24—This renunciation will bring you the truest happiness.

l. 25—*wonted joy*, the joy I have been used to.

l. 27–28—Tell boys from me that, if in their youth they had the wisdom of experience, their boyhood would be their happiest time.

46. JOLLY GOOD ALE AND OLD (William Stevenson).

The authorship is doubtful.

l. 4—*him that wears a hood*, him that is dressed properly (as I cannot afford to be).

48. WALSINGHAM (Sir Walter Ralegh).

This dialogue between a lover abandoned by his mistress and an unnamed pilgrim returning from the shrine of Walsingham in Norfolk is based on older ballads on this subject. It is probably, but not certainly, by Ralegh: if so, it is about the sorrow and bitterness he felt at his loss of favour with Queen Elizabeth. Walsingham, until its destruction in 1538, was the richest and one of the most famous of Catholic shrines in England.

l. 8—*That* probably refers back to line 6 ('many one').

l. 18—*as unknown*, as if she had never known me.

l. 31—*list*, likes.

l. 32—And is never firm in faith.

l. 33—This stanza is a bitter reflection on the shallowness of woman's love: He desires ephemeral happiness and joy that cannot be depended on. He is won only after infinite despair and lost by some trifle.

l. 37–40—The sense is that by the abuse of love as felt by women they make excuses for childish wishes and fancies.

l. 41–44—A description of true or ideal love, by contrast.

50. WHEN FLOWERED MY JOYFUL SPRING (Edmund Spenser).

Although partly adapted from a French poet, these lines probably recall Spenser's own boyhood. Compare Wordsworth's *Nutting* (p. 175).

51. ONE DAY I WROTE HER NAME UPON THE STRAND (Edmund Spenser). Compare Landor's *Well I Remember How You Smiled* (p. 201).

52. A BALLAD OF AGINCOURT (Michael Drayton).

v. 6—*our grandsire,* Edward III; *lopp'd the French lilies,* humbled French pride: the *fleur-de-lys* was the emblem of the French king.

v. 13—*a maiden knight,* one with no previous experience of battle.

57. LAMENT FOR ZENOCRATE (Christopher Marlowe).

Spoken by Tamburlaine in *The Second Part of Tamburlaine the Great,* when his wife Zenocrate is dying.

l. 18—*Apollo, Cynthia,* the sun and moon. Notice the combination of classical and Christian allusions.

l. 35—*empyreal heaven,* the highest realm, the abode of God and the angels.

58. BLOW, BLOW, THOU WINTER WIND (William Shakespeare).

A song from *As You Like It,* expressing the exiled courtiers' sense of grievance against the world from which they have been banished. See *Introduction* (p. xxx).

59. WHERE THE BEE SUCKS (William Shakespeare).

One of Ariel's songs from *The Tempest.* Ariel is an airy spirit who can change shape, form and size at will. He embodies the intangible magic of Prospero his master's island.

60. FULL FATHOM FIVE (William Shakespeare).

Another of Ariel's songs. See *Introduction* (p. xlv).

l. 4—*that doth fade,* that is mortal, subject to decay.

60. O MISTRESS MINE (William Shakespeare).

One of Feste the jester's songs from *Twelfth Night.* Compare Marvell's *To his Coy Mistress* (p. 118). *v.* 2—*Still,* always.

61. FEAR NO MORE THE HEAT O' THE SUN (William Shakespeare).

The dirge from *Cymberline.* Shakespeare's best songs exemplify the perfection of lyrical utterance—that is, of the expression of a mood or a feeling. This cannot be achieved through either meaning or sound alone. It requires the combination of both. It is impossible to *explain* how Shakespeare fuses sense and sound to create mood, but by reading and knowing the poems well it is possible to *feel* that he does so. The mood in this poem is one of resignation, of the consolations of death, and this mood is conveyed as much by the music and movement of the verse as through its meaning. For example, the general movement of the lines is trochaic, and this contributes to their heavy, dirge-like quality. Compare the opening of *A Lyke-Wake Dirge* (p. 1).

v. 2—*all follows this*; some editors think Shakespeare wrote *thee*.

v. 3—*thunderstone*, thunderbolt. It was once thought that a stone accompanied the lightning flash when a person was struck dead; *consign to thee*, agree to accept the same fate as you.

v. 4—*exorciser*, one who calls up spirits; *consummation*, final end.

62. Shall I Compare Thee to a Summer's Day? (William Shakespeare).

This poem and the next five are chosen from Shakespeare's Sonnets, in which he expressed intense personal feeling, mainly inspired by love and friendship. Shakespeare thought and felt in metaphors drawn from many aspects of life (religion, war, the law, and navigation—among others); his sonnets are charged with compressed thought and feeling, and the stages in their progress are marked by changes of metaphor.

l. 4—*summer's lease*, etc., summer is too short: a legal metaphor.

l. 7—*every fair*, etc., everything beautiful loses its beauty.

l. 8—*untrimm'd*, deprived of its beauty.

l. 10—*owest*, ownest. Another allusion to the laws of property.

l. 13–14—Compare Spenser's *One day I wrote Her Name upon the Strand* (p. 51).

62. When to the Sessions of Sweet Silent Thought (William Shakespeare).

l. 1–2—*sessions . . . summon up*, a legal metaphor.

l. 6—*dateless*, eternal.

l. 8—*expense . . . sight*, loss of the sight of many friends, or the waste of many a sigh (of which word *sight* was an Elizabethan form).

l. 9—*foregone*, past.

l. 10—*tell*, count.

63. Tired with all these for Restful Death I Cry (William Shakespeare).

In eleven pointed and epigrammatic lines Shakespeare sums up his criticism of the age he lives in. Compare Dryden's second Song from *The Secular Masque* (p. 127).

l. 3—*needy, nothing,* those who deserve nothing; *trimmed in jollity,* splendidly adorned.

l. 5—*gilded honour,* etc., positions of honour, with all their rich insignia, conferred on the undeserving.

l. 6—*maiden virtue,* etc., maidenly honour brutally violated.

l. 8—*strength,* etc., men of strength thwarted by feeble men in positions of authority.

l. 9—*art made tongue-tied,* etc., art, learning and science hampered by censorship. (Official interference with the stage, for example, was frequent.)

l. 10—*doctor-like,* with the air of a learned man.

l. 11—*simple truth,* etc., innocent, truthful people called idiots.

l. 12—*captive good,* etc., good the slave to evil.

63. SINCE BRASS, NOR STONE, NOR EARTH, NOR BOUNDLESS SEA (William Shakespeare).

l. 1–4—These lines mean: Since there is neither brass nor stone nor earth nor sea so powerful that it cannot be overcome or destroyed by time (*sad mortality*), what chance has beauty (so weak and flower-like) of holding its own against the devouring rage of time? (*Hold a plea* is a legal expression on meaning 'make out a case'. *Action* continues the legal metaphor).

l. 7–8—Notice the suggestion of invincible strength in the repeated heavy sounds of *rocks impreg-, not so stout, steel so strong.*

l. 10—*Time's best jewel,* etc., human beauty, which time will try to store away in its treasure-chest.

64. WHEN IN THE CHRONICLE OF WASTED TIME (William Shakespeare).

l. 1—*wasted,* past.

l. 5—*blazon,* description.

l. 8—*master,* possess.

l. 10—*all you prefiguring,* all of them anticipating or prophesying you.

l. 11—*for they looked,* etc., because their picture of you was only guesswork.

65. LET ME NOT TO THE MARRIAGE OF TRUE MINDS (William Shakespeare).

The constancy of true love expressed in a closely-linked series of changing metaphors.

l. 1–2—I cannot acknowledge any hindrance to the union of constant souls. *Marriage* is used metaphorically, and the word *impediments* comes from the marriage service in the English Prayer Book. Shakespeare is writing, not of marriage in particular, but of any strong friendship.

l. 3—*alteration*, disordered condition, cause for altering.

l. 4—*bends with the remover to remove*, changes its course when one of the pair is unfaithful.

l. 5—*mark*, sea-mark, beacon.

l. 8—*whose worth's unknown*, etc., whose value is incalculable although its height may be measured. In other words, although we may make love our guide, as the pole-star is the guide to mariners, we shall never know its true worth.

l. 9—*Time's fool*, the sport of time.

l. 12—*bears it out*, survives.

l. 13—*upon me*, against me.

l. 14—*no man*, any man.

65. A Dream (William Shakespeare).

The Duke of Clarence's dream, the night before he is murdered. Compare *Full Fathom Five* (p. 60) for a similar imaginary picture without the horror.

66. Saint Crispin's Day (William Shakespeare).

Spoken by King Henry V on the eve of the battle of Agincourt, fought on October 25th, 1415.

l. 5—*we are enow to do our country loss*, we will be sufficient loss to our country (without wishing others with us).

l. 22—*crowns for convoy*, money for the journey.

l. 35—*with advantages*, with additions, exaggerations.

l. 47–48—*be he ne'er so vile*, however low-born he may be, he will be raised to the rank of gentleman.

68. The Death of Kings (William Shakespeare).

King Richard II, deposed by Bolinbroke and imprisoned in Pontefract Castle, laments the miserable fate to which even Kings are subject.

l. 11—*and kill with looks*, have absolute power of life and death over his subjects. An allusion to the basilisk, an imaginary reptile supposed to be able to kill with looks. It had a crown-shaped mark and was therefore associated with royalty.

68. Sleep (William Shakespeare).

l. 23—*partial*, unfair, prejudiced (in favour of the poor).

l. 26—*with a appliances*, etc., with all possible comforts and means of assistance.

69. Music (William Shakespeare).

Lorenzo and Jessica, in *The Merchant of Venice*, are keeping house for Portia in Belmont. Portia is on her way home. While awaiting her arrival, Lorenzo explains to Jessica the theory of 'the music of the spheres'—that the stars (*orbs*) as they revolve sing together in harmony and their music is audible to angels (*cherubins*) but not to mortals enclosed in the gross and corruptible covering of flesh (*muddy vesture of decay*).

l. 4—*touches*, sounds (made by touching strings).

l. 6—*patens*, small gilt or gold plates (either small moonlit clouds or the stars themselves).

l. 13—*Come, ho!* Here Lorenzo calls to the musicians in the house; *Diana*, the moon goddess.

l. 14—*your mistress*, i.e. Portia.

l. 24—*make a mutual stand*, come to a standstill as if by agreement.

l. 26—*the poet*, i.e. Ovid (in *Metamorphoses* X, XI).

l. 28—*stockish*, dull, stupid.

l. 34—*affections*, emotions, sensibilities; *Erebus*, the darkest region of Hades.

71. SOUNDS AND SWEET AIRS (William Shakespeare).

Caliban, a deformed monster inhabiting Prospero's island in *The Tempest*, warns two newcomers not to be afraid when they hear Ariel's music or any other unearthly sounds.

71. THE DEATH OF CLEOPATRA (William Shakespeare).

After the death of her lover Antony, Cleopatra is closely watched by Octavius' guards in case she tries to kill herself and so cheat him of the triumph of capturing her. She is too cunning for him, however, and kills herself with poisonous snakes which she gets a countryman to bring her concealed in a basket of grapes. Iras and Charmian are her attendants.

l. 7—*Caesar*, i.e. Octavius.

l. 10—*I am fire, and air*; it was believed that human beings were composed of four elements, fire, air, earth and water.

l. 11—*have you done?* have you finished arranging my royal robes.

l. 14—*aspic*, asp, snake.

l. 25—*intrinsicate*, entangled.

73. IRRESOLUTION (William Shakespeare, *Hamlet*).

Hamlet has sworn to avenge the murder of his father by killing the murderer, his usurping uncle, Claudius. The tragedy is largely the story of his irresolution and the disasters so caused. The 'occasion' of this soliloquy is his encounter with a force of soldiers under Fortinbras, nephew to the King of Norway, on their way to fight for a worthless plot of land in Poland. The fight that is to ensue is for mere glory.

Hamlet here bitterly contrasts his own lack of purpose in a justifiable cause with the Norwegians' courage and resolution in an empty one.

l. 3—*market*, i.e. what he spends his time on.

l. 5—*discourse*, power of thought.

l. 6—*Looking before and after*, Having (unlike beasts) the capacity to think about the past and the future.

l. 8—*fust*, moulder.

l. 10—*event*, consequences.

l. 13—*This thing's to do*, the killing of my uncle is still to be done.

l. 15—Examples (of resolute courage), as obvious as the earth itself, urge me on.

l. 16—*charge*, cost.

l. 19—Makes defiant grimaces at the as yet undecided outcome.

l. 20—i.e. risking this frail mortal body.

l. 24—*egg-shell*, i.e. something of no worth.

l. 22–25—The *not* of 23 presents a difficulty, but the general meaning must be: True greatness consists, not in acting under great provocation, but in finding provocation in a mere trifle when honour is at stake.

l. 26—Who have a dead father and a dishonoured mother.

l. 30—who for a mere dream or trifle.

l. 33—*continent*, receptacle.

74. Bessy and Jamie (Thomas Campian).

The pagan pastoralism of this song is in contrast to the courtly artificiality of some Elizabethan love-songs. Campian was a lutenist-poet of genius.

l. 12—*dump*, fit of the sulks.

l. 21—*sleight*, trick.

75. In Time of Pestilence (Thomas Nashe).

During the medieval and Tudor periods London was constantly menaced by outbreaks of the bubonic plague. This poem is remarkable not for originality of thought—there are many echoes from other poems—but for the beauty of its language and for a solemn yet urgent note in its movement; this is due partly to the broken character of the verses, of which only the last two contain sentences of more than one line in length.

v. 1—*fond are*, etc., life's pleasures are mere foolishness; *toys*, vanities.

v. 2—*physic himself*, etc., even doctors must die.

v. 3—*brightness falls from the air*, the beauty of the sunlight fades from the sky. (But it seems likely that in the original poem the word was 'hair', which would certainly fit the context better); *Helen*, ideal human beauty.

v. 4—*Hector*, ideal courage.

v. 5—*wit with his wantonness*, clever people with their scandal and smart talk; *Hell's executioner*, death; *art*, skill or learning. (Compare Gray's *Elegy*: 'Nor flattery soothe the dull, cold ear of death').

v. 6—*each degree*, people of every rank and station in life.

77. HYMN TO DIANA (Ben Jonson).

Diana, or Cynthia, in classical mythology was the goddess of the moon, whose silver 'bow', when new, suggested the idea of a huntress. Diana was thought of also as a virgin, the goddess of chastity.

v. 1—*Hesperus*, the evening star.

78. INVITING A FRIEND TO SUPPER (Ben Jonson).

l. 5—With those that come, i.e. In the eyes of the other guests.

l. 7–8—It is the acceptance of an invitation in a congenial spirit, not the quality of the food and drink, that makes an entertainment perfect.

l. 13—*coney*, rabbit.

l. 15—*clerks*, scholars, experts.

l. 16—The sky not falling, Unless the weather breaks up entirely.

l. 19—godwit, a marsh-bird once accounted a great delicacy.

l. 20—*Knat*, species of sandpiper; *raile*, either the land- or the water-rail; *ruff*, another species of the sandpiper.

l. 24–26—Difficult lines: the sense appears to be that Jonson promises not to bore the company by reading any of his own verses; but if they should turn up by accident, it will be because the pie has been cased in them. It was a traditional joke among literary men that discarded poems were used by pastrycooks for baking or wrapping pies.

l. 28—*take*, enchant.

l. 29—*Canary-wine*, light, sweet wine from the Canary Islands.

l. 30—*the Mermaid*, Jonson's local.

l. 31—*Horace* . . . *Anacreon*, a Latin and a Greek poet who wrote in praise of drinking.

l. 33–34—Compared with canary-wine tobacco, the wine of the Gods and tragic poetry are no better than German beer.

l. 36—Robert Pooly was present at the death of the poet Marlowe, and his presence at Jonson's feast would surely be an ill omen. Parrot has not been identified.

l. 39—*Simple*, single.

79. THAT WOMEN ARE BUT MEN'S SHADOWS (Ben Jonson).

This ingenious argument, not to be taken too seriously, reminds us that Jonson was writing in an age in which both the wit and neatness of the Cavalier poets and the ingenuity and artificiality of the Metaphysicals were in evidence.

l. 6—*styl'd*, called.

80. Song (Ben Jonson).

l. 1—*Still*, Always.

l. 11—*th' adulteries of art*, the false attractions of the cosmetic art.

80. I Will Lift Up Mine Eyes unto the Hills (Psalm 121).

One of the songs sung by Jewish pilgrims when going up to Mount Zion for religious celebrations. Zion was the hill in Jerusalem on which the city of David was built, and it became the centre of Jewish religion.

l. 6—*the moon*, belief in the evil influence of the moon was widespread.

81. The Earth is the Lord's (Psalm 24).

l. 12—*Jacob*, i.e. the God of Jacob.

l. 13—*gates*, i.e. of Zion (see note on previous Psalm).

83. Four Things (Proverbs).

l. 3—*conies*, rabbits.

83. The War Horse (Job).

In these lines God is speaking to Job of his own power as the creator of all animal life.

84. David's Lament (II Samuel).

The Israelites were beaten in a disastrous battle at Mount Gilboa by their enemies the Philistines. Saul and three of his sons, including Jonathan, were killed. This lamentation, which is the expression of passionate personal grief and patriotic bitterness in defeat, is thought to have been originally the genuine work of David.

l. 4–5—*Gath, Askelon*, cites of the Philistines.

l. 7—*the uncircumcised*, i.e. the Philistines (regarded by the Israelites as unclean).

l. 9—*nor fields of offerings*: the meaning is obscure; scholars suggest that the original means *ye fields of death.*

85. Vanity of Vanities (Ecclesiastes).

The approach of old age is described metaphorically as the coming of a storm.

l. 10–15—A description of failing physical powers. *The keepers of the house* have been explained *as the arms*; *the strong men* as *the legs*; *the grinders* as *the teeth*; *those that look out of the window* as *the eyes*, and *the doors* as *the lips*.

l. 16—*he shall rise up*, etc., i.e. he cannot sleep.

l. 17—*the daughters of music*, etc. (possibly), he can no longer take pleasure in music.

l. 18—*they shall be afraid*, etc., they will be afraid to climb heights (because of bodily feebleness).

l. 20—*the almond-tree shall flourish* (either), his hair shall whiten (or), he shall wake early (the almond being traditionally the first tree to blossom in spring).

l. 21—*the grasshopper*, etc., even such a tiny insect as the grasshopper becomes a burden.

l. 25—*the silver cord*, the cord from which the lamp of life (*the golden bowl*) is suspended.

l. 27–28—*the fountain, the cistern*, the well of life.

86. The Valley of Dry Bones (Ezekiel).

In 586 B.C. the Chaldeans under Nebuchadnezzar destroyed Jerusalem and carried off the remnant of the Hebrew inhabitants into exile in Babylonia. In their despair they thought of themselves as the mere dead bones of a great people. In a vision their prophet Ezekiel saw them delivered from their graves (i.e. captivity) and restored to power through the spirit of God.

87. Fain would I change that Note (Tobias Hume).

It is not certain that Captain Hume wrote this poem, which is preserved only in his musical setting of it. It is one of the most perfect songs in English, and is rarely sung in public or broadcast.

l. 2—*fond*, foolish.

l. 3—*by rote*, mechanically.

88. Death, be not Proud (John Donne).

Donne's passionate and restless intellect found its most characteristic expression in contradictions and paradoxes. The last line of this sonnet is typical. It was customary in the age of Donne to address Death as if it were all-powerful (e.g. in Shirley's *The Glories of our Blood and State*, p. 104), but Donne delights in taking the opposite point of view. Far from being all-powerful, Donne says, Death is 'slave to fate, chance, kings and desperate men'—that is, all these agencies *make use of*, and hence command, Death to carry out their designs.

89. At the Round Earth's Imagined Corners (John Donne).

Donne imagines four angels blowing their trumpets to summon the living and the dead to the last judgement. Then he pleads for delay in order that he may repent of his sins, which he says exceed those of all other men.

l. 5—*and fire shall o'erthrow*, one of the beliefs concerning the end of the world was that it would be accompanied by universal fire.

l. 7–8—*and you, whose eyes*, etc.; it was believed that people still alive on the day of judgement would pass directly into life everlasting without dying a mortal death.

89. The Anniversary (John Donne).

In notes to this and the following three poems by Donne I quote the summaries given in my *Selected Poems of John Donne* (Heinemann Educational Books).

'It is a year since we first fell in love. Everything except our love is a year nearer to final destruction. When we die, our bodies will be separated, but our souls, in which our love alone lives, will leave our bodies. We shall then enjoy perfect happiness—but no more than anyone else. It is here on earth, while we are still alive, that our true greatness appears. We two are each other's kings: and no other king ever had such subjects, nor was so safe from treason. Let us have no fears, real or imaginary, but live to enjoy a long and happy life.'

l. 18—*inmate*, lodger, visitor.

90. The Expiration (John Donne).

'We must part; let us not wait till someone comes to part us; we asked no one's leave to love, nor need we be beholden to anyone for the word of parting. Go, then; and if you still have life, kill me by telling me to go. If you are dead already, may my own word kill me, your murderer—unless I am already doubly dead by parting from you and telling you to go.'

91. A Valediction: Forbidding Mourning (John Donne).

Said to have been given to his wife on leaving for the Continent in 1611. 'Let our parting be silent and imperceptible, like the dying breath of a good man; let not violent sorrow show the world how much we love. Mere earthquakes cause fear and alarm: when the whole of creation moves, the movement is greater but causes no shock. The love of ordinary lovers is only of the senses, and is destroyed if absence separate their bodies. But our love is of so pure an essence, being assured of existence in each other's minds, that it is less disturbed by the separation of our bodies. Our two souls are one: my parting does not divide, but rather expands, them, like gold beaten out thin. We are like the two legs of a pair of compasses, yours the fixed one in the centre. The further my soul goes from yours, the more yours leans towards mine; and as mine comes home, so yours revives. Your soul is the centre of my being, and keeps mine constant as it circles around you.'

92. The Good-Morrow (John Donne).

'Our love is unique. All other pleasures are mere fancies, and all previous experience as unreal as a dream. We are, each to each, a complete world, like the two hemispheres, but without change or decline. Our love cannot change, because it is equal on both sides.'

l. 4—*the seven sleepers.* of Ephesus slept in a cave for 187 years.

93. A Dirge (John Webster).

A lament from Webster's tragedy *The White Devil*, embodying current beliefs about certain animals, e.g. the birds and the wolf.

94. To his son, Vincent Corbet (Richard Corbet).

Compare two other poems, Waley's *On the Birth of his Son* (p. 316) and Graves's *To Lucia at Birth* (p. 321). All three poems contain strong social criticism incorporated in their wishes for the child's future.

l. 12—*places*, positions in public life. Richard Corbet became a bishop.

95. A Complaint (Henry Farley).

A Puritan's condemnation of his age. References to the popular love of oddities and spectacles among the Elizabethans are common in the literature of the time.

l. 4—*engine*, any sort of mechanical contrivance.

l. 6—*Mad Tom*, Tom o' Bedlam, a beggar masquerading as a madman and singing ballads for charity; *roundelay*, a ballad with a chorus.

l. 8—*the Hope*, a theatre in Southwark used for bear-baiting.

l. 13—*motion*, proposal.

96. This World a Hunting is (William Drummond).

l. 2—*Nimrod*, proverbial name for a mighty hunter (from *The Book of Genesis*).

96. To Anthea who may Command Him Any Thing (Robert Herrick)

v. 1—*Protestant*, devoted champion.

v. 5—*cypress*, a tree symbolic of mourning.

98. Corinna's Going a Maying (Robert Herrick).

May Day (May 1st) was celebrated throughout England as the beginning of summer; houses were decked with flowers, the May Queen was chosen, the maypole was set up and there was dancing and feasting. Herrick describes this ceremony, not for the sake of its picturesque qualities, but partly also to draw a moral, and this is expressed in the last verse. Compare Shakespeare's *O Mistress Mine* (p. 60).

v. 1—*the blooming morn*, etc., Aurora, goddess of dawn, rises in the east, revealing the sun-god Apollo with his rays cut short by the mists; *fresh-quilted*, newly mingled; *each flower has wept*, in classical mythology dew-drops were the tears wept by flowers when ravished each morning by the rising sun; *the birds have matins said*, the birds, especially larks, worshipped the sun each morning; *profanation*, desecrating an occasion which should be holy.

v. 2—*foliage*, traditional may-day dress for girls was green; *Flora*, goddess of flowers; *orient pearls*, dew-drops; *Titan*, another name for the sun-god; *beads*, prayers counted on a rosary.

v. 3—*an ark, a tabernacle*, a basket-like structure or tent made of interwoven branches; *white-thorn*, hawthorn (i.e. 'may').

v. 4—*many a green gown*, etc., many 'engagements' have been made; *many a jest*, etc., many stories have been told about lovers' secret meetings.

v. 5—*take*, take advantage of.

100. VIRTUE (George Herbert).

v. 2—*angry and brave*, red as with anger, and bright.

v. 3—*sweets compacted lie*, sweet things are crowded together; *my music shows*, etc., the beauties of spring must end, like phrases or movements in music.

v. 4—*gives*, yields, breaks under pressure; *turn to coal*, become fuel, i.e. at the day of judgement.

Compare Donne's *At the Round Earth's Imagined Corners* (p. 89).

101. JORDAN II (George Herbert).

It is not quite certain why this poem is entitled *Jordan*, but the implication is that it is connected with Herbert's conversion from a worldly youth to a serious concern with religion. This poem is a plea for simplicity and a turning away from artificiality and contrivance in poetry.

l. 6—embellishing my meaning as if it were for sale.

l. 9—*blotted*, cancelled.

l. 10—Such and such a word or phrase was not lively enough, and such and such was dead.

l. 11–12—No words were rich enough to describe natural beauty, much less heavenly pleasures which far outdo pleasure in nature.

l. 14—In this way I made my poems a vehicle for mere self-expression, for the display of my own cleverness.

102. THE PULLEY (George Herbert).

Herbert imagines God, at the creation of man, having all the world's blessings (strength, beauty, etc.) in a single vessel and pouring them upon him so that they are concentrated into a man's lifetime. But he withholds the final gift of peace of mind, for if he had this, he would worship, not God, but God's gifts. As it is, there is a chance that the need for rest may send him back to God; rest is the pulley by means of which man is drawn to God.

102. THE QUIP (George Herbert).

The pleasures of the world, says Herbert, came to jeer at him for his religious devotion. He was tempted in turn by beauty, wealth, worldly glory and frivolous social intercourse, who each asked him whom he belonged to. He concluded by saying that God would answer for him and that the answer would be that he belonged to God.

l. 15—He gave me no more than a glance (so taken up was he with his own glory).

104. THE GLORIES OF OUR BLOOD AND STATE (James Shirley).

v. 1—*blood and state*, mortal condition, probably with other associated meanings (e.g. state can mean also nobility or rank, and civil state or commonwealth); *scythe and spade*, farm labourers.

v. 2—*plant fresh laurels*, etc., gain new glory from killing the enemy, *still*, always.

105. THE BUILDING OF PANDEMONIUM (John Milton).

When Satan and the other rebel angels were driven out of Heaven, one of the first things they did in Hell was to build an assembly hall, Pandemonium (All Demons).

l. 4—*womb*, interior.

l. 5—*the work of sulphur*, it was believed that sulphur converted earth into metal.

l. 10—*least erected*, basest.

l. 17—*centre*, i.e. of the earth.

l. 21—*admire*, be surprised.

l. 23—*bane*, deadly evil.

l. 25—*Babel*, Babylon; *Memphian*, Egyptian.

l. 33—*sluiced from the lake*, caused to flow from a lake of liquid fire near-by.

l. 34–35—*founded the massy ore*, etc., melted down the heavy ore and skimmed the impurities off the molten metal.

l. 42—*exhalation*, vapour.

l. 45—*Doric*, plain, severe; *overlaid*, surmounted.

l. 49—*Alcairo*, city in Egypt founded by the Assyrian conquerors.

l. 51—*Belus, Serapis*, gods of the Assyrians.

l. 63—*the architect*, Mammon.

l. 70—*Ausonian land*, Italy.

l. 71—*Mulciber*, another name for Vulcan.

107. THEY ERR WHO COUNT IT GLORIOUS TO SUBDUE (John Milton).

In *Paradise Regained* Satan tries to tempt Christ to accept worldly power and glory. Christ answers by distinguishing between the false glory of those who seek power by force of arms and the true glory of those who patiently accept God's will (like Job) and are prepared to suffer and even die for truth (like Socrates). Compare Shirley's *The Glories of our Blood and State* (p. 104) and Shelley's *Ozymandias* (p. 202).

l. 4—*worthies,* Milton refers ironically to the Nine Worthies of the ancient world, who were all renowned for military glory.

l. 14—*one is the son of Jove,* etc., the sort of names by which great conquerors called themselves, or were called.

l. 23—*thy wrongs,* i.e. the trials to which Satan subjected Job.

l. 26—*Socrates,* the Greek teacher and philosopher who was condemned to death in 399 B.C. on charges of impiety towards the gods, fabricated by his enemies and rivals.

108. SAMSON BLIND (John Milton).

Samson, captured by the Philistines, has had his eyes put out and is in prison, lamenting his fate among the enemies of his people. Milton himself had gone blind before writing his dramatic poem on Samson, and this passage is strongly autobiographical.

l. 4—*prime,* first.

l. 19—Why am I deprived of the benefit of God's first enactment?

l. 23—Milton here imagines the moon as retiring into a cave when it is not visible on earth. The sun is to Samson no more visible than the moon at such times.

110. TO THE LORD GENERAL CROMWELL, MAY 1652 (John Milton).

One of Milton's politico-religious propaganda sonnets. While expressing admiration of Cromwell after the success of the Parliamentarian cause in the Civil War, naming three of the Protector's victories, Milton warns him of what he foresaw as a danger to 'free conscience' in certain reactionary proposals put before the Committee for the Propagation of the Gospel. One proposal was aimed at Non-conformists, whose freedom to preach would be in the hands of the 'hireling wolves', i.e. the repressive and rapacious priests in the Church of England.

110. GRATIANA DANCING AND SINGING (Richard Lovelace).

v. 1—*that gave each winding,* etc., as she sang, her voice appeared to regulate the winding movements of her body.

v. 2—As her feet danced upon the floor (pavement), Gratiana, being like a star, made it like a heaven (firmament), which ceased therefore to envy the roof. In its pride the floor rose up like Atlas (who bore the heavens upon his shoulders), and heaven and all the Gods were combined in the person of Gratiana.

v. 4—*the harmonious spheres*: it was believed that as the stars circulated in their orbits (spheres), they made music which was inaudible to mortal ears.

111. Of the Death of Mr. William Hervey (Abraham Cowley).

v. 3—*where their hid treasures lie*, ghosts were supposed to haunt any place where they had hidden treasure when on earth.

v. 4—*Ledaean stars*, Castor and Pollux, the twin stars, were sons of Zeus and Leda; *toys*, foolish pastimes; *philosophy*, science. Notice how in the seventeenth century scientists were not specialists, but were interested also in poetry and the arts.

v. 5—*join*, pronounced 'jine' at that time.

v. 8—*yet never did his God*, etc., even in his mirth he never talked blasphemy or scandal.

v. 10—*the place now only free from those*, Heaven is now the only place free from ignorance and hypocrisy.

114. The Mower, to the Glow-worms (Andrew Marvell).

v. 2—*Ye country comets*, etc., comets were supposed to portend the coming death of a king; the glow-worms foretoid nothing more serious than the fall of the grass beneath the mower's scythe.

v. 3—*officious*, helpful; *foolish fires*, the will o' the wisp (Latin: *ignis fatuus*).

115. The Garden (Andrew Marvell).

Marvell took a prominent part in public affairs on the Parliament side. This poem expresses his feeling about an age of strife and civil war.

v. 1—*amaze*, trouble, bewilder; *palm*, *oak*, *bays*, tokens of victory in sport, war and art; *single*, poor, unimportant; *does prudently*, etc., in effect, nature appears to be saying to men, 'Are the rewards of your labour worth all your efforts? Would it not be better to enjoy the restfulness of nature?'

v. 3—Green trees are more worthy of love than women with their white skins and red lips.

v. 6—The mind withdraws from the outer world and loses consciousness of reality, the imagination creating an ideal world of perfect peace and beauty.

v. 7—*My soul*, etc., like a bird preparing for flight, my soul withdraws from the body's covering (vest) and prepares for its final destination.

v. 9—*this dial*, the garden is compared to a clock-face, on which the opening and closing flowers mark the progress of the day; *zodiac*, the series of constellations through which the sun is said to pass as the seasons progress, here represented by different flowers; *computes*, the bee, as it goes from flower to flower, appears to be calculating the time of day, so that it knows when to 'knock off'.

118. TO HIS COY MISTRESS (Andrew Marvell).

The 'moral' of this poem is the same as that of Herrick's *Corinna's Going a Maying* (p. 98). Marvell combines wit, passion and formal perfection in a way different from that of all other poets. The first section is an elaborately ironical account of the slow progress of love if the lady continues to be disdainful (*coy*); the second describes the uselessness of beauty and desire after death; the third section is a plea that they should enjoy their passion while they have life.

l. 10—*the conversion of the Jews*, to Christianity—that is, never.

l. 19—*state*, slow and stately adoration.

l. 20—*at lower rate*, on any less exalted terms.

l. 29—*quaint*, delicate, refined.

l. 40—*slow-chapt*, slow-jawed. The image is that of being devoured by time.

119. MAN (Henry Vaughan).

Vaughan contrasts the restlessness of men with the ordered regularity of nature. Compare Marvell's *The Garden* (p. 115) and Whitman's *Animals* (p. 231).

v. 1—*state*, orderly existence; *intercourse of times divide*, divide up their day with clockwork regularity.

v. 2—*the birds nor sow nor reap*, etc., the reference is to the Sermon on the Mount (Matt. VI 26–29).

v. 3—*still*, always; *toys*, vain pursuits.

v. 4—*some stones*, the loadstone, magnetic iron ore; *these looms*, the cares and complexities of life.

120. THE WORLD OF LIGHT (Henry Vaughan).

Like Dunbar in the *Lament for the Makers*, Vaughan mourns the death of others; but whereas Dunbar mourns because he himself must die too, Vaughan laments because his friends have gone to Heaven and he is left on earth. Vaughan was an intensely spiritual man, and his passionate desire to know what Heaven was like appears constantly in his poems. Contrast with this poem Hardy's *Friends Beyond* (p. 259).

v. 6—*well*, spring.

v. 7—Just as angels sometimes appear to us in dreams, so our thoughts may come upon some sudden revelation of Heaven.

v. 8—The idea of Heaven, like a star entombed, can illuminate our life; but when we are freed from life, how much more brightly will the vision shine.

v. 9—*resume*, take back.

v. 10—*perspective, glass*, telescope, i.e. imperfect human imagination which can gain only a dim and misty idea of Heaven.

122. A PASTORAL HYMN (John Hall).

v. 1—*rebound*, resound (in praise).

v. 3—*as rent*, the idea of rent is suggested by the similarity of autumn leaves to gold coins; *purple*, can also mean crimson.

123. SONG FOR ST. CECILIA'S DAY (John Dryden).

A song in honour of music, especially church music, of which Cecilia was patron saint.

v. 1—This verse refers to the ancient theory of the origin of the universe, according to which there was originally nothing but a disordered mass of atoms (of four types—hot, cold, moist and dry) which were reduced to order under the harmonising influence of music; *stations*, proper places; *the diapason*, etc., the majestic series of harmonious sounds concluding with the creation of man.

v. 2—*Jubal*, according to the book of Genesis, the father of harp and organ music; *corded shell*, a hollow shell with strings stretched across it, a more or less imaginary form of the lyre.

v. 4—*lute*, an instrument whose strings are plucked with the fingers, the usual accompaniment to a love-song in the seventeenth century. Its note is of the twanging, rather than warbling kind.

v. 6—*mend*, improve.

v. 7—*Orpheus*, according to Greek mythology, played his lyre so sweetly that beasts, and even inanimate objects, followed him; *sequacious* in pursuit.

v. 8—*untune* just as music assisted at the ordering of the universe at the time of creation, so it will also assist in the final disintegration on the day of judgement.

125. ACHITOPHEL (John Dryden).

Absalom and Achitophel is a satirical poem which describes, under biblical disguise, the rebellion of the Duke of Monmouth (*Absalom*) assisted by Lord Shaftesbury (*Achitophel*).

l. 1—*these*, the members of Monmouth's party.

l. 3—*close*, secret.

l. 9—*o'er informed*, etc., overanimated his body to the point of exhaustion.

l. 26—*the triple bond*, the alliance of England, Sweden and Holland against France.

l. 27—*Israel*, England.

127. SONGS FROM 'THE SECULAR MASQUE' (John Dryden).

A masque was a sort of miniature opera having a ceremonial or social purpose and based as a rule on some mythological subject. *The Secular Masque*, performed in 1700, celebrated the end of the century, and contained in satirical form Dryden's condemnation of the war-like and profligate age he had lived in. These two songs, sung by Momus, the god of mockery, contain the pith of his criticism. For social criticism of different periods, compare Shakespeare's *Tired with all these for Restful Death I Cry* (p. 63), Farley's *A Complaint* (p. 95), Wordsworth's *The World is too much with Us* (p. 173), and Hopkins' *The Sea and the Skylark* (p. 264). (1)—*cost and care*, expense and trouble. (2)—*thy chase had a beast in view*: addressed to Diana, goddess of hunting, who represents sport—the futile sport of chasing mere animals; *thy lovers were all untrue*; addressed to Venus, who represents the promiscuous love-making of court circles in Dryden's day.

128. A CATCH (Henry Aldrich).

A catch is a sort of humorous round for several voices. It was a popular amusement in the seventeenth century. Aldrich was a scholar. a theologian and Dean of Christ Church, Oxford.

128. LOVE AND LIFE (John Wilmot, Earl of Rochester).

This ingenious argument is typical of Restoration love poetry at its best—light, elegant, amoral and not certainly insincere. The present moment is all the life I can call mine and is wholly devoted to Phillis. It is therefore impossible to accuse me of infidelity. It is as much as we can expect that I should be faithful to you for this minute.

129. MARY THE COOK-MAID'S LETTER TO DR. SHERIDAN (Jonathan Swift).

The Rev. Dr. Sheridan, who kept a school, was one of Swift's Dublin companions. This mock protest was part of a kind of running game of wit carried on between the friends. What at first might strike a casual reader as mere doggerel shows the acuteness of Swift's ear for racy Irish speech and his sympathetic understanding of humble people. It is not great poetry, but it is humane.

l. 9—Note Mary's fondness for traditional wisdom.

l. 10—*hoddy doddy*, a short, squat fellow.

l. 16—*come-rogues*, drinking companions—Mary's corruption of 'comrades'.

l. 23—To 'tell the truth and shame the devil' is another proverbial expression.

l. 27—*Saunders,* Swift's name for his manservant, Alexander McGee.

l. 33—*direct,* address.

131. A Description of a City Shower (Jonathan Swift).

This admirably concrete and graphic piece of description is a blend of simple and natural writing with elements of satire in passages where Swift is parodying the high-flown, artificial style of much of the descriptive poetry of his time.

l. 2—*prognostics,* signs, portents.

l. 3—*depends,* is imminent.

l. 5—*sink,* probably the sewer.

l. 10—*aches,* then pronounced as two syllables—aitches.

l. 11—*Delman,* an imaginary name for a grumbler.

l. 14—Throws a black cloud over the sky.

l. 20—*flirts,* flicks.

l. 32—*devoted,* doomed as by the gods.

l. 33—*Daggled,* mud-splashed.

l. 34—*cheapen,* bargain for.

l. 38—*umbrella,* made of oiled silk, this was considered fit only for use by women.

l. 51—*Laoco'n,* see *Aeneid Book,* II 50–53.

l. 53—*kennels,* gutters.

l. 58—*Smithfield or St. Pulchre's,* the cattle-market or St. Sepulchre's Church near Holborn conduit. Here waters from Smithfield and Snow Hill join and fall into Fleet Ditch.

133. Where'er You Walk (Alexander Pope).

The pastoral convention in poetry, derived from the Greek poet Theocritus, was employed by the majority of English poets from the early sixteenth to the mid-eighteenth century. It enabled them to write about real life in a setting of artificial rural simplicity, and to disguise themselves, their friends and the people around them as shepherds and shepherdesses with classical names.

l. 2—*Elisium,* the abode of the gods.

l. 3—*Adonis,* a beautiful youth loved by Venus, goddess of love.

l. 4—*Diana,* goddess of chastity, the moon goddess.

l. 5—*lovely nymph,* the maiden with whom the shepherd Alexis is in love.

l. 8—*Ceres,* goddess of the corn.

l. 15–18—*Where'er you walk,* etc., these four lines were incorporated in Handel's opera *Semele.*

l. 20—*invoke the Muses*, call upon the spirit of poetry for aid.

134. The Faithless Lover (Alexander Pope).

v. 3—*Arcturus*, one of the constellation Boötes.

v. 4—*Pan*, god of shepherds.

136. Sporus (Alexander Pope).

Pope's satirical portrait of Lord Hervey, a personal and political enemy. Compare Dryden's portrait of Shaftesbury (*Achitophel*, p. 125).

l. 1—'*What? that thing of silk*', the passage in quotation-marks is supposed to be said by Pope's friend Arbuthnot.

l. 2—*ass's milk*, prescribed as a tonic for weak constitutions.

l. 4—*who breaks a butterfly*, etc., i.e. why use powerful satire to destroy such a flimsy adversary?

l. 6—*painted child*, Hervey was a fop who used rouge.

l. 7—*whose buzz*, he was a notorious scandal-monger.

l. 10—*mumbling*, mouthing.

l. 15—*Eve*, Queen Caroline.

l. 25—*now trips a lady*, minces like a lady (a reference to Hervey's effeminate manner).

l. 26—*Rabbins*, Hebrew writers. (It is not known where they thus describe Satan.)

l. 28—*parts* talents, abilities.

137. Epistle to Miss Blount (Alexander Pope).

These lines, originally intended for Teresa Blount, but later addressed to her younger sister Martha (who, unlike Teresa, did not attend the coronation of George I in London in 1714) are a very good example of the witty and familiar *vers de société* produced by eighteenth century poets.

l. 4—*spark*, gay and flirtatious young man (the 'dear man' of the next line).

l. 7—*Zephalinda*, an imaginary name for Miss Blount.

l. 13—*assembly*, fashionable town gatherings

l. 15—*Bohea*, a kind of tea.

l. 18—*exact at noon*, the main meal of the day was earlier in the country. In London it might be as late as 3 p.m.

l. 23—*rack*, torment.

l. 24—*whisk*, whist; *sack*, dry white wine.

l. 26—*smacking buss*, resounding kiss

l. 38—*flirt*, flick or whisk (of the fan).

l. 41—*your slave*, i.e. the writer, Pope.

l. 45—*points*, visualises.

l. 46—*Parthenia*, a different girl.

l. 47—*Gay*, the poet John Gay was a close friend of Pope.

l. 28—*coxcombs*, foolish town gallants.

139. ON THE DEATH OF MR. ROBERT LEVET, A PRACTISER IN PHYSIC (Samuel Johnson).

Levet was surgeon to Johnson's household. Johnson was always profoundly affected by the death of friends and himself had a morbid fear of death.

l. 7—*officious*, helpful, considerate (not the same meaning as now).

l. 10—*obscurely wise*, Levet's knowledge was not recognised in medical circles.

l. 11—*letter'd arrogance*, the arrogance of doctors with official qualifications. Levet had no letters after his name.

l. 22—He was not too proud to accept small fees.

l. 27–28—It is certain that God found Levet's modest abilities made the most of. The reference is to the parable of the talents.

140. ELEGY WRITTEN IN A COUNTRY CHURCHYARD (Thomas Gray).

v. 7—*glebe*, ploughland.

v. 8—*ambition*, ambitious people; *grandeur*, people of rank and importance.

v. 9—*the boast of heraldry*, etc., the pride of noble ancestry, the ceremony associated with positions of power in public life; *th' inevitable hour*, death.

v. 11—*can storied urn*, etc., can elaborate funeral monuments bring back the dead to life?

v. 12—*pregnant with celestial fire*, full of divine inspiration; *hands that the rod of empire*, etc., one who might have been a great ruler or a great poet.

v. 13—*penury*, poverty.

v. 15—*Hampden*, an M.P. and a man of national importance; *some Cromwell*, a potential national leader who might not have engaged in civil war.

v. 16—*list'ning senates*, legislative assemblies (such as the British House of Commons).

v. 17—*nor circumscribed alone*, etc., their obscurity prevented them not only from making the most of their good qualities, but also from committing public crimes.

v. 18—*the struggling pangs*, etc., their obscure fate also prevented them from becoming liars and hypocrites, and from living a life of luxury and display, flattered by poets (followers of the Muses). This applies to some of the great men of Gray's time.

v. 19—*the noiseless tenour of their way*, the uneventful course of their lives.

v. 21—*spelt by th' unlettered Muse*, etc., the clumsy gravestones of the poor, with their illiterate inscriptions, replace the elaborate monuments of the great, and the biblical texts inscribed on them reconcile rustic readers to the thought of death.

v. 24–29—Gray is thinking of himself as the writer of 'these lines' in memory of 'th' unhonoured dead', and imagines some old countryman telling the passer-by (*some kindred spirit*) how he used to notice the poet in his wanderings or frequenting the beech-woods.

v. 30–32—Gray's epitaph on a somewhat fanciful picture of himself.

145. My Cat Jeoffry (Christopher Smart).

At the age of 34 Smart, a failed Cambridge don and conventional minor poet, was confined in a madhouse, suffering from some kind of religious mania, harmless enough except to the susceptibilities of workaday people. Here he wrote his two great religious poems, *Song to David* and *Jubilate Agno*. These represent a complete break with tradition. They show startling originality and imaginative power, and are consequently labelled 'naïve' by academic critics. Anyone who has lived with and observed cats will recognise the strength, truth and humour of this passage from *Jubilate Agno*.

148. The Loss of the 'Royal George' (William Cowper).

Written in answer to a request for words to fit the melody of Handel's March from *Scipio*, this poem is based on an actual disaster. (The facts are more or less as Cowper gives them, but the official explanation, that the ship over-balanced, was not true; what really happened was that the bottom of the ship was rotten and fell out. This was not known to Cowper and has no bearing on the poem.) It is a poem which strikes some readers as supremely commonplace, others as a masterpiece. These facts should be noticed: the language is extremely simple (count the number of words of more than one syllable), the story is told with absolute straightforwardness and no false emotion or rhetoric, the verse-form is managed with practically no distortion of the natural word-order.

v. 1—*fast by*, close by (i.e. in Portsmouth harbour).

v. 4—*Kempenfelt*, the *Royal George* was the admiral's flagship.

v. 7—*weigh the vessel up*, an unsuccessful attempt was later made to salvage the ship.

149. To Mary (William Cowper).

The melancholy warmth of this poem derives from Cowper's real love of and regard for the widow, Mary Unwin, who looked after him and helped to preserve, as far as possible, his mental balance during his latter years. They were engaged in 1773 but, as usually happened when Cowper was about to take any decisive step, he had a mental breakdown. He never married. Mary became paralysed in 1791. In this poem and especially the next, *The Shrubbery*, Cowper demonstrates his power to express real feeling within the confines of form and diction of late Augustan poetry.

154. THE TYGER (William Blake).

Notice that there is not a single statement in this poem. In a series of urgent, half-incoherent questions, Blake expresses what to him was one of the central mysteries of creation. How could a creator who made the lamb, symbol of defenceless innocence, also make something so terrifying, cruel and deadly as the tiger? This is the question Blake asks, but he is not concerned here with the answer; the poem is simply the passionate expression of his sense of mystery and terror. It may be that the Tyger and the Lamb represent two aspects of Christ—the Christ who brought 'not peace but a sword' and the Christ who went 'as a Lamb to the slaughter'. But it is not necessary to understand all the possible implications of Blake's imagery in order to appreciate the force and splendour of the poem.

v. 3—*and what dread feet?* It may help us to understand what was in Blake's mind, if we read the line that follows this in another version of the poem:

Could fetch it from the furnace deep?

v. 5—*When the stars threw down their spears*, etc. This seems to mean, When the stars gave up their task of guarding heaven and began to weep, so terrible was the newly created beast, how could God show pleasure at what he had done? (The earlier version reads, 'Dare he laugh his work to see?') Or *spears* may mean simply 'rays', and *threw down their spears* would thus mean 'ceased to shed light'. In either case, the general sense is that the stars showed consternation at God's action.

155. A POISON TREE (William Blake).

The story in this poem is not intended to be taken in any literal sense; the feeling that Blake conveys is of the deadly power of anger when concealed and allowed to increase by means of fear and deceit. No amount of explanation can make us accept the terrible force of this lesson; we can only feel it.

156. THE SWORD AND THE SICKLE (William Blake).

See *Introduction* (p. xliv).

156. AND DID THOSE FEET IN ANCIENT TIME (William Blake).

v. 2—*mills,* factories.

157. AH! SUN-FLOWER (William Blake).

Of this poem F. W. Bateson says: 'There is a golden world beyond and above the iron world of experience, where the frustrations of sex will no longer make themselves felt.'

157. LONDON (William Blake).

An apocalyptic vision of the terrible fate of London as a result of restrictions on liberty, poverty, pollution by the smoke of industry, war, prostitution and disease.

l. 1–2—*chartered,* restricted by charters giving power over the city to the corporation.

l. 7—*ban,* Bateson points out that this means, not 'restriction' but 'bane' or 'curse'.

l. 8—*mind-gorged,* forged *for* (not 'by') men's minds.

158–159. HOLY THURSDAY (from *Songs of Innocence* and of *Experience*—William Blake).

Two parallel poems on the annual services held on Ascension Day in St. Paul's Cathedral for children attending London's many charity schools.

161. I MURDER HATE BY FIELD OR FLOOD (Robert Burns).

This witty and rumbustious poem exemplifies the side of Burns which his Victorian admirers liked to suppress. Its meaning is summed up in the contemporary slogan 'Make love, not war'.

l. 9—*Socrates* committed suicide because he would not compromise his political principles.

l. 11—*Leonidas,* the Spartan general, was killed while opposing the Persians at Thermopylae.

l. 12—*Cato* was a Roman patriot who opposed Caesar and committed suicide when the anti-Caesar cause was lost.

l. 15–16—*Zimri* the Israelite during the time of Moses was slain by one of his countrymen when in the arms of the Midianite woman Cozbi (*Numbers* h. 25).

162. ANNA (Robert Burns).

One of Burn's poems in the Lowland Scots dialect.

l. 10—The Indus is in Asia, the Savannah in South America—the line thus means 'From east to west'.

l. 18—*Diana,* the moon, goddess of night.

l. 19—*Ilk,* each.

WALY, WALY THE SEEDS OF LOVE THE LOWLANDS OF HOLLAND

These three examples of English anonymous traditional verse at its best are given a place towards the end of the 18th century, because this seems to have been about the time when these songs took their present form. All true folk songs are found in many different versions, and there are versions of these three which can be traced back to a period far earlier than the 18th century. It will be noted that all three are concerned with love from the woman's point of view, and are distinguished by natural and true feeling, simplicity and directness, and beauty of imagery.

164. WALY WALY: the significance of this title is not known.

165. THE SEEDS OF LOVE.

l. 5—*gardener,* possibly Cupid is meant.

l. 7—The violet was traditionally a symbol of modesty, the lily of chastity, and the pink of courtesy.

l. 13—The rose was a symbol of uncontrolled passion.

l. 16—The willow was traditionally associated with desertion by a lover.

l. 21–24—This consoling last stanza does not appear in all versions.

167. STRANGE FITS OF PASSION HAVE I KNOWN (William Wordsworth).

Nothing is known for certain as to whether Lucy, the subject of this poem and the next two, really existed.

v. 1—*fits,* sudden delusions.

v. 7—*fond,* foolish.

168. SHE DWELT AMONG THE UNTRODDEN WAYS (William Wordsworth).

Wordsworth believed that poetry should be, as nearly as possible, the direct expression of feeling, unadorned by poetic diction and free from stock images. He expresses his feeling for Lucy with the utmost simplicity; but simplicity like this does not come naturally, it comes only from intense thought and careful self-discipline. Contrast with these poems the love-poems of Shakespeare, Herrick and Marvell.

v. 1—*Dove,* a river in Westmoreland.

v. 2—The simile of the violet and the star are introduced not because of a vague suggestion of something beautiful, but because of certain quite precise qualities which Wordsworth associates with Lucy. What are these qualities?

173. THE WORLD IS TOO MUCH WITH US (William Wordsworth).

l. 1—*The world is too much with us,* we are too much concerned with material things.

l. 3—*little we see,* etc., we cannot truly possess the beauty of nature (because we are preoccupied with worldly cares).

l. 4—*a sordid boon,* a doubtful benefit, since our hearts are so mean and worldly.

l. 10—*Pagan,* i.e. Greek of pre-Christian times.

l. 13–14—*Proteus, Triton,* sea-deities of the ancient Greeks; *wreathed,* curled in a spiral.

173. SKATING (William Wordsworth).

This passage is from a long autobiographical poem, *The Prelude.* Wordsworth presents the scene to our eyes and ears with exactness and vividness, but his purpose is far from being merely descriptive. In his imagery and his rhythm he conveys also the rapture he had experienced as a boy and the sense of union with nature which he later regarded as his most important formative influence. Notice how, for example, in the last picture Wordsworth is concerned, not with mere physical sensation, but with the feeling of being for a few moments at the very centre of the universe.

l. 26—*reflex,* reflection.

175. NUTTING (William Wordsworth).

Wordsworth writes of his early love of nature as of a feeling more passionate and personal than any other poet ever experienced towards nature. Contrast, for example, Spenser's lines on the same subject, *When Flowered My Joyful Spring* (p. 50). He writes of nature here as of a maiden whom, in tearing a branch from a tree, he attacks with brutal exultation. He expresses his sense of guilt and shame and appeals to the guardian spirit of nature to heal the wounds he has caused.

l. 11—*by exhortation,* etc., as my thrifty mother had bidden me.

l. 12—*motley accoutrement,* etc., an assortment of clothes well able to defy thorns and undergrowth.

177. KUBLA KHAN (Samuel Taylor Coleridge).

Much has been made of two matters which have nothing to do with our appreciation of this poem: first, the various sources of Coleridge's information about the historical Kubla and his palace of pleasure; secondly, the circumstances in which the poem was composed. It is interesting to know that it is only a fragment of a poem dreamed by Coleridge under the effects of opium, and that the rest of the poem is irrecoverably lost owing to an untimely interruption. But we must read and appreciate the poem as we have it, remembering Coleridge's own words, 'nothing can permanently please which does not contain in itself the reason why it is so, and not otherwise.' In short, we must value *Kubla Khan*, not for any incidental interest in its origin, but for the beauty and completeness of the poetic world it creates.

l. 1–5—See *Introduction* (p. xxxi); *Kubla Khan*, a thirteenth-century Mongolian ruler.

l. 13—*athwart a cedarn cover*, across a cedar wood.

l. 15–16—*as e'er beneath a waning moon*, etc., Coleridge here introduces the romantic and magical associations of the folk-lore on which are based some of the old ballads, see *The Daemon Lover* (p. 12).

l. 19—*momently* in sudden, short bursts.

l. 25—*five miles meandering*, etc., it is worth while studying this line as an example of Coleridge's command of sound-effects. The long open vowels and the alliterative use of the letter 'm' compel the reader to slow down his pace and linger on the line, in exact imitation of the scene described.

l. 33—*measure*, music.

l. 37—*dulcimer*, a stringed instrument (here introduced for the musical quality of its name and for its biblical associations).

l. 41—*Abora*, mountain in Abyssinia (mentioned for its general suggestion of remoteness and strangeness rather than with any geographical precision). Coleridge is carefully building up a picture of an ideal world of delight and harmony, full of varied associations with whatever is romantically distant, both in time and in space, from the ordinary, everyday world.

l. 42—*Could I revive within me*, etc., these lines contain the real meaning of the poem, the significance of the dream picture. It now becomes clear that what Coleridge is expressing is his conviction of the power of poetry—or rather, of what should be the power of poetry. 'Had I the power to enchant, as the Abyssinian maid enchanted me in my vision, I would be able to re-create the perfect beauty of Kubla's palace. I would be acclaimed by all as a prophet divinely inspired, drawing nourishment direct from Paradise, the original source of ideal happiness.'

179. THE RIME OF THE ANCIENT MARINER (Samuel Taylor Coleridge).

Coleridge has a supernatural and romantic story to tell, far removed (like *Kubla Khan*) from the everyday world. In order to make his story acceptable to modern readers and to achieve 'that willing suspension of disbelief for the moment, which constitutes poetic faith', Coleridge composed his story in the form and manner of the old ballads. Thus his readers could feel they were entering into a different, but not less real, world. So brilliant is the descriptive imagery, so passionate and urgent the expressions of emotion (guilt, horror, repentance, thankfulness and so on), that the reader has no difficulty in accepting the reality of the experience described. Had Coleridge been a lesser poet, the poem would have been a failure, like most modern 'mock-ballads'. But *The Ancient Mariner* is no mock-ballad; it is a profoundly real and moving story of certain phases of Coleridge's experience, and in that of most sensitive people. Yet there is no need to regard the poem in the first place as the story of 'a soul in agony'; it can also have intense excitement for a reader who looks for no more than a supernatural tale, told in strikingly original language, full of music and colour.

Part I, *v.* 3—*loon*, idiot; *eftsoons*, at once.

v. 14—*clifts*, cliffs; *ken*, recognise.

v. 15—*swound*, swoon, fainting-fit.

v. 19—*vespers*, evenings.

v. 20—Notice how the guest's interruption prepares for the mariner's dramatic climax.

Part II, *v.* 3—*averr'd*, asserted.

v. 4—*uprist*, rose. Coleridge's marginal note to this verse is important.

Part III, *v.* 2—*wist*, thought.

v. 9—*gossameres*, spiders' webs.

v. 12—The meaning of this passage is that the mariner's companions are destined to die from hunger, thirst and exposure, while the mariner himself is to undergo a living death, an agony of pain and loneliness, a sort of paralysis of the soul. (The condition is known nowadays as neurasthenia or nervous breakdown.)

v. 17—*like the whizz of my cross-bow*: why does Coleridge introduce this comparison, so daring as to verge on the ridiculous?

Part IV, *v.* 14–15—The soul of the mariner begins to be healed as soon as he is able to give a spontaneous blessing to the water-snakes: no sooner is he able to recognise and feel thankful for the beauty of life in other creatures, than he begins to feel life revive in himself.

Part V, *v.* 5—*sere*, withered and brown, like autumn leaves.

v. 6—*fire-flags sheen*, lightning-flashes shone.

Part VI, *v.* 7—*charnel dungeon*, prison vault in which dead bodies were placed.

v. 20—*rood*, cross, *seraph*, angel of light and love.

v. 25—*shrieve*, pardon.

Part VII, *v.* 5—*ivy-tod*, clump or bush of ivy.

202. OZYMANDIAS (Percy Bysshe Shelley).

l. 7—*these lifeless things*, the remains of the statue.

l. 8—*the hand that mocked them*, the sculptor's hand that mocked the passions of Ozymandias. ('Hand' is the object of the verb 'survived'); *the heart that fed*, the heart of Ozymandias which nourished his passions.

l. 11—*Look on my works, ye Mighty*, etc., the irony of this line contains the point of the poem. Ozymandias of course meant, 'Despair of ever rivalling my works'. Shelley means, 'Despair of defying the ravages of time by works of mere material grandeur'.

l. 14—Notice the effect of the open vowels and the alliterations in this line.

203. ODE TO THE WEST WIND (Percy Bysshe Shelley).

Poets of the Romantic period thought of the world of men as sordid and materialistic. Wordsworth's sonnet, *The World is too much with Us*, expresses this point of view. They regarded the old kingdoms of Europe as the relics of a corrupt and bankrupt social order. Revolutionary ideas had spread from America and France, and idealistic dreams of the regeneration of mankind were in the air. Shelley believed passionately in the importance of the poet's part in this regeneration, and the *Ode to the West Wind* is his expression of this belief. The west wind in autumn strips the old foliage from the trees and scatters the seeds of future growth: 'Let me', he says at the end of the poem, 'be the voice of the west wind, spreading among mankind the prophecy of a new and better world.'

Stanza I, *l.* 4—*hectic*, feverish.

l. 11—*driving sweet buds*, the spring wind forces open the buds, as lambs are driven out into open pasture.

Stanza II, *l.* 4—*angels*, messengers, forerunners.

l. 7—*Maenad*, in Greek mythology a wild, half insane spirit of the woods and mountains who followed the god Dionysos, her head crowned with ivy or snakes.

l. 8—*zenith*, the highest point of the sky.

l. 9–14—*Thou dirge*, etc. The west wind is called a lament for the dying year, of which the last night will be an immense tomb filled with black clouds pouring out rain, lightning and hail.

Stanza III, *l.* 4—*pumice*, lava (from Vesuvius). *Baiae*, on the gulf of Naples.

l. 11—*the sea-blooms*, etc., according to Shelley's note, 'The vegetation at the bottom of the sea, of rivers, and of lakes, sympathises with that of the land in the change of seasons, and is consequently influenced by the winds which announce it.'

l. 14—*despoil themselves*, shed their foliage.

206. Pleasant Sounds (John Clare).

This poem, found among the manuscript copies of the poems written by Clare while he was in Northampton Asylum, is not certainly by Clare. But it shows the minute and accurate observation of nature which is typical of him, and the simple, exquisite pleasure which he found in the life of birds and small animals. It is a very early example of the kind of writing known as impressionism, which aims at conveying as faithfully as possible the sensuous impressions derived from appearances, without reference to thoughts about, or intellectual knowledge of, the things described. Contrast an earlier writer Herrick *Corinna's going a Maying*, (p. 98) who sees nature with the eyes of a classical scholar. To Clare a dew-drop is a dew-drop, not a tear wept by a flower when ravished by the sun-god Apollo; a lark is a lark, not a chorister singing at the gate of Heaven. With this attitude to nature goes complete freedom from any fixed verse-form; Clare uses the rhythm of everyday speech in order to convey with greater accuracy and spontaneity the precise impression he aims at. Compare the free verse of later writers, Whitman, Lawrence and others.

207. Autumn (John Clare).

In contrast to the previous one, this poem is composed in an elaborate verse-form; the metre is anapaestic and there are internal rhymes.

v. 2—*gossamers twitter*, spiders' webs tremble.

v. 3—*Eternity*: with the grass burnt up by the drought and the soil parched and cracked, the earth looks, not like the familiar ever-changing earth we know, but like some vision of eternity, changeless and inhuman.

207. Badger (John Clare).

Clare was not a propagandist against cruelty, but a poet—a man of his time concerned with the passions of his fellow men. What he does here is to record with graphic objectivity one of the crueller country sports of his time, but it is impossible not to feel that his sympathies are engaged on the side of the hunted creature. His entire avoidance of sentimentality is characteristic.

209. Country Letter (John Clare).

A deeply sympathetic picture of a country household upset by the absence and apparent neglect of one of its members. This is achieved without condescension, false sentiment or overstatement.

l. 29–30—Letters had to be collected from coach stations, and were not delivered to the door.

210. I Am (John Clare).

Written in Northampton County Asylum, this is an expression of the utter isolation and desolation of Clare's last 27 years.

211. ODE TO AUTUMN (John Keats).

A blend of impressionism (see note on Clare's *Pleasant Sounds*) and the personification so common in eighteenth-century poetry (see verse II). Compare Keats' thought in the last verse with that of Shelley's *Ode to the West Wind* (p. 203); compare also Clare's picture of autumn in the poem immediately before this one, and Hulme's *Autumn* (p. 297).

v. I—*gourd*, fleshy fruit like a melon or marrow.

v. II—*winnowing*, that separates chaff from grain; *swath*, row of corn cut by the scythe; *gleaner*, one who collected stray stalks of corn left by the reapers. The sheaf of gleanings would be carried home on the head.

v. III—*bàrred clouds*, making what is called a mackerel sky; *sallows*, willows; *hilly bourn*, hillside that bounds the view; *croft*, enclosed land by a house.

212. LA BELLE DAME SANS MERCI (John Keats).

In this poem Keats does not merely imitate the form and style of the old ballads, he expresses the sense of romance and mystery produced in a modern reader by thoughts of the medieval world of chivalry. The title (meaning 'The Pitiless Fair Lady') is also that of a medieval French poem.

v. 4—*meads*, meadows.

v. 5—*zone*, girdle.

v. 7—*mannadew*, a sweet secretion from the bark of certain trees.

v. 8—*grot*, cave.

v. 9—*latest*, last.

214. IN A DREAR-NIGHTED DECEMBER (John Keats).

v. 1—*the north cannot undo them*, they cannot feel the keen north wind; *nor frozen thawings*, etc., they cannot be prevented from budding in spring by ice formed from snow which has melted and fallen on them.

v. 2—*Apollo's summer look*, the look of the sun in summer; *they stay their crystal fretting*, their clear rippling ceases; *petting*, complaining.

v. 3—*was never said in rhyme*, no poet ever expressed the sense of pain which comes from the consciousness of lost happiness.

215. [SONNET] WRITTEN ON A BLANK PAGE IN SHAKESPEARE'S POEMS (John Keats).

l. 4—*eremite*, hermit.

216. To a Friend (Hartley Coleridge).

Hartley, son of Samuel Taylor Coleridge, was one of the best sonnet writers in English. He is here regretting the loss of the unself-conscious happiness of childhood, when he was in love with a companion without being aware of it. Love for a human being has replaced the love of nature.

l. 5—The subject of 'subdued' is 'peace' (line 3). Any tendency to wilfulness on our part was controlled by the sense of peace derived from nature. Hartley was brought up in the English Lake District.

216. 'Tis Strange To Me . . . (Hartley Coleridge).

To remove from the country, where I was part of a familiar community, to a big city gives me a sense of isolation and alienation.

218. Now Fades the Last Long Streak of Snow (Alfred, Lord Tennyson).

Section CXIV of the long poem *In Memoriam*, in which Tennyson mourns the death of his friend Arthur Hallam.

v. 1—*burgeons*, bud or sprout; *maze of quick*, thicket of hawthorn or other hedging shrub. The choice of the word 'quick' suggests also the other meaning, 'sensitive', 'painful to the touch', and this gives a clue to the writer's state of mind; *violets*, symbol of faithfulness.

v. 3—*lights*, probably sunlight passing through moving branches.

v. 4—*greening gleam*, an effect of sunlight on the sea; *brood*, sit on their eggs.

v. 5—*violet*, in comparing his grief with the violet, Tennyson recalls the image in *v.* 1. The contrast between the happy, purposeful activities of the spring creatures and the pain of reawakening grief is left unstated, and is all the more poignant because of the *superficial* resemblance between the two.

219. Tithonus (Alfred, Lord Tennyson).

Tithonus, son of one of the kings of Troy, married Aurora, goddess of dawn. In answer to his request she gave him immortality, but he forgot to ask for eternal youth; in consequence he grew older and more and more decrepit; finally Aurora turned him into a grasshopper. Tennyson imagines him in extreme old age, lamenting the weariness and wretchedness of life, and begging that he may die like other men. Compare *Vanity of Vanities* (p. 85).

l. 18—*thy strong Hours*, time is imagined as indignant at the granting of immortality to a mortal.

l. 21—*in presence of immortal youth*, i.e. with Aurora, who as a goddess would have the gift of immortal youth.

l. 30—*pass beyond the goal*, etc., live longer than the time allowed to men by the laws (ordinance) of nature.

l. 34—*the old mysterious glimmer*, the light of dawn.

l. 39—*blind the stars*, cause the stars to fade; *the wild team*, the horses which draw the chariot of dawn.

l. 44—*before thine answer given*, before you give your answer to my repeated request to lose my immortality.

l. 63—*Ilion*, Troy.

l. 76—*silver wheels*, i.e. of her chariot.

221. ULYSSES (Alfred, Lord Tennyson).

Tennyson expresses, through the lips of the aged Ulysses, man's unfailing desire for change, for discovery, for new experience. Ulysses, king of Ithaca, is here imagined as weary of the years of inactivity which followed his return from the voyage described in Homer's *Odyssey*, and about to start on a new voyage to the extreme west of the known world.

l. 3–4—*mete and dole Unequal laws*, administer unjust laws.

l. 10—*Hyades*, seven stars supposed to bring rain.

l. 24–28—*Life piled on life*, etc., many successive lives would be too short to taste all experience: I have only one life, and that is nearly over. But each hour left to me is not only an hour saved from the silence of eternal death, but also a bringer of new experience.

l. 29—*suns*, summers (Ulysses thinks he may have three more years to live).

l. 47—*frolic*, light-hearted.

l. 63—*Happy Isles*, Hesperia, land of the blest, where the souls of heroes went, supposed to be at the extreme west of the Mediterranean.

l. 64—*Achilles*, Greek hero during the Trojan war. Accounts of his death vary.

l. 66—*strength*, strong company.

l. 68—*one equal temper*, etc., men of equal courage and determination.

224. A TOCCATA OF GALUPPI'S (Robert Browning).

Baldassare Galuppi was an eighteenth-century Venetian composer and musician. A toccata is a piece of music for a keyboard instrument, intended to show off dexterity of touch; it has a lively rhythm which Browning here imitates. Browning imagines himself hearing this composition, which calls up the vain, frivolous life of eighteenth-century Venice; a pair of lovers break off their conversation to listen to the master with an air of condescension. They and all they stood for have long been extinct. As Browning meditates on their fate, he imagines the dead composer passing severe judgment on his Venetian contemporaries; and yet, he thinks, among these foolish, worldly people there had after all been beauty, charm and the warmth of life; he has not the heart to condemn, and suddenly feels old and chilly.

v. 1—*misconceive*, misunderstand.

v. 2—*St. Mark's*, the Cathedral (where Galuppi was in charge of the music); *the Doges*, every year the Doge (chief magistrate) performed a symbolic marriage ceremony with the sea (indicative of the sea-power of the Venetian republic) by dropping a ring over the side of his state barge.

v. 3—*Shylock's bridge*, the Rialto Bridge; *it's as if I saw it all*, Galuppi's music calls up a picture of Venetian life.

v. 6—*clavichord*, Browning possibly means harpsichord, of which Galuppi was a celebrated player. The clavichord is also a keyboard instrument, popular at this time.

v. 7—In this and the next two verses Browning interprets some imaginary musical passages in terms of human feelings. *Lesser* (minor) *thirds, diminished sixths, suspensions, solutions, the dominant, octave*—all these are harmonic effects suggestive of the moods Browning attributes to them.

v. 8—A lovers' dialogue suggested by the music.

v. 12–14—The dead Galuppi tells Browning how the fops and coquettes of his Venice were, like butterflies, doomed to extinction (dust and ashes), while no doubt he (Browning) with his knowledge of science would never die.

v. 15—And yet, Browning concludes, were they not beautiful, and do not I, in spite of all my knowledge and philosophy, lack youth and warmth?

227. MY LAST DUCHESS (Robert Browning).

The unnamed Duke of Ferrara in Lombardy is bargaining with the Count's envoy about the dowry to be paid by the Count on the proposed marriage of his daughter with the Duke. In censuring his last Duchess, whom he has had murdered ('I gave commands') for no other fault than her instinctive delight in beautiful things and her free expression of gratitude to those who gave her them, he unconsciously reveals his own jealous, proud and greedy nature. The painter, Frà Pandolf, and the sculptor, Claus of Innsbruck, are imaginary.

l. 8—*glance*: the Duchess's look is evidently one of innocent delight, an expression which the jealous Duke disapproves of. Evidently the sitter expressed in her face the pleasure that some casual compliment by the painter had evoked.

Note: for a critical questionnaire on this poem, see *Inside Poetry* (Reeves and Seymour-Smith, H.E.B.).

230. Beginning My Studies (Walt Whitman).

Like Wordsworth earlier, and Lawrence later, Whitman mistrusted the *mind* of civilised man; he here expresses delight in the senses, and the desire to express in his poems simply the joy given by the world around him. The free-verse form preserves the freshness of his utterance. Compare Clare's *Pleasant Sounds* (p. 206).

230. After the Sea-ship (Walt Whitman).

An attempt to convey the *feeling* of the sea, without drawing any conclusions from the impressions described. This poem should be read aloud. Compare Lawrence's *Spray* (p. 298).

231. Animals (Walt Whitman).

Compare Wordsworth's *Lines Written in Early Spring* (p. 169).

232. Native Moments (Walt Whitman).

This expression of the desire to throw off all inhibition is the kind of poem which has made Whitman the founding father of the hippy verse of Alan Ginsberg and his associates in the present century.

233. A Sight in Camp in the Daybreak Gray and Dim (Walt Whitman).

Whitman joined the Confederate army and was a male nurse during the Civil War.

no! — Republican army!

234. There is no God (Arthur Hugh Clough).

Clough, the friend of Matthew Arnold, was a rebel against Victorian pietistic hypocrisy.

236. The Maldive Shark (Herman Melville).

l. 5—*charnel of maw*, the slaughterhouse of his stomach.

l. 8—*Gorgonian*, monstrous.

237. The Gods Are Happy (Matthew Arnold).

v. 2—*Asopus*, river of Boeotia in central Greece; *Tiresias*, a blind Theban prophet; *inly revolving*, inwardly considering; *the doom of Thebes*, fate of Thebes (city of Boeotia involved in wars against the seven heroes).

v. 3—*the Centaurs*, a fabulous race, half man, half horse, living in Thessaly (northern Greece) in which was Mount Pelion.

v. 5—*Scythian*, nomadic inhabitant of ancient region of what is now central Russia; *saffron*, autumn crocus.

v. 6—*Chorasmian stream*, the Oxus (Chorasmia was to the east of the Caspian); *balsam*, healing oil.

v. 7—*Heroes*, companions of Jason in the Argo; *Happy Islands*, see note to *Ulysses l.* 63 (p. 367).

239. The Forsaken Merman (Matthew Arnold).

This is more than a fairy story about a merman. It expresses a profound regret at the passing of the old pagan world (here represented by the kingdom under the sea), and the loss of the beautiful and carefree life which paganism meant to Arnold, in favour of organised religion (as represented by the return of the merman's mortal wife to her old home and especially its church). Compare the last six lines of Wordsworth's sonnet *The World is too much with Us* (p. 173) which also express wistful grief for the lost beauty and romance of the ancient world.

v. 1—*white horses*, foamy waves.

v. 4—*spent lights*, light enfeebled by passing through sea water.

244. Lovesight (Dante Gabriel Rossetti).

A good example of Rossetti's Victorian romantic manner. The general sense is: Do I see you better in the full light of day, when I gaze at your face, or when we are making love at dusk? Then, without answering his question, the poet asserts that if his love were to die, it would be the end of all hope for him.

245. On the Site of a Mulberry-tree (Dante Gabriel Rossetti).

Rossetti's boundless admiration for Shakespeare is expressed in a hyperbolically fierce denunciation of the man who was supposed to have cut down a tree planted by him.

l. 4—*frailer than his laurel-wreath*, unlike the symbolic wreath of Shakespeare's immortal fame, the tree he planted was destructible.

l. 7–8—Even on the gallows, from which they hang, the highwaymen, Jack Sheppard and Dick Turpin, plead to have restored the breath which should have been taken by hanging the Rev. Gastrell.

l. 11—*deaf drudge*, Gastrell is likened to a beast of burden, a donkey whose ears are deaf to the music of Shakespeare.

l. 14—Starveling is the tailor in *A Midsummer Night's Dream*, and there is a proverbial expression 'It takes nine tailors to make a man'. The implication is that Gastrell is only one ninth of a man.

246. Success is Counted Sweetest (Emily Dickinson).

Emily Dickinson, one of the best and most original of American poets, was remarkable for the compression of her poems and their paradoxical irony. Here she is saying that success can only be fully understood by one who has failed.

l. 3—*nectar*, wine of the gods, i.e. the best wine.

l. 5—*purple host*, victors in a battle (the American Civil War was being fought at the time of Emily Dickinson's best productive period).

246. I KNOW SOME LONELY HOUSES . . . (Emily Dickinson).

l. 17—*so*, so long as.

l. 35—*Chanticleer*, the cock.

248. I LIKE TO SEE IT LAP THE MILES (Emily Dickinson).

Written in the early days of American railroads, this poem describes the progress of a train as if it were a live animal, not a machine.

l. 8—And then slice out a cutting for itself on a hilltop.

l. 14—*Boanerges*, in Mark 3.17 the sons of Zebedee are called Boanerges, meaning 'sons of thunder'. Emily Dickinson here refers to Boanerges as if it were a horse.

249. IT DROPPED SO LOW IN MY REGARD (Emily Dickinson).

We are not told what 'it' is in line 1. It does not matter. The poet is blaming herself for overvaluing something or someone—mistaking for solid silver what was only plate.

249. A NARROW FELLOW IN THE GRASS (Emily Dickinson).

A vividly graphic realisation of a grass-snake and the shudder of fear ('zero at the bone') produced whenever it is encountered.

l. 11—Emily Dickinson always refers to herself when a child as 'a boy'.

l. 14—*unbraiding*, untwisting.

250. SUMMER (Christina Rossetti).

v. 1—*yea and nay*, undecided (whether to be fine or not).

252. JABBERWOCKY (Lewis Carroll).

This is the poem from the book which Alice found when she got *Through the Looking-Glass*. 'Somehow it seems to fill my head with ideas (she remarked)—only I don't exactly know what they are!' Lewis Carroll uses the sound-associations of language to invent new words (neologisms) or portmanteau words (combinations of parts of real words) in order to convey ideas and feelings not quite expressed by any existing words. Later in the book Humpty Dumpty explains some of the neologisms, and Lewis Carroll gave a few further notes in the preface to another book. The following are the explanations given:

v. 1—*brillig*, four o'clock in the afternoon ('the time when you're *broiling* things for dinner'); *slithy* (pronounced with long 'i' as in 'writhe'), lithe and slimy (a portmanteau word); *toves* (pronounced to rhyme with 'groves'), a creature resembling a badger, a lizard and a corkscrew, that nests under sun-dials and lives on cheese; *gyre*, 'go round and round like a gyroscope'; *gimble*, 'make holes like a gimlet'; *wabe*, the grass plot round a sun-dial. ('It's called "*wabe*" you know, because it goes a long way before it, and a long way behind it—' 'And a long way beyond it on each side.'); *mimsy*, flimsy and miserable; *borogoves*, 'a thin shabby-looking bird with its feathers sticking out all round—something like a live mop'; *mome raths*, 'a "*rath*" is a sort of green pig: but "*mome*" I'm not certain about. I think it's short for "from home"—meaning that they'd lost their way, you know'; *outgrabe*, made a noise 'something between bellowing and whistling, with a kind of sneeze in the middle.'

253. THE BURGHERS' BATTLE (William Morris).

The citizens (burghers) of a medieval town tell how they feel as they go out to fight. The picture of a solid, prosperous life is slowly built up, and the chorus-line runs through it, adding a persistent note of sadness to underline, and contrast with, the peaceful contentment of the picture. Notice how Morris deals with the difficulty of finding a rhyme for the chorus-line in fourteen verses.

v. 1—*erst*, formerly.

v. 2—*Ruddy Fox, Running Ox*, signs on the burghers' battle standards.

v. 5—*close*, walled garden.

v. 6—*yore*, olden days.

v. 9—*scarlet*, robes of the aldermen.

v. 13—*wain*, farm-wagon.

255. IN PRISON (William Morris).

The mood and atmosphere are conveyed unmistakably in almost every phrase. Notice how the dactyllic rhythm is used to reinforce the effect. Can you account for the difference in pace between the first two lines of this poem and Shakespeare's *Merrily, merrily, shall I live now*, which appears to have the same rhythm?

v. 2—*loophole's spark*, small amount of light visible through the slit in the wall.

257. OLD FURNITURE (Thomas Hardy).

v. 4—*in the wont of*, in the habit of, like.

v. 5—*viol*, stringed instrument similar to and superseded by violin, viola and 'cello; *whilom*, formerly; *nut*, ridge on a stringed instrument over which strings are stretched at upper end.

v. 6—*tinder,* dry substance used before invention of phosphorus matches for getting a light from flint and steel; *linten,* of flax-waste (used as tinder).

259. Friends Beyond (Thomas Hardy).

v. 1—*Tranter,* carrier.

v. 2—*leads,* flat leaded roofs.

v. 3—*stillicide,* dripping of water from roof of cave to form stalactites and stalagmites. (It is this 'muted, measured note' which Hardy suggests in the rhythm of the poem).

v. 4—*we have triumphed* etc., we have achieved peace, and this reconciles us to the troubles of life.

v. 5—*terrestrial stress,* the strain of earthly life; *detraction,* blame, disapproval.

v. 6—*bass-viol,* precursor of the 'cello; *hold the manse in fee,* have absolute possession of the manor.

v. 8—*charlock,* mustard; *grinterns,* compartments in a granary; *blue china,* set of willow-pattern ware; *ho,* worry.

v. 11—*Trine,* Trinity (God); *witteth,* knows.

261. Afterwards (Thomas Hardy).

Each verse contains a piece of delicate observation which Hardy hopes that others, after he is dead, will think of as characteristic of him. Hardy wrote many poems in which he thinks of the local people as ghosts; here it is almost as if he thought of himself as a ghost.

v. 5—*bell of my quittance,* the passing bell tolling to signify that I have quitted the world.

262. Regret Not Me (Thomas Hardy).

Hardy thinks of himself as resigned to death, like the characters in *Friends Beyond*; not because, like them, he found life full of troubles, but because he has lived a happy life.

v. 7—*junketings,* merry-making.

263. Hurrahing in Harvest (Gerard Manley Hopkins).

Hopkins was perhaps the most original poet who ever wrote in English. His poems owe less than any others to established forms and traditional diction and imagery. It is true that he wrote many sonnets, but the sonnet was the mere outward frame or shape for his thought. Language is used in its most elemental way, as the direct expression of sensation and feeling. That is why his poems appear to go back to the very beginning of English poetry; the nearest approach to them in the poetry of the past is that of the Anglo-Saxon age. Hopkins was original, not for the sake of originality—indeed his 'oddness' sometimes troubled him—but because his experiences were to him absolutely fresh and personal; his manner of expressing them, therefore, had to be fresh and personal. This is what makes his poems 'difficult'. But they are not so much difficult as exacting. They demand that we shall read each phrase, each word, not with a mind trained by the reading of other poems, but with senses much more than ordinarily alert to experience things as they really are. (Another modern poet who can often give this sense of experiencing naked reality, unobscured by a veil of poetic language, is D. H. Lawrence. But Lawrence rarely troubled to work his poems into a finished, satisfying shape, as Hopkins did). To appreciate a poem by Hopkins is exacting, but it gives the feeling of never having completely experienced nature before. Many readers are dissatisfied or disturbed by a first reading of Hopkins. This is a good sign, for a completely new experience is always disturbing. Hopkins' originality took the direction first, of inventing new rhythms—what he called 'sprung rhythm' or the free rhythm of repose speech, designed to place the stresses where they would most help the sense; secondly, of using old words in new ways and in new combinations. He often coupled words by means of a hyphen so as to make what was virtually a new word. The sense of these is sometimes not at first clear, but always yields to an effort of the imagination. *Hurrahing in Harvest* is an expression of sheer rapture at the beauty of creation: it is as if the poet were seeing it for the first time. (Compare *I Will Lift Up Mine Eyes*, p. 80).

l. 1—*barbarous*, wild, shaggy.

l. 3–4—*has wilder, wilful wavier*, etc., the clouds as they form (mould) and break up (melt), are compared to drifts of meal or flour, wild and wavy in a wilful or original, everchanging way.

l. 6—*to glean our Saviour*, as gleaners gather corn from the harvest-fields, so the poet imagines himself gathering (in the sense of knowing, understanding) Christ by searching among the clouds.

l. 7–8—What living person ever gave to the eyes and heart of a lover more real and rapturous replies than the clouds gave me as I questioned them about Christ?

l. 9–14—*the azurous hung hills*, etc., the blue hills, hung as it were from Heaven, are the majestic shoulder (sturdy as a stallion and sweet as a violet) upon which God bears the world. These things have existed for ever, only I have failed to see them, to appreciate them fully; as soon as I do so, my heart seems to grow wings which, as they become bolder, raise me towards Heaven and seem to cast the earth away under my feet.

l. 14—*for him*, i.e. for the beholder.

264. The Sea and the Skylark (Gerard Manley Hopkins).

l. 2—*trench*, cut or break in on.

l. 2—*ramps*, rears itself up (like a rampant beast).

l. 6–7—*His rash-fresh re-winded*, etc.; this was the subject of a long explanation by Hopkins. The meaning is: (I hear) his headlong and exciting song (*score* means the printed notes in music) whirl (through the air), like a skein of new silk running off the reel (*winch*) on which it has been re-wound.

l. 10—*how ring right out*, how the sea and the skylark out-ring (as a coin or a bell made of pure metal out-rings a counterfeit).

l. 11—*crown*, we (men) are the crown or summit of creation.

l. 12—*cheer*, comely appearance; *earth's past prime*, the beauty of early creation (of which the sea and the skylark are still a part).

l. 13–14—Mankind and all its works are disintegrating, hastening onwards to their final destruction and backwards to the original slime out of which man was created.

265. Felix Randal (Gerard Manley Hopkins).

l. 1—*farrier*, shoe-smith; *my duty all ended*, Hopkins was a Catholic priest, and his duty was to bring the comforts of religion to the sick man and to administer the last sacrament.

l. 5–8—*impatient he cursed*, etc., at first he uttered impatient curses because of his fatal sickness, but his disposition improved after he had received the supreme unction (part of the Catholic last sacrament); although he had begun to have more heavenly thoughts some months before, when I had talked to him of Christ, the pardon and ransom of mankind.

l. 10—*thee*, notice how, as Hopkins' pity for the dead farrier increases and becomes more intimate, more personal, he addresses him directly (instead of referring to him in the third person, as hitherto). It is as if the *endearing* spoken of in *l.* 9 had suddenly taken this form; *all road ever*, in whatever way.

l. 12—*how far from then*, etc., you did not foresee your days of sickness and misery when you were strong and boisterous at the blacksmith's forge.

l. 13—*random*, meaning uncertain, but probably casual, careless, not thinking about heaven or death; *peers*, equals (equally powerful men, or possibly horses).

l. 14—*fettle*, put in order; *sandal*, Hopkins' pity and tenderness touch even the iron horse-shoe and it is transformed into something soft and gentle.

266. Thou Art Indeed Just, Lord (Gerard Manley Hopkins).

Hopkins' ms. of this poem is prefaced by a quotation, in Latin, from Chapter 12 of *The Book of Jeremiah*: 'Righteous art thou, O Lord, when I plead with thee; yet let me talk with thee of thy judgements: Wherefore doth the way of the wicked prosper? wherefore are all they happy that deal very treacherously? Thou hast planted them, yea, they have taken root: they grow, yea, they bring forth fruit: thou art near in their mouth, and far from their reins.' Compare the first lines of Coleridge's sonnet, *Work without Hope*:

All Nature seems at work. Slugs leave their lair—
The bees are stirring—birds are on the wing—
And Winter slumbering in the open air,
Wears on his smiling face a dream of Spring!
And I the while, the sole unbusy thing,
Nor honey make, nor pair, nor build, nor sing.

l. 10—*lacèd*, interlaced, or decorated with lace.

l. 11—*fretty chervil*, cow-parsley whose leaves are lace-work or fret-work.

266. IN HONOUR OF ST. ALPHONSUS RODRIGUEZ (Gerard Manley Hopkins).

Because of its originality and the compactness of its thought, this is a difficult poem, but its meaning will be revealed to careful study. St. Alphonsus was a Catholic saint who for forty years acted as hall porter in the Jesuit college in Palma, Majorca, and was said to be much troubled by evil spirits. This sonnet praises the virtue of inner fortitude (a virtue for which Hopkins himself was remarkable, though there were few to remark it). In spite of the saint's outwardly uneventful forty years, God (patient creator of natural forms) crowded his inner life with victory over evil spirits.

l. 1–4—The meaning is that external and bloody conflicts rightly win renown. The contrasting argument is introduced by the 'but' of line 6.

267. SPRING AND FALL (Gerard Manley Hopkins).

This poem expresses the idea of the 'sad mortality' of man and nature alike. The child that weeps because of the golden leaves falling in autumn really mourns, though she does not yet know it, her own mortality.

l. 8—Though you see whole worlds of pale, fallen leaves.

268. IN VALLEYS GREEN AND STILL (Alfred Edward Housman).

Housman's poems have the classical virtues of compression and understatement: they say much in a small space, and they leave the reader to infer the full meaning. Emotion and passion are disciplined within the bounds of fairly rigid formal pattern, and the reader's attention is held by beauty of form and melody and appropriateness of diction. He should, while appreciating these aspects of the poems, feel also the urgency and strength of the underlying emotions. In this poem the pity and pathos of the particular situation described are focused in the line 'And both are sighing'. Each of the two lovers sighs for several reasons, and the sum of these reasons constitutes the human situation for which the reader's pity is evoked.

269. ON WENLOCK EDGE (Alfred Edward Housman).

v. 1—*Wenlock Edge* is an escarpment to the south, and *the Wrekin* a hill to the north of the River Severn.

v. 2—*holt,* wood, copse; *hanger,* wood on a steep slope; *Uricon,* Roman settlement on the Severn.

v. 3—*yeoman,* farmer, countryman.

270. THE CHESTNUT CASTS HIS FLAMBEAUX ... (Alfred Edward Housman).

This poem is a powerful statement of fatalistic and stoical resignation to the fate of humanity and the malignity of the creator.

l. 22—To-morrow it will move on to remoter errands. The general sense is that if today we are afflicted by evil weather, tomorrow it will be others' turn.

271. OTHERS, I AM NOT THE FIRST (Alfred Edward Housman).

l. 7—*reins,* loins.

273. THE HOUR BEFORE DAWN (William Butler Yeats).

A narrative poem in which the two characters stand for contrasting attitudes to life. 'Red-head' believes in avoiding all trouble, as well as all experience, by sleeping for ever; the beggar indignantly denounces 'Red-heads's' philosophy and believes in living his life to the full, even though it has little to offer him, and he is a half-blind cripple.

l. 3—*Cruachan,* a rugged hill in Connaught (western Ireland).

l. 8—*Queen Maeve's nine Maines.* Maeve, in Celtic mythology, was Queen of Connaught; she had seven (in Yeat's story, nine) sons called the Maines.

l. 28—*outlandish,* i.e. in a fashion many centuries old.

l. 52—*Goban,* founder of artistry and handicraft, armourer to the ancient Celtic Gods and kings.

l. 79—*upon his hunkers,* squatting.

276. AN IRISH AIRMAN FORESEES HIS DEATH (William Butler Yeats).

277. THE THREE MONUMENTS (William Butler Yeats).

These two poems have in common a certain disillusion with accepted notions of patriotism, but the first is a serious expression of the political attitude of Irishmen towards Britain, while the second is an ironical comment on the honesty of politicians.

280. THE VILLAIN (William Henry Davies).

Compare Blunden's *The Ballast-Hole* (p. 322). The question that Blunden asks in his first line—'Can malice live in natural forms?'—might also have prefaced this poem of W. H. Davies. Both poems are based on an experience common among those who observe nature—a sudden feeling of the presence of guilt or evil lurking in outwardly innocent objects.

281. FAREWELL (Walter de la Mare).

v. 2—*traveller's joy*, a wild clematis, also called old man's beard. (The choice of this particular flower was not accidental: its name is related to the thought of the poem).

282. BY ORDER! (Walter De la Mare).

The Poet is contemplating the nearness of his death, represented by a closed gate leading to 'dark fields'. The world, to him once familiar, now seems more and more incomprehensible, and he experiences a growing sense of unreality.

l. 6—*phantasmata*, (accent on second syllable), fantasies, projections.

282. DRY AUGUST BURNED (Walter De la Mare).

l. 12—*limber*, detachable front of gun-carriage.

283. DRUGGED (Walter De la Mare).

It is possible that the drug may have been alcohol, but it is more likely to have been the opium in liquid form drunk by early addicts such as Coleridge.

284. ROBERT FROST, for the last twenty years or so of his long life, was a kind of unofficial American Poet Laureate. His deceptively simple, even homely style, based on the country speech of the eastern seaboard, conceals much craft, subtelty and individuality. He often expresses his meaning obliquely. In *The Road not Taken*, for instance, are we intended to take the meaning symbolically? *Not to Keep* is a typically economical compression of a whole story—that of a week's leave in wartime.

289. THE BLOWING OF THE HORN (John Masefield).

An English version of part of the medieval French *Chanson de Roland*, according to which Roland, one of the noblest of the French king Charlemain's knights, was ambushed in the pass of Roncesvalles by an enemy force, while Charlemain's army was returning into France after an expedition against the Saracens in Spain. He refused, out of pride, to blow his horn for help until it was too late.

v. 1—*thirty leagues thence*, the horn, called Olivant, was magic; *Count Guenes*, Ganelon, the traitor, in league with the Saracens (Mohammedan conquerors of Spain).

v. 2—*Naimes*, one of Charlemain's knights; *Franks*, French.

v. 3—*Noples*, a Spanish fortress; *Durendal*, Roland's magic sword, supposed to have belonged to Hector of Troy; *horn a hare*, follow a mere hare with his hunting-horn; *gabbing*, chattering boastfully.

v. 4—*by my hope of gain*, as I hope for salvation; *he here*, i.e. Guenes; *who did so feign*, who pretended (to be loyal).

v. 5—*hawberks*, coats of mail.

291. The Owl (Edward Thomas).

l. 10—Thomas is here referring to Shakespeare's song *When icicles hang by the wall*, where the cry of the owl is called 'a merry note'.

293. The Daniel Jazz (Nicholas Vachel Lindsay).

Jazz is the kind of syncopated dance-music introduced by American negroes. This poem is a 'jazz' version of the story from the Book of Daniel (Ch. vi) re-told as a modern American negro might imagine it.

l. 22–23—*St. Peter, Judas*, the simple mind of the negro introduces these New Testament figures anachronistically.

l. 24—*Beelzebub*, a devil.

296. Disillusionment of Ten O'Clock (Wallace Stevens).

Stevens was a highly individual and original poet. This is a surrealistic evocation of conventionality, in which white-night-gowned early-to-bedders do not have irrational dreams, and the only exponent of the unconventional and irrational is a drunken sailor asleep.

l. 9—*ceintures*, girdles.

297. Autumn (Thomas Ernest Hulme).

See *Introduction* (p. xliii).

298. Salutation (Ezra Pound).

A simple protest against the smugness of bourgeois life—an early hippy poem perhaps.

298. Spray (David Herbert Lawrence).

Much of Lawrence's poetry is described by Wordsworth's famous saying, 'Poetry is the spontaneous overflow of powerful feelings'. This poem and the next two come from a book called *Pansies* from the French *pensées*—thoughts. 'So I should wish these "PANSIES" to be taken,' Lawrence says in the Preface, 'as thoughts rather than anything else; casual thoughts that are true while they are true and irrelevant when the mood and circumstance changes.' Prose thoughts, he says, tend to be dogmatic and assertive, so he has chosen a verse-form; but the verse is free verse, which allows for greater spontaneity and freshness than rhyme and metre, Lawrence uses a more formal verse pattern in *Piano* (p. 302). Compare Whitman's *After the Sea-ship* (p. 230).

299. POVERTY (David Herbert Lawrence).

l. 3—*St. Francis* of Assisi, founder of the Franciscan order of friars in the early thirteenth century, who practised and preached worldly poverty.

300. BAT (David Herbert Lawrence).

l. 6—*Ponte Vecchio*, the Old Bridge in Florence.

l. 11—*spools of dark thread*, compare the images describing the skylark in Hopkins' *The Sea and the Skylark* (p. 264).

l. 12—*circle*, i.e. circular.

l. 34—*Pipistrello*, Italian for bat (literally 'little piper').

302. PIANO (David Herbert Lawrence).

This poem recalls the rest of the quotation from Wordsworth given above (see note on *Spray*). Poetry, he says, 'takes its origin from emotion recollected in tranquillity'.

v. 3—*appassionato*, being played passionately (a term from music).

302. LAST SNOW (Andrew Young).

l. 6—*spathe*, outer sheath protecting certain plants as they appear through the earth.

304. TO ANY DEAD OFFICER (Siegfried Sassoon).

A characteristic protest against the wastefulness and futility of the first World War, in which men were used simply as cannon-fodder, and in which the fighting men continually complained of the actions of the politicians who mismanaged the war from back home.

305. THE RETURN (Edwin Muir).

As the story is told in Homer's *Odyssey*, Ulysses (Odysseus) took ten years to return home to the island of Ithaca after the ten years' siege of Troy. Meanwhile it was assumed that he was dead, which his wife Penelope refused to believe. The palace was occupied and misused by various local princes, suitors for her hand. She undertook to choose one of them when the tapestry she was weaving was completed. She kept them off by unweaving at night what she had woven the previous day.

307. RANNOCH, BY GLENCOE (Thomas Stearns Eliot).

A type of poem whose meaning is easier to feel than to explain. The moorland scene round Loch Rannoch in the Scottish highlands evokes memories of Scottish history, particularly of the brutal and treacherous massacre of the inhabitants of Glencoe in 1692 by the orders of the English king, William III. Their chief had failed to take the oath of allegiance by the appointed date.

l. 2—*the rifle*, i.e. of sporting visitors.

l. 5—*moon cold or moon hot*, like the moon, of no certain temperature; *the road winds*, etc., the winding roads suggest the slow progress of the armies who used, and possibly made them in olden days.

l. 9–12—The sense is, that although Scottish national pride was broken, the memory of injustice outlasts human life (*the bone*); pride lives on, in the scene of disgrace (the pass of Glencoe), and here there is no *concurrence*, no agreement, no acceptance (of English sovereignty).

308. THE JOURNEY OF THE MAGI (Thomas Stearns Eliot).

Magi, the three wise men who came from the east to bring gifts to Christ, whose birth had been reported from Jerusalem.

l. 10—*sherbert*, a cooling fruit drink.

l. 38–39—*this Birth was . . . like Death, our death*, the knowledge of the birth of Christ brought to the magi a sense of loss, a feeling that their old selves had died, so that when they got back to their own people and their idolatry, they experienced dissatisfaction and weariness with life.

309. RHAPSODY ON A WINDY NIGHT (T. S. Eliot).

On the surface this poem describes a walk home in the small hours, its successive stages marked by the passing of the hours and by the street lamps which focus a number of sordid images. The reader then notices that these images from present reality recall images from the speaker's memory, to which they are compared. These 'twisted' mental images objectify the speaker's state of mind. The 'lunar synthesis' which gives unity to the external night scene also temporarily upsets the normal structure of memory and re-orders it in a new synthesis, until the return home (the door-key, toothbrush, etc.) restores the actuality of the daily routine. For much of his method and diction Eliot draw on the French symbolist poets, especially Jules Laforgue.

313. PIAZZA PIECE (John Crowe Ransom).

A variation on the theme of 'Death and the Maiden'.

313. BLUE GIRLS (John Crowe Ransom).

This poem may be taken as a variation on the theme of 'Carpe diem' or 'Gather ye rosebuds while ye may'.

314. FIGHTING SOUTH OF THE CASTLE (Arthur Waley).

This poem and the others by Arthur Waley are translated from the Chinese; but they are far more than just translations. They are among the best of twentieth century English poems. The original of this one is an anonymous epitaph of about 124 B.C.

l. 12—*By the bridge there was a house.* 'There is no trace of it left. This passage describes the havoc of war. The harvest has not been gathered: therefore corn-offerings cannot be made to the spirits of the dead.' (Translator's note.)

315. BURIAL SONGS (Arthur Waley).

Anonymous poems of the Han Dynasty (200 B.C.—A.D. 220). Compare these Chinese dirges with their English counterparts—*A Lyke-Wake Dirge* (p. 1), *Fear No More the Heat o' the Sun* (p. 61), and *The Glories of our Blood and State* (p. 104).

316. ON THE BIRTH OF HIS SON (Arthur Waley).

From the Chinese of Su Tung-p'o (A.D. 1036–1101). Contrast Corbet's *To his Son* (p. 94) and Graves's *To Lucia at Birth* (p. 321).

316. THE HAT GIVEN TO THE POET BY LI CHIEN (Arthur Waley).

From the Chinese of Po-Chü-i (A.D. 772–846). The pathos evoked by homely things has never been more movingly expressed. The ideas occur in pairs, as in some Hebrew poetry (e.g. *The War Horse*, p. 83).

316. A LOVE SONG (Arthur Waley).

An anonymous Chinese poem. (See note on next poem.)

317. PLUCKING THE RUSHES (Arthur Waley).

An anonymous poem of the fourth century A.D. In this and the preceding poem depth of feeling is combined with delicacy of expression to create an appearance of simplicity unmatched outside Chinese art. The love-poetry nearest to this in English for intensity and simplicity is Wordsworth's 'Lucy' poems (e.g. *She Dwelt Among the Untrodden Ways*, p. 168).

320. 1805 (Robert Graves).

v. 3—*runt*, term of contempt for an undersized person.

v. 4—*one arm, one peeper*, Nelson lost his right eye in 1794 and his right arm in 1797; *plain moll*, mere harlot.

v. 6—*we tried to box him down*, the Admiralty tried to prevent Nelson's promotion.

v. 7—*Copenhagen*, where under Admiral Parker Nelson achieved a brilliant victory in 1801; he put the telescope to his blind eye and so failed to see the signal to discontinue the attack.

v. 9—*the seas are England's now*, by his decisive victory over Napoleon's fleet at Trafalgar, Nelson secured for England the control of the seas.

321. To Lucia at Birth (Robert Graves).

Wishes for the future of a new-born girl, in which she is warned of the evils of the world in the symbolism of the child's rhyme of 'The lion and the unicorn'. The unicorn is a symbol of lust, and the lion of war and destruction. In a world driven mad by this 'outrageous company' may the child strive to keep her dignity and integrity. Compare Corbet's *To his Son* (p. 94) and Waley's *On the Birth of his Son* (p. 316).

322. The Ballast-hole (Edmund Blunden).

Compare W. H. Davies' *The Villain* (p. 280) and see note on that poem (p. 378). *Ballast-hole*, hole made by excavating sand or gravel (here filled with water).

l. 4—*fangy*, like a fang (tooth of carnivorous animal, or poison-tooth of snake). Compare Shakespeare's expression in *Twelfth Night*, 'by the very fangs of malice'.

l. 8—*snarling*, recalls the previous adjective *fangy* with its suggestion of the jaws of some malicious beast.

322. Report on Experience (Edmund Blunden).

In the first three stanzas Blunden expresses a vision of corruption—a righteous man forsaken, a country ravaged by war (Blunden was in the trenches in World War I), a woman become corrupt. The last stanza despite the irony of its reference to God, holds out some ultimate hope.

323. It Would be Strange (Cecil Day Lewis).

v. 1—The picture is of men undergoing questioning by 'third degree' methods. How strange if they found their confidence 'at a crucial question', and refused to answer.

v. 2—*construction*, method of nest-building; *seamless*, faultless. (The starling is a bad nest-builder and singer.)

v. 3—*consternation*, overthrow, destruction.

v. 4—Just as it would be strange for terrified men, or birds, or ants, to learn new and better ways, so it would be even more strange if we learnt to forgive others instead of hate them. Hatred is the 'devil' we raise to revenge ourselves on others for our own weakness, envy and grief.

326. THE FORCE THAT THROUGH THE GREEN FUSE DRIVES THE FLOWER (Dylan Thomas).

It is not easy, and perhaps not possible, to be precise about the meaning of every line. The poem conveys in a cryptic and visionary way a sense of the poet's oneness with the outer world, both in its aspects of living growth and ever-recurring death.

Index of First Lines

A cold coming we had of it 308
A discreet householder exclaims on the grandsire 312
A narrow fellow in the grass 249
A one-legged, one-armed, one-eyed man 273
A sight in camp in the daybreak gray and dim 233
A touch of cold in the Autumn night 297
A widow bird sate mourning for her love 202
About the shark, phlegmatical one 236
Above the quiet dock in midnight 297
Adieu! farewell earth's bliss! 75
After the sea-ship, after the whistling winds 230
Ah, my bones ache, my limbs be sore 39
Ah! Sun-flower, weary of time 157
All, all of a piece throughout 127
All Kings, and all their favourites 89
All my past life is mine no more 128
Although the snow still lingers 302
And David lamented with this lamentation 84
And did those feet in ancient time 156
And in the frosty season, when the sun 173
As I was walking all alane 6
As some fond virgin, whom her mother's care 137
As virtuous men pass mildly away 91
As you came from the holy land 48
At evening, sitting on this terrace 300
At the round earth's imagined corners, blow 89
At Viscount Nelson's lavish funeral 320

Be not afeard, the isle is full of noises 71
Beginning my studies the first step pleas'd me so much 230
Behold her, single in the field 172
Bid me to live, and I will live 96
Black is the beauty of the brightest day 57
Blow, blow, thou winter wind 58

Boney was a warrior 21
Bright Star, would I were stedfast as thou art— 215
But, chief of all 108
By Saint Mary, my lady 40
By the bivouac's fitful flame 234

Call for the robin-redbreast and the wren 93
Can malice live in natural forms 322
Careful observers may foretell the hour 131
Careless and still 284
Come all you young fellows that carry a gun 19
Come, come away, to the tavern I say 21
Come, dear children, let us away 239
Condemn'd to Hope's delusive mine 139
Cromwell, our chief of men, who through a cloud 110

Darius the Mede was a king and a wonder 293
Dear brother Robin, this comes from us all 209
Death, be not proud, though some have called thee 88
Do others waking in the morning hear 325
Down in the meadows the other day 164
Downhill I came, hungry, and yet not starved 291
Dry August burned. A harvest hare 282

Fain would I change that note 87
Fair stood the wind for France 52
Families, when a child is born 316
Fear no more the heat o' the sun 61
Felix Randal, the farrier, O he is dead then? my duty all ended 265
Flee fro the prees, and dwelle with sothfastnesse 34
Follow a shadow, it still flies you 79
For God's sake, let us sit upon the ground 68
For I will consider my cat Jeoffry 145
Four men stood by the grave of a man 26
From harmony, from heavenly harmony 123
Full fathom five thy father lies 60

Get up, get up for shame, the blooming morn 98
Give me my robe, put on my crown, I have 71
Green rushes with red shoots 317

Had we but world enough, and time 118

Happy choristers of air 122
Hast thou given the horse strength? 83
He that dwelleth in the secret place of the most High 82
Here the crow starves, here the patient stag 307
His golden locks Time hath to silver turned 51
Honour is flashed off exploit, so we say 266
How all occasions do inform against me 73
How many thousand of my poorest subjects 68
How sweet the moonlight sleeps upon this bank! 69
How swiftly it dries 315
How vainly men themselves amaze 115

I am a gentleman in a dustcoat trying 313
I am the only being whose doom 229
I am: yet what I am none cares or knows 210
I cannot eat but little meat 46
I have been young, and now am not too old 322
I heard a thousand blended notes 169
I heard my love was going to Yang-chou 316
I know not how it may be with others 257
I know some lonely houses off the road 246
I know that I shall meet my fate 276
I like to see it lap the miles 248
I met a traveller from an antique land 202
I murder hate by field or flood 161
I saw a creature sally with booty 27
I sing of a maiden 18
I sowed the seeds of love 165
I that in heill was and gladness 35
I think I could turn and live with animals 231
I travelled among unknown men 169
I wander though each chartered street 157
I was angry with my friend 155
I will lift up mine eyes unto the hills 80
I wish I were where Helen lies 10
I wish people, when you sit near them 299
I wonder by my troth, what thou, and I 92
If all be true that I do think 128
In a drear-nighted December 214
In valleys green and still 268
In Xanadu did Kubla Khan 177
Inert in his chair 283

Is this a holy thing to see 158
It dropped so low in my regard 249
It fell on a summer's day 74
It is a wonder foam is so beautiful 298
It is an ancient Mariner 179
It little profits that an idle king 221
It seems a day 175
It was a dismal and a fearful night 111
It would be strange 323

Laid in my quiet bed, in study as I were 45
Let me not to the marriage of true minds 65
Let Sporus tremble—'What? that thing of silk' 136
Let the boy try along this bayonet blade 318
Long ago to a white-haired gentleman 316
Lord, Lord! methought, what pain it was to drown! 65

Madam, withouten many words 43
Margaret, are you grieving 267
Merry Margaret 41
Move him into the sun 317
Mrs. Someone's been to Asia 287
My enemy had bidden me as guest 324
My mother bore me in the southern wild 153

Native moments—when you come upon me—ah you are here now 232
Now fades the last long streak of snow 218
Now first, as I shut the door 292
Now welcom somer, with thy sonnë softe 30

O blithe new-comer! I have heard 170
O Generation of the thoroughly smug and thoroughly uncomfortable 298
O mistress mine, where are you roaming? 60
O my love is like a red, red rose 160
O that we now had here 66
O what can ail thee, knight-at-arms 212
O where hae ye been, Lord Randal, my son? 14
O where have you been, my long, long love 12
O wild West Wind, thou breath of Autumn's being 203
O yesterday I was married, last night I went to bed 166

Of an old soldier of the Queen's 20
Of these the false Achitophel was first 125
Oh, Galuppi, Baldassaro, this is very sad to find! 224
Oh happy shades! to me unblest 151
On ear and ear two noises too old to end 264
On Wenlock Edge the wood's in trouble 269
One day I wrote her name upon the strand 51
One evenin' as the sun went down 24
One fine morning in May I was tilling the land 22
One night when I went down 279
Others, I am not the first 271
Out of the wood of thoughts that grow by night 292

Queen and huntress, chaste and fair 77

Regret not me 262
Remember now thy Creator in the days of thy youth 85
Resound, ye hills, resound my mournful strain! 134
Roland gripped his horn with might and main 289

Season of mists and mellow fruitfulness 211
See what delights in sylvan scenes appear! 133
See! with what constant motion 110
Shall I compare thee to a summer's day? 62
She dwelt among the untrodden ways 168
Since brass, nor stone, nor earth, nor boundless sea 63
Slant sunshine and these naked fields once more 282
Snow falling and night falling fast, oh, fast 288
So Abram rose, and clave the wood, and went 318
So, so, break off this last lamenting kiss 90
Softly, in the dusk, a woman is singing to me 302
Still to be neat, still to be dressed 80
Strange fits of passion have I known 167
Success is counted sweetest 246
Summer ends now; now, barbarous in beauty, the stooks arise 263
Sweet, be not proud of those two eyes 97
Sweet cyder is a great thing 256
Sweet day, so cool, so calm, so bright 100

That's my last Duchess painted on the wall 227
The chestnut casts his flambeaux, and the flowers 270
The curfew tolls the knell of parting day 140

The doors flapped open in Ulysses' house 305
The earth is the Lord's, and the fulness thereof 81
The force that through the green fuse drives the flower 326
The glories of our blood and state 104
The Gods are happy 237
The hand of the Lord was upon me 86
The houses are haunted 296
The king sits in Dunfermline town 7
The Kirk an' State may join, and tell 163
The laws of God, the laws of man 272
The merry world did on a day 102
The only people I ever heard talk about My Lady Poverty 299
The rustling of leaves under the feet 206
The splendour falls on castle walls 217
The sword sung on the barren heath 156
The thistle down's flying, though the winds are all still 207
The twentieth year is well-nigh past 149
The winter evening settles down 306
The woods decay, the woods decay and fall 219
The world is too much with us; late and soon 173
There be four things which are little upon the earth 83
'There is no God,' the wicked saith 234
There lived a wife at Usher's Well 2
There stood a hill not far, whose grisly top 105
They are all gone into the world of light! 120
They err who count it glorious to subdue 107
They fought south of the Castle 314
They hold their public meetings where 277
They sent him back to her. The letter came 286
Thick rise the spear-shafts o'er the land 253
This ae nighte, this ae nighte 1
This life is sweetest; in this wood 278
This sely widwe, and eek hir doghtres two 33
This tree, here fall'n, no common birth or death 245
This winter's weather it waxeth cold 15
This world a hunting is 96
Thou art indeed just, Lord, if I contend 266
Though the moon beaming matronly and bland 321
Though ye suppose all jeopardies are passed 40
Throughout the world if it were sought 44
Thy sword within the scabbard keep 127
Tired with all these for restful death I cry 63

'Tis strange to me, who long have seen no face 216
To explain the nature of fishes in craft of verse 27
To see a strange outlandish fowl 95
Toll for the brave! 148
To-night, grave sir, both my poor house, and I 78
'Twas brillig, and the slithy toves 252
'Twas on a Holy Thursday, their innocent faces clean 159
Twelve o'clock 309
Twirling your blue skirts, travelling the sward 313
Two roads diverged in a yellow wood 285
Tyger! Tyger! burning bright 154

Under an hill there is a cave 28

Wearily, drearily 255
Weighing the stedfastness and state 119
Well, how are things in heaven? I wish you'd say 304
Well I remember how you smiled 201
Well; if ever I saw such another man since my mother bound my head, 129
What I shall leave thee none can tell 94
What man's land is the graveyard 315
What passing bells for these who die as cattle? 319
When do I see thee most, beloved one? 244
When first my lines of heav'nly joys made mention 101
When God at first made man 102
When I heard the learn'd astronomer 232
When I lie where shades of darkness 281
When in the chronicle of wasted time 64
When midnight comes a host of dogs and men 207
When the green woods laugh with the voice of joy 152
When the Present has latched its postern behind my tremulous stay 261
When to the sessions of sweet silent thought 62
When we were idlers with the loitering rills 216
Where the bee sucks, there suck I 59
While joy gave clouds the light of stars 280
Whilome in youth, when flowered my joyful spring 50
Whoso list to hunt, I know where is an hind 43
Why do you lie with your legs ungainly huddled 303
Why does your brand sae drop wi' blude 4
William Dewey, Tranter Reuben, Farmer Ledlow late at plough 259

Winter is cold-hearted 250
With him ther was his sone, a yong Squyer 32
With that my hond in his he took anoon 31

Ye living lamps, by whose dear light 114
Yestreen I had a pint o' wine 162